The International Business Environment and National Identity

Globalisation influences every aspect of post-modern social reality. How-ever, little empirical research has considered how it affects people's percep-tion of their national attachments. This book explores the nature of national identity in our increasingly globalised society. "Who are you?" is the ques-tion that it addressed in conversations with international business travellers whose exposure to different cultures, languages and values through their business travel and interactions with their foreign colleagues brings a new slant on their vision of the world. How does it influence their understanding of themselves?

The International Business Environment and National Identity is based on interviews with Russian and British business travellers whose views on their national identity and the role of global business in shaping it offer a new insight on our understanding of the impact of global forces on contem-porary society. The book discusses the respondents' practical experiences of their international encounters, their impact on shaping their personal identi-fication and highlights differences and similarities in people's articulation of their national belonging. The issues of understanding the self and the effects of globalisation on business people's professional and personal lives are at the core of the book's investigation.

The International Business Environment and National Identity will appeal to students and researchers of international management and cross-cultural management as well as those studying intercultural communication and globalisation.

Tatiana Gladkikh is a Senior Lecturer in Business Management at the Uni-versity of Winchester, UK.

Routledge Studies in International Business and the World Economy

For a full list of titles in this series, please visit www.routledge.com

The International Business Environment and National Identity

Tatiana Gladkikh Ph.D.

Routledge
Taylor & Francis Group

LONDON AND NEW YORK

First published 2018 by Routledge

2 Park Square, Milton Park, Abingdon, Oxfordshire OX14 4RN
52 Vanderbilt Avenue, New York, NY 10017

Routledge is an imprint of the Taylor & Francis Group, an informa business

First issued in paperback 2019

Copyright © 2018 Taylor & Francis

Library of Congress Cataloging-in-Publication Data
Names: Gladkikh, Tatiana (Lecturer in business management), author.
Title: The international business environment and national identity / by
    Tatiana Gladkikh.
Description: New York : Routledge, 2017. | Includes index.
Identifiers: LCCN 2017020330 | ISBN 9781138667266 (hardback) |
    ISBN 9781315618999 (ebook)
Subjects: LCSH: International business enterprises—Employees. |
    International travel—Social aspects. | Business travel—Social
    aspects. | Nationalism. | Group identity.
Classification: LCC HF5549.5.E45 G53 2017 | DDC 306.3/6—dc23
LC record available at https://lccn.loc.gov/2017020330

ISBN: 978-1-138-66726-6 (hbk)
ISBN: 978-0-367-87780-4 (pbk)

Typeset in Sabon
by Apex CoVantage, LLC

To Vicka,
my source of love, life and energy

Contents

Table

Acknowledgements

I should like to thank all those people who contributed to this book, directly or indirectly. I am deeply grateful to Professor Julian M Cooper OBE, my academic critic and a wise supporter, Dr Paul Sheeran and Dr William Sheward for their belief in my success and Dr Patrick Osborne, for being my tireless editor and advisor.

I thank all my research participants in Britain and Russia, who generously gave me their precious time and talked to me during and between their business travel in offices, cafes, homes and airports. Their thoughts, memories and feelings produced rich accounts of our social reality that was a great pleasure to work with. I am very lucky to have made some very good friends during my work on the book.

My special thanks go to De La Rue Plc and personally to Martin Allen and Vera Linetskaya, who assisted with organising interviews with some of the De La Rue staff. Many thanks to the Russo-British Chamber of Commerce (RBCC) and personally to its Executive Director at the time, Stephen Dalziel, for welcoming me to work with RBCC's library material and for use of their networking resources. I am grateful to the staff from the Office of the Chief Scientific Advisor of the Scottish Government and particularly to my senior colleagues Ben Dipper and Isabel Bruce OBE for their help with interviewing business travellers in Scotland. Many thanks to EventScotland and its Chief Operating Officer, Paul Bush OBE, who also generously assisted with interviewing their staff.

My very warm thanks to all my friends in Britain and Russia whose contacts and willingness to help with my book produced a wide network of respondents from different spheres of life. Many thanks to Karen Aberdeen, Olga Andrianova, Sofia Borisova, Tim Colman, Maria Craig, Olga Day, Elena Leschen, Will Leschen, Walter Speirs and Galina Westwood.

I thank the Economic and Social Research Council for their financial assistance.

And, finally, my very special thanks to my daughter Victoria, who gives me faith in everything I do.

1 Introduction

Flying from an international airport, be it in Britain, Russia or anywhere else in the world, can be a fascinating experience. On weekdays, holiday-makers and leisure travellers are heavily dominated by businesspeople, easily identifiable by their charcoal-grey business dress, determined and focused behaviour and a must-have set of business accessories: mobile phones and laptops. These people do not fuss. They know their way around. They are not there to enjoy the experience. They are on business. They are working. Airports can be seen as the hub for a worldwide business network that accommodates nationals of numerous countries performing the role of the global business traveller who constantly keeps connected via email or telephone with his or her colleagues across the globe and is totally mobile. He (more rarely, she) feels comfortable communicating with foreign partners and operates with ease in any country.

This book addresses the complexity of identity construction of the contemporary international business traveller: the intermix of the openness to the global business environment and inclusivity of national belonging. The book does not intend to examine in depth contemporary features of nationalism; rather, the focus is on the influences of global exposure on international business travellers' constructions of their national self. The aim is to understand whether these people's national attachments are becoming reinforced or, on the contrary, less pronounced and therefore substituted by a newly emerging cosmopolitan vision of self. Is the erosion of national identity taking place in the global business arena?

This book is fuelled by the concern that there has been a lack of inquiry into the effects of international travel beyond understanding its "functionality and role in getting the job done" (Beaverstock *et al.*, 2009). Thus, this read is a response to this challenge. It takes place within the global business arena, a broad platform for further development of contemporary business practices and for shaping the social interactions of those involved in them. The book holds that globalisation affects people's understanding of their national self in two opposing directions. On the one hand, people are becoming more international, while on the other, they are reaffirming their national belonging. The book particularly concentrates on British and

Russian businesspeople who are actively involved in international business operations through interactions with their colleagues from different countries, frequently travelling abroad for business and spending significant amount of time away from their countries of origin.

This book consists of five chapters, each of them beginning with a brief introductory section that sets out the direction of its discussion. Chapter 2 ("Identity in the Global World") outlines the academic environment in which the book takes place by addressing four major themes that are important to consider in this context: different approaches to understanding the concept of national identity that can be found in the academic literature; the importance of understanding and theorising globalisation; an overview of the literature on transnationalism, the transnational business community and cosmopolitanism; and a discussion of the psychological dimension in studying national identities and the role that psychology can play in understanding issues of national belonging. Chapter 2 highlights that the emphasis of this book is on the national identity of British and Russian international business travellers.

Chapter 3 ("The International Business Traveller") opens with the methodology employed for collecting empirical evidence to inform the book. The analysis of the empirical evidence that follows is split into four consecutive parts, spanning the following sections: Part One focuses on the international business traveller and introduces some definitions of the global business traveller that can be found in the contemporary literature. It then proceeds to establish a generalised image of the international business traveller based on the discourses of the 60 international business travellers whose interviews informed the book.

The analysis addresses such characteristics as age, gender, education, foreign language skills and professional ambition to travel abroad. It also explores the business travellers' discourse on their willingness and ability to be immersed into foreign cultures; formation of social networks and, in particular, friendships with foreign nationals; feeling of comfort or discomfort while on business trips abroad; feeling a foreigner in non-home countries; ways and efficiency of communication with their foreign counterparts; and feelings and degrees of satisfaction or dissatisfaction with their busy lifestyles. The section acknowledges the pitfalls of generalisations in qualitative research and admits that the image of the global business traveller that transpires from this study is by no means inclusive of all international business travellers.

The following parts analyse, respectively, national identity construction by international business travellers interviewed in England, Scotland and Russia. The book focuses on how national identities are being understood, interpreted and articulated. By deliberately not placing national identity in any particular context and not conditioning its construction by any limiting factors, this section of the book aims to uncover what elements of people's lives constitute their national identity and whether the national explanation of self occupies an important role in their day-to-day activities or remains insignificant and distant from factual reality.

Having analysed national identity construction as an abstract concept, the book continues by exploring the nature of national identity in Chapter 4 ("Identity Claims in a Cross-Cultural Perspective"), where the subject of discussion is placed in two different contexts. Part One ("The Significance of National Identity from International Business Travellers' Perspective") adopts a cross-cultural approach for identifying the similarities and differences in the international business travellers' articulations of their national identity and provides further insight into how national identities are created and manifested by people of different national and ethnic origins. The major identity constructs which have been identified in this book are tested against A.D. Smith's national identity theory (1991) in order to examine potential theoretical developments in the way national identity is lived, understood, performed and theorised.

Part Two ("National Identity and the International Business Environment: The Analysis of Trends and Tendencies Towards Change") positions the discussion in the context of the international business environment in order to assess whether erosion of national identity is taking place in the global era. Firstly, it provides an overview of the different approaches to understanding globalisation that can be found in the academic literature. It then investigates the nature of globalisation as it is understood by the business travellers in order to consider what their empirical understanding of globalisation can do for globalisation theory today. Secondly, building on the business travellers' discourse on globalisation, this part examines the dynamics of national identity in the context of the contemporary international business environment. It pays particular attention to the international business travellers' understanding of themselves in the global arena: Do they preserve their attachment to their national roots, or do they associate themselves with much broader geographical, political and political and economic landscapes? How does globalisation affect their sense of national belonging?

Finally, Chapter 5 ("Erosion of National Identity?—Searching for Answers") summarises the main discussion points from the previous chapters in order to provide the answer to the book's main question. This concluding chapter also presents the author's self-reflection on this work.

References

Beaverstock, J.V., Derudder, B., Faulconbridge, J. and Witlox, F. (2009) International Business Travel: Some Explorations. *Geografiska Annaler: Series B, Human Geography*, 91 (3), pp. 193–202.

Smith, A.D. (1991) *National Identity*. London: Penguin Books.

2   Identity in the Global World

This chapter seeks to set out the academic context in which the investigation of the erosion of national identity takes place. Owing to the nature of the enquiry, it is important to address a wide range of areas that directly affect the issue of the book. Thus, it firstly considers the concept of national identity by discussing different approaches to its understanding and establishing the theoretical framework which will guide this discussion. It then emphasises the importance of understanding and theorising globalisation as the environment in which the erosion of national identity is potentially taking place. Thirdly, it presents an overview of the literature on transnationalism, the transnational business community and cosmopolitanism. This appears important if we are to understand the social group who transcend national borders in their business activities and adopt cosmopolitan views on the world as an effect of their international interactions. The book then introduces a discussion of the psychological dimension in studying national identities and highlights the role that psychology can play in understanding issues of national belonging. In conclusion, it emphasises the need for a deeper understanding of local and cosmopolitan orientations of contemporary business travellers that currently has not received the desired level of academic attention. By highlighting that the emphasis of this examination is on the national identity of British and Russian international business travellers, the book raises its main research question that will be guiding its discussion.

Identity and National Identity

This section addresses the issue of national identity as a component of a complex organisation of human social identity (Tajfel, 1982). In this respect, it is useful to distinguish national identity from other types of social identity and to understand how identity changes depending on the context in which it is considered.

The Multifaceted Character of Identity

Identity as a term originated in ancient Greece and since then has had a long history in Western philosophy. However, it acquired the more intensive social-analytical use in the United States in the 1960s. It appeared highly popular and diffused rapidly across academic disciplines and state borders. It was quickly adopted in the journalistic lexicon and the language of social and political practice and analysis. "Identity talk" continues to flourish, with many authors whose main interest lies outside the traditional "identity field" publishing extensively on identity (Brubaker and Cooper, 2000).

Wodak *et al.* (1999) assert that identity is a topic of wide variety. Echoing this view, Brubaker and Cooper (2000) claim that as an analytical category it is "heavily burdened and is deeply ambiguous" (p. 8). The term is used and abused in both social sciences and humanities and this "affects not only the language of social analysis but also—inseparably—its substance" (Brubaker and Cooper, 2000: 2). Thus, in order to avoid political and intellectual costs, it requires conceptual clarity.

Identity as a Concept

Identity as a term can be characterised by a broad spectrum of approaches depending on the context in which it is studied, e.g., national identity and advertising (Morris, 2005), questions of Englishness and Britishness (Byrne, 2007), multiculturalism (Parekh, 2000), national identity and geopolitics (Dijkink, 1996). Identity can be accessed from different levels of enquiry, e.g. from lived and felt identities of individuals (identity at a personal level) to identities of nations and organisations (identity at a structural level) and from identities of nations or countries to group identities, such as European identity.

The concept of identity is non-static and changing, positioned in the flow of time and involved in other processes. Therefore, it is wrong to assume "that people belong to a solid, unchanging, intrinsic collective unit because of a specific history which they supposedly have in common, and that as a consequence they feel obliged to act and react as a group when they are threatened" (Wodak *et al.*, 1999: 11). Identity can be perceived as a "relational term" and thus is defined as "the relationship between two or more related entities in a manner that asserts a sameness or equality" (Wodak *et al.*, 1999: 11).

With the analytical complexities attached to the term, it is claimed that "identity" is harder to understand than we suppose. We all seem to have multiple identities and therefore the question arises: What determines which identity is silent at any given time? Mandler (2006) stresses that identity is not fixed and not being formed by any one particular process. In order to understand how identity is shaped, we need to understand the context in which this process is taking place.

Identity as Sameness and Identity as Selfhood

Ricoeur (1992) attempted to untangle the semantic jungle of the sub-components of the term "identity": identity as sameness and identity as selfhood. "Sameness" is seen as a concept of relation and as a relation of relations (Ricoeur, 1992: 116), whereas the concept of "selfhood" is identi-fied with what can also be referred to as the "ego identity" in other theories. For example, Goffman (1990) defines "ego identity" as "one's own subjec-tive feeling about one's own situation and one's own continuity and unique-ness" (Goffman, 1990: 129).

According to Ricoeur (1992), sameness and selfhood are in a relationship with each other, with "narrative" identity taking an intermediate position between those two identity elements. Narrative identity is an identity of a character (*personage*).

> Narrative identity allows various, different, partly contradictory cir-cumstances and experiences to be integrated into a coherent temporal structure, thus making it possible to sketch a person's identity against the background of a dynamic constancy model which does justice to the coherence of a human life. Thus the concept of narrative identity can go beyond the one-sided model of an invariant, self-identical thing. It can take into account the ideas that the self can never be grasped without the other, without the change.
>
> (Wodak et al., 1999: 14)

Identity as a Category of Practice and a Category of Analysis

Brubaker and Cooper (2000) assert that it is important to differentiate iden-tity as a category of practice from identity as a category of analysis. As a category of practice it is used by lay actors in everyday settings to under-stand themselves, their actions and their similarities and differences relative to others. Identity as a category of practice can also be used by politicians in the course of their political activities to make people make sense of them-selves, relate and differentiate themselves from others in order to organise and direct collective response of people in a particular way.

Identity, when used as a category of analysis, assists in explaining social processes. However, one should avoid adopting—even unintentionally—the use of categories of practice as well as categories of analysis. This is not to say that the same term cannot qualify as a category of practice and as a cat-egory of analysis at the same time. For example, "nation", "race" and "iden-tity" are used both analytically and in practice, for they do exist and people do have "nationality", "race" and "identity" (Brubaker and Cooper, 2000).

In seeking to bring some analytical clarity to the term identity, Brubaker and Cooper (2000) distinguished five uses of the term:

- Identity as a ground of social or political action, often opposed to "interest"
- Identity as a collective phenomenon ("identity" in this case presuppos-ing sameness among members of a group or category)
- Identity as a core aspect of "selfhood" emphasising something very deep, basic and foundational

- Identity as a product of political action, highlighting collective self-understanding, solidarity or "groupness"
- Identity as the evanescent product of multiple and competing discourses: "identity" demonstrates the unstable, multiple, fragmented, fluctuating nature of the contemporary "self" (Brubaker and Cooper, 2000: 6–8).

Individual and Collective Identity

Identity can be classed as individual and collective (or system-related) (Wodak *et al.*, 1999). Individual identity is understood as an identity with an individual person in focus. This notion is sometimes referred to as "social identity". The object of identification possesses such social characteristics as age, class and sex and has certain external attributes, for example, a particular role, which one takes on in one's visions of oneself. Collective identity considers identity in relation to systems. Here, groups, organisations, classes and cultures are the object of identification, but not individual people. Wodak *et al.* (1999) point out, referring to Holzinger (1993: 12), that "individual-related and system-related identities overlap a great deal in the identity of an individual".

Therefore, individuals as well as collective groups such as nations cannot possess pure homogeneous identities. This simply cannot be realistic (Wodak *et al.*, 1999). Rather, individual identity and group identity are hybrids of identity that becomes even more complex in the era of global change influenced by cultural intermix (Hall, 1996a, 1996b). Thus, individuals or collective groups carry "multiple identities", of which national identity is only one component.

Collective identity, according to Peters (2002), should be understood as an area of culture, as a special class of cultural elements. The cultural elements of a social unit, such as its current state, its character, its problems, achievements, history or its future, taken all together make up a collective identity. Collective identity can have a narrow or "thin" character (e.g., where a group or organisation shares a small range of common interests or goals), or it may be rich or "thick" with considerable historical depth, detailed conceptions of group character, collective solidarity and so on.

"Strong" and "Weak" Identities

Similarly, Brubaker and Cooper (2000) present their vision of identity as a term that tends to mean too much or too little in different situations. They analyse identity from the point of view of "strong" and "weak" uses of the term. Thus, "strong" conceptions of identity emphasise sameness over time or across people, assuming that:

- Identity is something all people have or ought to have
- Identity is something all groups of people have or ought to have

- Identity is something people (or groups) can have without being aware of it
- Strong notions of collective identity imply strong notions of group boundness and homogeneity; a clear boundary between inside and outside (Brubaker and Cooper, 2000: 10).

A "weak" understanding of identity is quite contradictory to a "strong" one, implying that identity is "multiple, unstable, in flux, contingent, fragmented, constructed, negotiated and so on" (Brubaker and Cooper, 2000: 11). The authors see a problem with the "soft conception of identity, asking the question what is the point of using the term "identity" if the core meaning is repudiated? They also state that the "weak" conception of identity is too weak to do useful theoretical work. To them, the term is too elastic and therefore incapable of doing any serious analytical work (Brubaker and Cooper, 2000: 11).

National Identity and Collective Identity

The concepts "national identity" and "collective identity" are widely used and heavily contested in both social science and public discourse (Peters, 2002). Aiming to shed some analytical clarity on the term "identity", Peters (2002) provides a multidimensional analysis of elements of national identity and clarifies the meanings of "ethnic", "cultural" and "political". Two conceptions of nationhood are being distinguished: "ethnocultural" and "civic". *Ethnocultural* conception presupposes common genealogy and descent ties, a common history, shared cultural traditions and customs as constitutive elements of the nation or of national identity (p. 4). *Civic* conception understands nation as a political community, self-governing, democratic unity with legal and political equality among its citizen-members (Peters, 2002: 4, with reference to A.D. Smith, 1991: 11–13). The ethnocultural conception of nationhood can further be split into the "ethnic" and "cultural"; however, this separation is a bit fuzzy, as the ethnic part often relies on cultural commonalities.

Types of National Identity

It is suggested that four typologies of identity as a concept can serve for analytical clarity of the term (Peters, 2002):

- Ethnic conception
- Cultural conception
- Political conception
- "Class" conception

The "class" type is referred to as the most historically outdated type; thus, Peters (2002) chooses to leave it aside, arriving at a tripartite model. He refers here to the work of Eisenstadt and Giesen (1995), who had also distinguished three ideal types of collective identity: "primordial", "cultural" and "civic".

Developing the discussion about ethnocultural and civic identities, Peters (2002) mentions that in identity literature (Finkielkraut, 1987; Schnapper, 1991; Schnapper, 1995) France and the USA are treated as instances of civic visions of nationhood, while Germany has continuing influences of ethnic understandings. This model has been put to explanatory use in the area of immigration and naturalisation policies: "Ethnocultural identity" leads to restrictive exclusionist policies (Germany), while civic identity leads to inclusive immigration and naturalisation policies, either assimilationist (as in France) or a more multicultural type (USA, UK) (Peters, 2002: 6).

Peters (2002) suggests that certain combinations of civic, cultural and ethnic elements may support, or at least not hinder, each other. The inter-relation between the components of national identity can be understood differently depending on people's understanding of what these components are. Therefore, Peters (2002) advocates a "neutral" specification of national identity components in order to open them to empirical investigation.

National Identity as Part of the Public Culture of a Modern State

National collective identity consists of those elements of collective identity which are present or circulate among members of a state-bounded society. In this sense, national identity should be regarded as a specific part of the public culture of a modern state-bounded society (Peters, 2002: 12). However, it is not necessarily true that the same conception of national identity is shared by all members of the public; it does not mean that it is consensually accepted or internalised (Peters, 2002).

For Peters (2002), a nation is a political organisation and a political collectivity, where membership implies specific rights and duties. There are values and principles which specifically relate to the political order, but they rarely stand alone; rather they are intermixed with others (e.g., national economy, national scientific achievements, high culture and national cuisine). From a historical perspective, a nation is an entity with a past and a future which transcends individual life-spans. Peters (2002) makes interesting comments on acquiring cultural heritage through understanding, accepting, sharing and practicing it and also on collective orientations towards the future. This implies that people can actually acquire another's identity if they adopt it. Also in business (especially international), if there is a common vision for the future, then perhaps a common business identity can form?

Multiple National Identities

The same author, Peters (2002), claims that most people expect that their children and grandchildren will belong to the national society of their parents and grandparents. This is less so in the contemporary global environment with increased movement of people around the world, where the possibility of "multiple national identities" (Peters, 2002: 18) is not out of the question. For the first time in history, due to the development of communication technologies, individuals scattered around the world can now feel unity and belonging to a single imagined community in hyperspace (Anderson, 1998) where multiple identities can be created and reinvented.

An individual can have many identities; if one could sum them up, one perhaps could get the self (Mandler, 2006). People identify themselves with what they are not, by contrasting themselves against oppositions. Identities, according to Mandler (2006), can be "donned and doffed like hats" (p. 272). However, understanding of national identity has a different slant. It can be traced back to pre-modern periods, to the time when people were already defining themselves as members of groups that were similar to nations (ethnicities, cultures, rulerships) (Mandler, 2006: 272).

Challenges in Studying National Identity

Summing up lessons from previous works on what "national identity" is and what its role is in human minds and societies, Mandler (2006) criticises the social science of the 1950s and the 1960s for being too handicapped by its laboratory conditions. Although he does acknowledge the works published since the 1970s aimed at explaining collective identity (e.g., Tajfel, 1982; Stryker and Burke, 2000), Mandler (2006) still sees them as too laboratory orientated and not applicable to "real life", especially at macrolevels, such as national identity (p. 274).

Mandler (2006) refers to Phillip Gleason (1983), who in the 1980s raised warnings about distinguishing two very different meanings of national identity—psychological and sociological. Mandler (2006) claims that social scientists working with "identity", "have puzzled its possible meaning and utility" (p. 271). Therefore, Mandler (2006) attempts to look at what social scientists think "national identity" is and what its role is in human minds and societies.

For Mandler (2006), "identity" is just one form of national consciousness which exists alongside other forms, such as ideologies, patriotism, nationalism, the idea of national character, which may or may not be incorporated into identities (p. 276). Anthony Cohen (1986) distinguishes between the "private face" and "public face" of the group identification, which suggests that identity construction is both a psychological and a social process (Mandler, 2006: 278). Social psychologists argue that most of the time, people are in the state midway between consciousness of their individual uniqueness and consciousness of their group identities. "Nationhood . . . structures our everyday social reality on both an institutional and face-to-face level":

Identity is an important but elusive quality and "national identity" is even more so. What goes on in people's heads is very complicated and difficult for historians to pin down. We do have evidence at least about the "public faces" of people's identities. The processes by which those identities are constructed are themselves very complex, involving a number of psychological and sociological mechanisms, and varying according to context and situation.

(Reicher and Hopkins, 2001: 281)

In order to understand better the nature of national identity in the United Kingdom, Mandler (2006) offers a historiographical discussion of national identity in modern Britain driven by a renaissance of the "national question" initially in the 1970s and later, after the devolution of power to Scotland and Wales in 1998. An insight into the historical formation of British identity points out some curious views on the issue, for example, Sonya Rose's (2003) attitude to national identity in wartime Britain. To Rose (2003), national identity is a modern requirement, where nation is the fantasy structure through which society perceives itself as a homogeneous entity, which is impossible to achieve. Mandler (2006) perceives Rose's (2003) work as a rule for our times, which tells us that "we ought to stop striving for a "real" or "essential" Britishness, and accept that collective identities are no more than strategies for collective action which will always fall apart" (Rose, 2003: 290). Out of a war situation, identities are more fluid or are hidden altogether (Rose, 2003).

The Role of "The Other" in Understanding National Identity

Mandler (2006) also refers to Linda Colley's (1992) vision of national identity, which states that national identity is defined by a boundary dividing the self from the other: "Quite simply, we usually decide who we are by reference to who and what we are not" (Colley, 1992: 311). Another "back door" introduction of "national identity" against an "other" is given by Krishan Kumar (2003): "English national identity cannot be found from within the consciousness of the English themselves. We have to work from the outside in" (p. 62–63). Reflecting on psychological implications of national identity, Fiona Clampin (1999) describes it as a "fundamental means of self-definition" which forms part of our sub-consciousness. To her, any identity begins by establishing difference and the awareness of an "other" is a fundamental element in the construction of any national identity. Although identity is created and constructed, it is not necessarily false "as there is a constant agreement on the existence . . . of the nation as an entity" (Clampin, 1999: 68–69).

The Nation (State) and National Identity

For Robert Colls (2002), identities are never imposed; they require consent or accommodation. Nation-states, according to him, have to build up a collective identity as a counterweight to individualism. Colls (2002) claims that "people can be many things in different circumstances, but at some point they have to decide who they are *in sum*" (p. 174). For Richard Weight (2003), national identity is the sum of all the forms of national conscious- ness". Bourdieu (1994) asserts that a significant role in national identity formation is performed by the state:

> Through classificational systems (specially according to sex and age) inscribed in law, through bureaucratic procedures, educational struc- tures and social rituals (particularly salient in the case of Japan and England), the state moulds mental structures and imposes common principles of vision and division. . . . And it thereby contributes to the construction of what is commonly designated as national identity (or, in a more traditional language, national character).
>
> (Bourdieu, 1994: 7)

Thus, "national identity is shaped by state, political, institutional, media and everyday social practices, and the material and social conditions which emerge as their results, to which the individual is subjected" (Wodak *et al.*, 1999: 29). In the process of shaping national identity, it is important to recog- nise the role of national symbols in developing the spirit of national identity:

> National identity describes that condition in which a mass of people have made the same identification with national symbols—have internalised the symbols of the nation—so that they may act as one psychological group where there is a threat to, or the possibility of enhancement of, these symbols of national identity.
>
> (Bloom, 1990: 52)

National Identity Dynamic

William Bloom introduces the phrase *National Identity Dynamic*, which he explains as "the potential for action which resides in a mass which shares the same national identification" (Bloom, 1990: 53). It is closely linked to mass national mobilisation at a psychological level when, in order to find psychological security, critical for stability and emotional well-being of a person, individuals tend to maintain, protect and support their identity. Bloom states that this imperative is active and works from a very young age throughout all life up to old age. Identifications can be shared by groups, who tend to act in unison in order to enhance or protect their shared iden- tity (Bloom, 1990: 53).

The Approach to National Identity in This Book

As pointed out above, identity (and especially national identity) is a very complex and elusive concept. It has been demonstrated that in attempts to understand it, various approaches can be employed. For example, as part of social processes, national identity (acting as a category of analysis) can be seen as "strong" or "weak", individual or collective, or perceived as having potential for mobilising individuals for action.

In order to uncover how identity is used by lay actors in everyday settings to understand themselves, their actions and their similarities and differences relative to others, identity is analysed as a category of practice and can be approached from the position of "the other". In this book, identity is firstly addressed as a category of practice (i.e. how international business travellers understand and construct their own identity) and secondly employing the concept for understanding the influences of globalisation on contemporary society (i.e. is the erosion of national identity taking place in the global business world?).

In the discussion of different approaches to understanding identity and national identity discussed above, the issue is presented primarily as a category of analysis. However, in order to understand how national identities are constructed, it is important to consider a theoretical stance on national identity as a category of practice. In this respect, A.D. Smith's (1991) work appears particularly apposite for the purposes of this research as the author usefully theorises what constitutes national identity as a lived experience, i.e. uses the concept as a category of practice. This approach to understanding national identity differentiates itself from the attempts of other thinkers who see national identity as a tool to understand social processes, i.e. use the concept as a category of analysis (Goffman, 1990; Reicher and Hopkins, 2001; Peters, 2002; Kumar, 2003; Mandler, 2006).

National Identity Theory by A.D. Smith (1991)

A.D. Smith's work on nations and nationalism, echoed in identity literature (Wodak *et al.*, 1999; Peters, 2002; Bechhofer and McCrone, 2010; Savage *et al.*, 2010), asserts that national identity is a complex and abstract phenomenon which can be combined with other types of identity: class, religious or ethnic. It can also be influenced by ideology and is "fundamentally multi-dimensional; it can never be reduced to a single element, even by particular factions of nationalists, nor can it be easily or swiftly induced in a population by artificial means" (A.D. Smith, 1991: 14). A.D. Smith (1991), defining a nation as a "named human population sharing an historic territory, common myths and historical memories, a mass, public culture, a common economy and common legal rights and duties for all members" (p. 14), suggests five fundamental features of national identity display (that should not be assumed as fixed):

- historic territory or homeland
- common myths and historical memories
- common, mass public culture

- common legal rights and duties for all members
- common economy with territorial mobility for members

This breakdown of national identity into categories that constitute the concept appears especially useful for establishing the makeup of national identity of British and Russian businesspeople addressed in this book. Among other attempts to categorise the ways of articulating national identity (Hopkins and Moore, 2001; Popescu, 2006; Mansbach and Rhodes, 2007; McCrone and Bechhofer, 2008; Skey, 2010), it presents the most comprehensive and more generically applicable account of tropes through which national identity can be displayed. Therefore, A.D. Smith's (1991) national identity constructs will be employed in this book as a guiding theory in establishing what comprises the national identity of international business travellers in the era of globalisation.

National Identity in the Era of Globalisation

With the influences of global development on almost every sphere of human activity, the future of national identity is attracting heightened attention and is frequently debated. The idea of the emergence of a global identity becomes increasingly topical and occupies a prominent position in academic and political discourse on globalisation and national identity (A.D. Smith, 1995; Hetherington, 1998; Kennedy and Danks, 2001; Scholte, 2005; Freeland, 2007; The Economist, 2008). A.D. Smith (1991), for example, admitting that some elements of global culture and the effect of communication technologies on global interconnections provoke stronger ties between people in the world, suggests that

> there is no global "identity-in-the-making"; a global culture could only be a memory- less construct or break up into its constituent national elements. But a memory-less culture is a contradiction; any attempt to create such a global culture would simply accentuate the plurality of folk memories and identities that have been plundered in order to constitute this giant bricolage.
>
> (p. 159)

Therefore, global culture is no more than "a pastiche of the past underpinned by science and telecommunications" (p. 159).

In his later book, *Nations and Nationalism in the Global Era*, A.D. Smith (1995) continues his discussion of national identity in the age of globalisation. Analysing the paradox of emerging global culture and the rebirth of ethnic nationalism happening at the same time, he assesses three approaches to explain this phenomenon and admits that "narratives of national identity are becoming increasingly hybridized and ambivalent" and observes "the emergence . . . of looser polyethnic societies" (p. 3). However, none of the three approaches to explain this paradox appears satisfactory to A.D. Smith. He rejects the "global culture approach" as lacking evidence and failing "to grasp the import of proliferating ethnic nationalisms" (p. 6). Looking at the works of Marx, Engels and Hobsbawm, he points out that their approaches to understanding national identity and national culture at the time of rapid global changes are based on depoliticisation:

- separation of the cultural level of the nation from the political level of the state
- demilitarisation
- "normalization" and ritualisation of nationalism.

A.D. Smith criticises the vision of cultural nationalism and political nationalism as separate and unrelated to each other. He argues that "plural nations" have no ground for existence.

Discussing the idea of a "new imperialism", A.D. Smith (1995) acknowledges the dominant position of large transnational companies, which require a "transnational class of capitalists, powerful global ideology and culture of mass consumerism" (p. 16–17). However, this idea is subverted by strongly persisting power politics and national cultures. For A.D. Smith, global culture, cosmopolitan and rootless, causes fear and concern among people: Shallow and memory-less, it cannot offer common memories, myths, symbols, values and identities. A.D. Smith (1995) firmly concludes that no global identity in-the-making can be observed, remaining a dream to some intellectuals. People are still "divided into their habitual communities of class, gender, region, religion and culture" (p. 24).

Jan Aart Scholte (2005) continues the discussion of the effects of globalisation on identity in the book *Globalisation*, where identities are defined as "constructions of being, belonging and becoming—[they] hold key significance in terms of both defining the self and forging collective bonds with others". Scholte (2005) perceives contemporary globalisation as a process which has weakened the former neo-monopolistic power of nation-states in the construction of collective identities. From this point of view, globalisation has led to formation of national identities on scales other than states, such as substate, transworld and macro-regional. The growth of transworld places has encouraged the development of non-territorial identities on the grounds of faith, class, gender and race. Some tendencies towards hybridisation in the context of globalisation have also been noticed.

Globalisation can also be seen as a process that threatens national identity and at the same time provides possibilities for challenge and opportunity (Kennedy and Danks, 2001). This multifaceted social influence manifests itself through causing extreme difficulties for some nations, thus putting their identities in the state of "crisis" and "threat" (p. 21), whereas for others, it offers "a set of resources for empowering the reconstruction of identities in ways that enhance problem-solving and genuine hybridization without jeopardizing integrity or autonomy" (p. 21). Having examined different approaches to understanding influences of globalisation on national identity, this thesis adopts the view that globalisation affects people's understanding of their national self in two opposing directions. On the one hand, people are becoming more international, while on the other, they are reaffirming their national belonging.

Consequently, following the discussion above, this study endeavours to test its hypothesis by investigating how the understanding of one's national self is shaped by the international business environment, an arena in which globalisation, perhaps, has advanced the most. Responding to this challenge, and in order to understand what is special about "national identity"—historically, sociologically and psychologically—more detailed study of the specific contexts and situations in which "identity talk" takes place is first necessary.

Understanding Globalisation

For many centuries, international trade and commerce have been linking different parts of the world, providing an insight into foreign countries and cultures to those who were at the forefront of international businesses. As early as the 16th century, joint-stock companies were established to promote and facilitate international business interactions. One of the most impressive examples is the English Muscovy Company, also called Russian Company or Muscovy Trading Company, established in 1555. This company became the first major English joint-stock trading venture, enjoying the benefits of trade between England and Russia for a few centuries, up until 1917 (Mayers, 2005). After the Russian revolution of 1917, Russian-British business relations went through a time of decline and uncertainty. However, their rebuilding picked up in the late 1920s. *The Bank for Russian Trade Review* (1928) reported in June 1928 a success in important credit negotiations as the result of which some British firms had secured orders for textile machinery, electrical plant and equipment for power stations. "The new agreement for the purchases of machinery for the Soviet industry represents the first big orders of the Soviet Union in Great Britain since the break between the two countries" (*The Bank for Russian Trade Review*, 1928: 8).

Several Phases on the Path to Globalisation

It can be argued that the interconnection between societies, known in the contemporary world as globalisation (Baylis and Smith, 2006), is a process with a long history. Roland Robertson (1990) identifies several phases on the path to globalisation, starting with *the germinal phase*, which originated in Europe in the early 15th century and lasted until the middle of the 18th century. This phase could be marked by accentuation of concepts of humanity and the beginnings of modern geography. The following *phase of incipiency* also took place in Europe (middle of the 18th century till the 1870s) and is distinguished by the formalisation of international relations, development of the ideas of the homogeneous state leading to issues of nationalism and internationalism and the emergence of transnational regulations and communication.

The *take-off phase* accounts for the period from the 1870s to the 1920 and is characterised by further internationalisation of society, implementation of ideas about humanity and the increasing role of global communication. Global competitions, such as the Nobel Prize and the contemporary Olympic games, originated during this phase. At exactly the same time the world became enveloped by the First World War and the first transnational organisation, the League of Nations, was founded. The Gregorian Calendar experienced near-global acceptance. The take-off phase was followed by the *struggle for hegemony phase* (1920s–1960s), with the world immersing itself in a pool of multiple international conflicts threatening all forms of life. Issues of humanity were mainly focused on the Holocaust and atomic bombs. The United Nations Organisation was set up to take on the responsibilities of a transnational government (Robertson, 1990).

Finally, the *uncertainty phase* began in the early 1960s, to which we all are eye witnesses. Crisis tendencies of the 1990s resulted in the collapse of bipolarity which followed the end of the Cold War, making the international system more fluid. The spread of nuclear weapons is still concerning the world, as well as issues of human and gender rights, Third World and global consciousness. During this phase, the world witnessed active development of civil society; information generated by global media systems started being absorbed by millions of people across the globe; ordinary citizens of various countries became involved in transnational interactions and fast and easy global travel; and do not exclude the possibility of emergence of world citizenship. All this happened at a time when some countries were still underdeveloped in their economic and political advancement. There are still people in remote parts of our planet who have never seen or used a mobile phone (Robertson, 1990).

This phase of uncertainty is also a phase of living in a "liquid modern world" under conditions of constant change (Bauman, 2005).

> "Liquid modern" is a society in which the conditions under which its members act change faster than it takes the way of acting to consolidate into habits and routines. Liquidity of life and that of society feed and reinvigorate each other. Liquid life, just like modern liquid society, cannot keep its shape or stay on course for long.
>
> (Bauman, 2005: 1)

Liquid life proceeds in a fashion of "creative destruction", ruthlessly breaking traditional societies and throwing people into the race round a global track. Both those who have the most chances of winning this race (those at the top of the global pyramid enveloped by freedom to move, choose and change from what one now is into what one wants to be) and those whose chances in the race are painfully limited (those for whom new gates hardly ever open and exits seem to be permanently blocked, those for whom a duty to belong is an irreversible fate) find themselves in a maze of identity, which is itself a puzzle of similarity and difference (Hetherington, 1998). Those at the top end of the spectrum are puzzled by the choice of many identities on offer and the difficulty of picking the right one or skilfully assembling parts of different ones currently on offer. Those at the opposite end are challenged to hold on to the sole identity available and preserve it from crushing forces.

Those who find themselves in between the extremes are loaded with the moral weight of the two (Bauman, 2005). Indeed, those positioned by Zygmunt Bauman (2005) at the top end of the spectrum attract the close attention of academics with interest in transnational communities, the much-contested product of globalisation (Morgan, 2001; Carroll and Fennema, 2002; Carroll and Carson, 2003; Carroll and Fennema, 2004; Kentor and Jang, 2004; Kentor and Jang, 2006; Stone Sweet, 2006).

Theoretical Approaches to Understanding Globalisation

Analysing the complexity of different approaches to understanding globalisation, Peter Dicken (2003) distinguishes two opposite ends of the ideological spectrum: the *hyperglobalist* (or "globalist" later in the text) position and the *sceptical* position. Thus, following this theoretical framework, transnationalism for sceptics is simply wishful thinking (Schlesinger, 2007). Opposite to them are adherents of hyperglobalism (or "globalism" later in the text), who believe that contemporary society has created a new very distinctive social group of transnational people, the so-called transnational capitalist class (TCC) (Sklair, 2001). Recognising strong grounds supporting each of these two diametrically opposed theoretical perceptions of globalisation, it is difficult not to agree with Scholte (2005) and Peter Dicken (2003), who propose that the truth lies in neither. Those within an intermediate position accommodate their views in a transformationalist perspective. For them transnational communities are something quite probable in the making (Carroll and Fennema, 2002; Morgan, 2001).

Theoretical approaches to understanding globalisation as described by Dicken (2003) are a very useful tool to conceptualise manifestations of globalisation and place them into relevant perspectives. However, it is by no means an exhaustive attempt to theorise globalisation. For example, Douglas Kellner's (2002) critical theory of globalisation presents globalisation as a product of capitalism and democracy, as a set of forces imposed from above in conjunction with resistance from below. According to Martin *et al.* (2006), there is still no clarity among researchers as to how to approach globalisation itself: as a set of social processes common to (almost) all countries of the world (and more accurately, common to all relevant entities) and which are converging in the same direction, or as social phenomena that immediately present themselves as global and, surely, result from prior globalisation processes.

Whichever theoretical view one adopts, one should appreciate the potential need for new concepts and therefore be advised to approach the sociology of globalisation with caution (Martin *et al.*, 2006: 503). It is suggested that in order to assess social facts completely, "one needs to comprehend them wholly, i.e. from outside as an object, but an object with subjective perception . . . as we, as humans, would experience the fact as being native" (Mauss, 1997: xxviii). The call to comprehend globalisation processes fully implies approaching them simultaneously from "outside the world" and from "inside all its relevant entities" (Mauss, 1997: xxviii).

Terms and Concepts in the Globalisation Debate

Unification of the use of terms and concepts in academic debate on globalisation is another primary step on the route to conceptual clarity. Sklair (2001), Munck (2002) and Stone Sweet (2006) have commented on the interchangeable use of *global, transnational* and *international* in contemporary publications and, in order to avoid confusion, misunderstanding and misuse of these adjectives, Leslie Sklair (2001) effectively clarifies subtle linguistic nuances by clearly defining each of them. Thus, *international* in Sklair's *The Transnational Capitalist Class* (2001) "refers to forces, processes and institutions based on the pre-existing (even if changing) system of nation-states" (p. 2). *Transnational* presupposes "forces, processes and institutions that cross borders but do not derive their power and authority from the state". Power and authority derive from the transnational corporations owned by the transnational capitalist class. As for *global*, Sklair (2001) suggests narrowing the use of the term to "a very specific meaning, namely the goals to which processes of globalisation are leading. The most important of these goals are the establishment of a borderless global economy, the complete denationalization of all corporate procedures and activities, and the eradication of economic nationalism" (p. 3).

An Argument for the Universalist Approach in Research on Globalisation

Martin *et al.* (2006) reinforce the necessity to approach research on global social processes from a cross-national perspective. They acknowledge that although theoretical frameworks developed by scientists in different parts of the world might lead to a confrontation of interpretations (often burdened by cultural bias), scientific interdependence and exchange, they will nevertheless only stimulate internationalisation of social sciences. Therefore, the sociological conception of universalism, which is understood as the capacity to distance oneself from one's own culture and one's own history, appears able to accommodate the inclusion of all experiences aimed at understanding the world (Martin *et al.*, 2006).

As an example, research on influences of culture on Human Resource Management (HRM) is often concerned with internationalisation of the world economy and consequently increasing diversity of the members of business organisations (Cox, 1993; Stone-Romero *et al.*, 2003; Stone-Romero and Stone, 2007). Cultural norms, values and ideologies are among the most important dimensions of diversity of organisations, and in order to understand better how these various dimensions influence HRM processes and practices, research is needed across a wide range of countries (Adler and Bartholomew, 1992b).

Up to now, such research has been predominantly Western and is limited by including an extremely narrow range of cultures in any given study (Stone and Stone-Romero, 2008). Thus, it is anticipated that a wider Universalist approach will enhance existing knowledge on implications of culture on design of HRM policies, processes and practices across the globe. Universalism as a sociological conception can (and should) be applied to a wide range of social research projects, as it will contribute to a better understanding of social processes achieved through inclusion of all theories, perspectives and methodologies developed by researches from various countries, globalised or not. However, it is not the intention of this study to contribute to the enhancement of knowledge on HRM, but rather that the example from HRM is used to demonstrate the value of the Universalist approach in academic research.

Understanding Transnationalism and Cosmopolitanism

Transnational Communities and Networks

Universalism appears particularly relevant to studies of transnationalism and its implications and consequences on contemporary society, be it the future of nation-state, political processes, business practices or concerns of ordinary individuals. A number of publications address the issues of transnationalism from different slants, e.g., communities in cyberspace (Smith and Kollock, 1999), transnational governance (Stone Sweet, 2006) and future generations of contemporary transnational elites (Freeland, 2007). These studies use various theoretical approaches and methodologies from mere conceptualisation of cultural processes in the tradition of social anthropology, e.g., Ulf Hannerz's (1996) *Transnational Connections*, to developing the researchers' own theories, for example, Stone Sweet's (2006) theory of how new legal systems evolve, which combines "rationalist" and "constructivist" elements.

Discussions in the contemporary academic literature suggest that transnational business communities have indeed identified themselves as a unique social construct (Sklair, 2001; Morgan, 2001; Carroll and Fennema, 2002;

Carrol and Fennema, 2004; Kentor and Jang, 2004; Kennedy, 2005; Kentor and Jang, 2006; Schlesinger, 2007). The transnational business community is recognised as something certain, active and already with a history of more than 30 years (Stone Sweet, 2006). Sklair (2001) identifies this group as a Transnational Capitalist Class (TCC), while David Rothkopf (2008) characterises it as a superclass. Both authors, however, focus on new global elites, arguing that if nation-states at the point of their rise produced national elites, it would be logical to assume that the current economic integration could produce new global elites.

The TCC, according to Sklair (2001), comprises four fractions: "those who own and control major corporations and their local affiliates, globalizing bureaucrats and politicians, globalizing professionals, and consumerist elites. The TCC engages in a variety of activities that take place at all levels, including community, urban, national, and global politics and involve many different groups of actors" (Sklair, 2001: 144).

For Rothkopf (2008), these new global elites—the global ruling class—are businesspeople and financiers who run global companies and global politicians who lead supranational organisations. They are graduates of the same universities (usually Harvard, Stanford and the University of Chicago), they belong to the same clubs (the most popular one is the Council on Foreign Relations in New York) and they are on each other's Boards of Directors (*The Economist*, 2008). They live a truly cosmopolitan life, easily crossing national borders and public and private sectors. They have a global sense, described by Ulrich Beck (2006) as:

> . . . a sense of boundarylessness. An everyday, historically alert, reflexive awareness of ambivalence in a milieu of blurring differentiations and cultural contradictions. It reveals . . . the possibility of shaping one's life under conditions of cultural mixture.
>
> (Beck, 2006: 3)

Chrystia Freeland (2007) believes that this sense of living in "the global" is being passed on to the children of international corporate bosses and investment bankers, who during their childhood lived in various places of the world outside the country whose passport they hold and "recognise that they belong to a distinct and possibly new human tribe". They call themselves "cosmopolitan nomads" and, due to their peripatetic experience they had as children, cannot imagine staying in one place. The sense of global belonging and global responsibility is strongly developed in these global young people, and many of them want their children to develop the same feelings.

Five years earlier, Carroll and Fennema (2002) did not appear very confident about the existence of a transnational business community. Their paper "Is There a Transnational Business Community?" sought to provide more evidence on the issue by analysing linkages between international corporate governance and networks of interlocking directorates. Responding to

Sklair's (2001) claim that TCC operates from a global perspective, Carroll and Fennema (2002) stated that Sklair (2001) had not been clear about whether members of TCC have disengaged from their national identities. To Carroll and Fennema (2002), Sklair had not answered the question raised by Therborn (2000) in his introduction to *International Sociology*, specifically devoted to globalisation: "Is the world a system shaping the actors in it and directing their strivings, or is it an arena, where actors who were formed outside act and perform?" (Therborn, 2000: 155).

Therefore, their research attempts to fill this gap and comes to the conclusion that "the transnational network is a kind of superstructure that rests upon rather resilient national bases" (Carroll and Fennema, 2002: 414). They also conclude that ". . . corporate governance still takes place predominantly within a national framework" and ". . . business communities are still predominantly organised along national lines" (Carroll and Fennema, 2002: 414), thus emphasising the still prevalent importance of the nation-state in the globalising world order. However, their research does not completely deny development of a transnational business community. The authors provide evidence in support of the argument that a transnational business community *is* in the making: They emphasise increased efficiency and connectivity of the international network. As for the issue of national embeddedness and the weight of national cultures in transnational operations, Carroll and Fennema (2002) stress that "The vast reach of today's Transnational Corporations (TNCs) and the increasingly integrated financial markets may be global, but the governance of corporations and the life of the *haute bourgeoisie* remain in important ways embedded in national and regional (including transatlantic) structures and cultures" (p. 415).

Carroll and Fennema's publication of 2002 initiated the academic debate "Exchanges on the Transnational Business Community" with Jeffrey Kentor and Yong Suk Jang, which was published in *International Sociology* during 2004–2006. Thus, Kentor and Jang (2004) disagree with the methodology employed by Carroll and Fennema (2002), stating that their disproportionate stratified sample of 176 corporations between 1976 and 1996 was inappropriate for the study of characteristics of the global economy in its entirety and is more suitable for research of subgroups within a population. Kentor and Jang's (2004) own research design was based on samples drawn from the Fortune Global 500 in 1983 and 1998, which ranks the world's 500 largest firms by revenues, irrespective of economic sector or activity (Kentor and Jang, 2004: 358).

Kentor and Jang (2004) found an increased number of both transnational and domestic linkages, which suggests that the global corporate structure has become substantially more integrated during the last two decades of the 20th century. This means that the individuals who control transnational corporations may indeed constitute a global capitalist class. Kentor and Jang (2004) also noted the absence of transnational linkages with Japanese and Korean firms that highlights a local way of doing business in those countries and therefore indicates the importance of cultural and national influences on business operations.

Further publications by the two groups of researchers offer a debate over methodological assumptions and choices (Carroll and Fennema, 2004; Kentor and Jang, 2006). As Kentor and Jang (2006) pointed out, different questions lead to different answers. What remains important, however, is that both studies have confirmed the increasing interconnection of transnational interlocking directorates, which in its turn acts as evidence of an emerging transnational capitalist class. Echoing Kentor and Jang (2006), different questions, different answers. Nevertheless, the emergence of the transnational capitalist class does not seem to be in doubt any longer. However, taking the issue further, the question arises: To what extent has the transnational business community developed as a sovereign social group?

Glenn Morgan (2001) examined the concept of transnational communities in the course of The Transnational Communities Programme funded by the ESRC and running during 1997–2003. The transnational community was defined as

> consisting of structured interactions between social actors located in more than one national setting; these structured interactions are based not on contracts or markets but on the recognition of a shared set of interests within a specific transnational social space, interests that are distinctive from nationally based interests.
>
> (Morgan, 2001: 117)

Studies on contemporary identity construction often engage the concept of transnationalism when considering identity formation in the context of globalisation and particularly global migration (Velayutham and Wise, 2005; Batnitzky *et al.*, 2008; Conway *et al.*, 2008; Green, 2008). Based on studies of diaspora, transnationalism can be defined as a process in which migrants or diasporic populations build a social field that links together their countries of origin and settlement (Zhou and Tseng, 2001: 132). Carrol and Fennema (2002) characterise the transnational network as "a kind of superstructure" that rests on rather resilient national bases (p. 414). Conway *et al.* (2008) observed in the literature on transnationalism that "cross-border" lives "transcend the spatial constraints of one nation-state and widen . . . political, economic and social affinities to more than one sovereignty or territory" (p. 377). In contrast, Robinson and Harris (2000) propose that a fully transnational capitalist class with its "organic composition, objective position and subjective constitution . . . [is] no longer tied to the nation state" (p. 14).

It does not necessarily consist of people sharing the same national or ethnic identity; rather, the bond bridging these people is built on shared professional activities and interests. Members of this community experience a cosmopolitan way of living, crossing national borders with ease, speaking at least two languages, working and socialising with people from different national and cultural backgrounds and feeling at home anywhere in the world.

Understanding Cosmopolitanism

According to Robin Holton (2002), the concept of cosmopolitanism has been subject to remarkable transformations in recent years. The term initially emerged as a derivative from the Greek "cosmos" (association between the world as a whole) and "politics" (government of the political community). Seen as a desirable form of universalism, cosmopolitanism became an important component in Enlightenment thought. Through its development over the last 200 years, the meaning and application of the term continued to evolve. Related to various slants of the social world, it became synonymous with the tone of a positive moral, projecting the ideals of a better, unified world community (Holton, 2002: 154). Referring to Bruce Robbins (1998), Holton acknowledges a significant shift from "old" to "new" cosmopolitanism that has taken place recently through a movement from "exclusively Western liberal-democratic notions of cosmopolitan universalism associated with sovereign rational actors able to transcend particularities of communal origins, to a plural set of transnational attachments and experiences emerging in a more diverse range of social settings", including Africa and Asia as well as Europe (Holton, 2002: 153). He, however, points out the limitations of the idea of the new cosmopolitanism, among which is the difficulty of distinguishing between varieties of transnational identity, as they can vary in their degree of openness and inclusivity.

Robert Fine (2007) asserts that cosmopolitanism "does not expect that in the era of global interconnections people will or should live without local, immediate, concrete or exclusive bonds" (p. 135). In his book *Cosmopolitanism*, he also affirms the importance of the life of the mind in any vision of cosmopolitan order (Fine, 2007: 115–132). From that perspective, analysis of the cosmopolitan character of the international business traveller and examination of the evolution of his/her national identity would appear incomplete without considering an understanding of the national identity phenomenon from a psychological perspective. As people's behaviour is often influenced by their personal understanding of themselves (including their national selves), it is important to acknowledge the working of the mind in shaping people's understanding of their identity and, consequently, their behaviour. Here, psychology, as the scientific study of behaviour (Martin *et al.*, 2010) appears very useful in providing additional insight into how identities are formed, what they derive from, what they are influenced by and how they are conceptualised. In order to provide that additional background to our understanding of identity construction, I introduce a discussion of the role of psychology in national identity debate. The material presented below is not exhaustive but provides an overview of the interrelation between national identity and social psychology in stimulating better understanding of interaction between the individual and group.

National Identity and Psychology

As it has been discussed above, national identity (nationality) is a concept usually surrounded by paradoxes, contradictions and vagueness (Cameron, 1999). It is also often used interchangeably with culture. This is understandable as there is certainly a common perception of national cultures attributed to a particular nation-state, for example British, Russian, American, French culture. However, nationality is not culture (Matsumoto, 2000), and, interestingly, the distinction between the two categories is reflected in the degree of attention attributed to them by psychologists. Lonner and Malpass (1994) point out a strong interest in psychological research in cultural influences on people's behaviour, whereas Reicher and Hopkins (2001) have noticed rather weak engagement of psychologists with national identity issues:

> For all the huge and burgeoning literature on nations and nationalism… psychology is frequently excluded from the family of disciplines that are invited to discuss the nature of national phenomena.
>
> (p. 1)

Nevertheless, if culture is seen as a major influence on human behaviour, and culture and national identity are closely intertwined, the question arises: What role does national identity play in shaping people's behaviour, and how can this knowledge be related to improvement of performance of international business organisations employing staff from different national backgrounds?

Psychology as a Branch of Science

Psychology, defined as "the scientific study of behaviour and its causes" (Smith *et al.*, 1986: 4), is a relatively new area of scientific activity. Officially, its birthday was marked by the establishment by Wilhelm Wundt in 1879 of a research facility at the University of Leipzig, Germany, to study scientifically the structure of the mind (Smith *et al.*, 1986). This is not to say that inquiries into the workings of the human mind had not been done before; philosophers had discussed "the mind" for thousands of years (Hardy Leahey, 1996). Wundt, however, for the first time in history, applied basic methods of scientific investigation to the study of mental processes (Gross, 2001). Thus, psychology is defined as the science of mental life, its phenomena and their conditions. The psychological phenomena are such things as human feelings, desires, cognition, reasoning, decisions and the like (James, 1890).

Psychology and National Identity in Academic Publications

Reicher and Hopkins in their *Self and Nation*, published in 2001, invite their readers to explore how social psychology and national phenomena cannot just answer some questions about each other but also mutually gain from an explicit consideration of each other. Acknowledging that "nations, nationalism and national identity are all around us" (Reicher and Hopkins, 2001: ix), the authors argue that multiple definitions of national identity, which can be found in the booming literature on nations, represent not only different theoretical positions but are also used to sustain different projects, both current and future-orientated. The authors focus their research on constructions and use of the Scottish national identity in order to demonstrate the different consequences of the different ways of defining Scotland. In other words, they aim to explain national identity as a process of *becoming* as well as *being*, thus revealing the dynamic of the relationship between the way "in which our self-understandings create the world and the way in which the world creates our self-understandings" (Reicher and Hopkins, 2001: ix).

The authors argue that people's awareness of a relationship between events and identities has profound emotional consequences. The nature of emotions is caused by the relationship that has been involved, e.g., the affirmation of an identity provokes joy, whereas an attack on identity spawns anger towards the offending agent (p. 221). Considering the implications of their conclusion and drawing on the discussion of the opposition between rationality and irrationality, Reicher and Hopkins (2001) point out that identity is neither rational, nor irrational but constitutes the core of people's rationality. They go on to say that "it (identity) defines what we value, it provides a model of the social world which allows us to plan how to get what we value" (p. 221). This explains why people have strong emotional reactions to events undermining our identities.

Reicher and Hopkins (2001) believe that the banality and the extremity of national identity should not be seen as opposing or competing with each other. Most of the time identities are taken for granted and stay unnoticed until particular events position our identities in question, suddenly placing them in the focus. The implications of the relationship between identity and events resulting in emotional consequences, identified and discussed by the authors, are important not only because they demonstrate close links between psychology and national identity, but also because of their applicability to group management. Awareness of implications of such relationships is a powerful tool for explaining human emotions, reactions and actions, but also for manipulating people's behaviour.

Self and Nation is an attempt to attract the closer attention of social psychologists to national identity. Back in 2001, Reicher and Hopkins pointed out that "students of psychology have ignored the nation" (p. 2). Has the situation changed since then? A computer search of psychology databases

(Psychology and Behavioural Sciences Collection, PsycINFO, PsycARTI-CLES, PsycBOOKS) conducted in February 2009 on articles on national identity showed only seven publications (four journal articles and three book reviews) still mirroring negligible interest in national identity as a prime focus of study in psychological research. This is not to say that issues of identity are totally neglected. They do appear in the academic literature as dependent or independent variables in plentiful numbers (e.g., Oakes, 2002; Davies *et al*, 2008; Papadopoulos, 2008; Wakslak *et al.*, 2008); however, national identity still rarely appears as the main topic of interest in psychology.

Those journal papers published after 2001 that do place their focus on national identity address the issue from different perspectives: category construction and construction of place (Abell *et al.*, 2006; Wallwork and Dixon, 2004), nation- and democracy building (Eaton, 2002) and basis for conflicts (Muldoon *et al.*, 2007). Liberty Eaton (2002), reiterating Reicher and Hopkins (2001), acknowledges the scarcity of national identity research by social psychologists and aims to encourage local social psychologists "to take a renewed interest in national identification processes" (p. 45).

All these publications, however different in their approaches to identity, explore the issue within a certain political arena. Wallwork and Dixon (2004), for example, view the British rural landscape as a rhetorical construction which is invoked for influencing social relations. The rhetoric of common characteristics becomes particularly important in the process of mass mobilisation, helping to unite disparate populations under a common identity. Landscapes, according to Wallwork and Dixon (2004), illustrate their role as a powerful signifier of national identity which designates a common orientation or rootedness in place (Wallwork and Dixon, 2004). Everyday discourse facilitates the tighter connection between identities and "qualities" of places, making "social categories such as 'nation' become imaginable" (p. 36).

Echoing Wallwork and Dixon (2004), Abell *et al.* (2006) design their research in the context of the British political environment. They use the image of Britain as "an island" in order to investigate the constructions of citizenship and national identity. Through the analysis of interviews conducted in Scotland and England, their research shows that recognition of application of territorial references to social categorical representation ("people like us") (Abell *et al.*, 2006: 223) may contribute to "our understanding of the general phenomenon of stereotype suppression" and also "expand the remit of current social psychological work on the 'flexibility' of social categorical representation" (p. 223). Evaluating the role of the "cultural dimension" in political psychology advocated by Haste (2004), the authors' analysis of very different orientations displayed by people in England and Scotland, and those who moved from England to Scotland, concludes that concepts of "culture" and "nation-state" cannot be easily equated. While adopting a "cultural" approach to psychological research, it should not be assumed that "cultures will present themselves as conveniently pre-packaged in ways that correspond exactly with the territorial boundaries of extant polities" (p. 224).

Another "territorial" study was conducted by Muldoon *et al.* (2007). In their article "Religious and National Identity after the Belfast Good Friday Agreement" published in *Political Psychology*, the authors focus on two dimensions of collective identity, namely religion and nationality, with a view to attending "to content and processes that underlie collective identity self-categorisation in Northern Ireland after the Belfast Good Friday Agreement" (p. 92). The paper builds upon two studies: The first one comprises in-depth qualitative interviews with nine adult participants across three generations (grandparents, parents and young adults) from the border region of Northern Ireland and 14 interviewees from mixed Protestant-Catholic marriages. The second study analyses 115 essays written by boys and girls aged between 13 and 17 from both urban and rural areas and from both Catholic and Protestant backgrounds.

Both studies demonstrate a significant importance of national identity, however interviews with adults (study 1) also drew emphasis on religion in their identity construction. Often, the identification process is associated with political conflict and largely identities "continue to be structured as oppositional and negatively interdependent" (p. 101). The authors point to the overlap between national and religious identities, especially among young respondents, and also notice extensive political and strategic use of identity in adults' discourse. Drawing attention to the interrelation between identities, conflict and structural and institutional division in Northern Ireland, the paper concludes that "the post-Agreement landscape would be better served by reducing the influence of the political, national, religious, and historical structures that divide Northern Ireland" (Muldoon *et al.*, 2007: 101). Thus, identity is seen as an influential force in policy-making and nation-building.

Liberty Eaton (2002) echoes this view on identity as an issue of practical social importance. Her paper "South-African National Identity: A Research Agenda for Social Psychologists" advocates a renewed interest in national identity research among psychologists in South Africa (approaching the subject once again from the nation-state perspective). Sadly, neglected by social psychologists of her country, national identity, according to Eaton, should receive revived attention in South African social psychology. Apart from having "intrinsic academic interest", it is also seen as able to offer valuable practical knowledge contributing to "the establishment of 'national legitimacy' and stable democracy" (Eaton, 2002: 52). Eaton argues that knowledge on how people construct their national identity and broader political community can be an invaluable addendum in influencing government policy and constructing "healthy democracy" (Eaton, 2002: 101).

As evidenced from the literature reviewed above, national identity (or nationality) is an important complex social category. Analysis of its construction and use, approached from different slants, generates creative intrinsic research that contributes to the existing academic knowledge on the subject and also encourages its practical impact on political processes. It can be argued that similar influence of psychological knowledge on national identity can be translated onto other areas of social life. For example, strategic planning in large organisations can only benefit from better understanding of employees' behaviour, decision-making, reasoning and emotions through social psychological explanations of how national identities are constructed and how they influence people's cognition and actions.

The analysis of the psychological inquiry on national identity reveals some significant observations. Firstly, it is important to distinguish culture from national identity (nationality). Although the two categories have common grounds and are often intertwined and observed within the same national boundaries, they are not the same. This is particularly important in the era of globalisation, characterised by an increased flow of goods, information and, more importantly, people around the globe. The "melting pot" of contemporary multinational society accommodates a plurality of cultures within a nation-state; however, this by no means should suggest that identification with a particular state necessarily implies full adoption of its dominant culture.

Secondly, identity is at the core of our rationality: It shapes our values and behaviour. Therefore, the ability of psychologists to provide explanations for people's motivations and actions is a valuable asset for effective group management. Findings of psychological research can be practically applied in day-to-day people management in various types of organisations of different sizes. As demonstrated by Wallwork and Dixon (2004) and Abell *et al.* (2006), stimulation of stronger ties with a particular place (group or organisation) could be carried out through knowledgeable employment of language and images as constructs, reinforcing people's need for belonging and attachment.

Thirdly, national identity is recognised as a powerful force in policy making and nation-building. This role of national identity could become critical in attempts to formulate new managerial initiatives in multinational organisations at the time of their strategic change, where the unity of organisations, comprising employees from various national backgrounds, could be strengthened by "downplaying" national differences and encouraging the creation of reinforced organisational identity. As Dimitris Papadopoulos (2008) argues, understanding individuality "is not simply a theoretical construction but an active constructive force of our social reality" (p. 140). Thus, psychology as science with its very core rooted in understanding of individuality comes to the fore (Danziger, 1997).

Thus, national identity, already an important and complex social category, is becoming even more multidimensional, more fluid and more malleable in the context of globalisation. Recognisably different from cultural identity, it lies at the core of our rationality and helps us form and govern our values and actions. As such, national identity is seen as strongly related to practical concerns of constructing communities and influencing policies. That certainly applies to the contemporary business world, which, during the 1990s, went through a period of accelerated change due to the wave of takeovers and restructuring. Extensive international business travel is the result of those changes that enforces the development of the business travel industry (Callan and Kyndt, 2001) and facilitates formation of transnational networks of business professionals (Rauch, 2001).

Identifying the Question

This overview of the academic debates on national identity, globalisation, cosmopolitanism and the role of psychology in studying national identity presented above leads us to conclude that national identity is a complex, fluid and elusive concept that becomes even more multifaceted and more ambiguous in the era of intensive global development, characterised by cosmopolitanisation of people's views, attitudes and behaviours. Understanding the dynamics of national identity in people's perception of their self can be a useful instrument in grasping social reality at the beginning of the 21st century. A more specific look at how national identities are constructed and understood by international business travellers can shed more light on international business travel which, despite being a necessity of today's global economy (Espino *et al.*, 2002), is recognised as having not attracted sufficient academic interest (Beaverstock *et al.*, 2009; Welch *et al.*, 2007).

Beaverstock *et al.* (2009) call for detailed empirical analysis (either quantitative or qualitative) that would contribute to our understanding of the business travel's "agency in the world of work and [its] impacts on economic development, individuals, household and the environment" (p. 193) that extends beyond business functionalities. Similarly, Per Gustafson (2009) emphasises the need for further sociological investigation of local and cosmopolitan orientations of frequent business travellers, while Glenn Morgan (2001) encourages further academic enquiries into "the degree to which a sense of being transnational communities, distinctive from their national origins, permeates their work practices and sense of identity" (p. 126–127).

This book, aiming to contribute to a better understanding of social processes in the global age, is a response to the academic concerns identified above. It stems from the view that globalisation affects people's understanding of their national self in two opposing directions. On the one hand, people are becoming more international, while on the other, they are reaffirming their national belonging. In order to test this hypothesis, the book seeks to explore how the national identities of British and Russian business travellers are being understood and constructed and how globalisation influences businesspeople's perceptions of their national belonging. Thus, it attempts to provide an answer to the question whether national identities are being eroded in the global business environment and what role globalisation plays in shaping the national identities of international businesspeople.

References

Abell, J., Condor, S. and Stevenson, C. (2006) "We Are an Island": Geographical Imagery in Accounts of Citizenship, Civil Society, and National Identity in Scotland and England. *Political Psychology*, 27 (2), pp. 207–226.

Adler, N.J. and Bartholomew, S. (1992b) Academic and Professional Communities in Discourse: Generating Knowledge on Transnational Human Resource Management. *Journal of International Business Studies*, 23 (3), pp. 551–569.

Anderson, B. (1998) *Imagined Communities: Reflections on the Origin and Spread of Nationalism*. London: Verso *The Bank for Russian Trade Review* (1928) March 1928. Volume 1(5). London.

Batnitzky, A., McDowell, L. and Dyer, L. (2008) A Middle-Class Global Mobility? The Working Lives of Indian Men in a West London Hotel. *Global Networks*, 8 (1), pp. 51–70.

Bauman, Z. (2005) *Liquid Life*. Cambridge: Polity Press.

Baylis, J. and Smith, S. (2006) *The Globalisation of World Politics* (3rd Ed). New York: Oxford University Press Inc.

Beaverstock, J.V., Derudder, B., Faulconbridge, J. and Witlox, F. (2009) International Business Travel: Some Explorations. *Geografiska Annaler: Series B, Human Geography*, 91 (3), pp. 193–202.

Bechhofer, F. and McCrone, D. (2010) Choosing National Identity. *Sociological Research Online*, 15 (3), p. 3. Available at: http://socresonline.org.uk/15/3/3.html.

Beck, U. (2006) *Cosmopolitan Vision*. Cambridge: Polity Press.

Bloom, W. (1990) *Personal Identity, National Identity and International Relations*. Cambridge: The Press Syndicate of the University of Cambridge.

Bourdieu, P. (1994) *Zur Soziologie der Symbolischen Formen* (5th Ed). Cited in Wodak, R., De Cillia, R., Reisigl, M. and Liebhart, K. (1999) *The Discursive Construction of National Identity*. Edinburgh: Edinburgh University Press Ltd.

Brubaker, R. and Cooper, F. (2000) Beyond "Identity". *Theory and Society*, 29 (1), pp. 1–47.

Byrne, B. (2007) England—Whose England? Narratives of Nostalgia, Emptiness and Evasion in Imaginations of National Identity. *The Sociological Review*, 55 (3), pp. 510–530.

Callan, R.J. and Kyndt, G. (2001) Business Travellers' Perception of Service Quality: A Prefatory Study of Two European City Centre Hotels. *International Journal of Tourism Research*, 3, pp. 313–323.

Cameron, K. (ed.) (1999) *National Identity*. Exeter: Intellect Books.

Carroll, W.K. and Carson, C. (2003) The Network of Global Corporations and Elite Policy Groups: A Structure for Transnational Capitalist Class Formation? *Global Networks*, 3 (1), pp. 29–57.

Carroll, W.K. and Fennema, M. (2002) Is There a Transnational Business Community? *International Sociology*, 17, pp. 393–419.

Carroll, W.K. and Fennema, M. (2004) Problems in the Study of the Transnational Business Community: A Reply to Kentor and Jang. *International Sociology*, 19, pp. 369–378.

Clampin, F. (1999) Those Blue Remembered Hills . . . National Identity in English Music (1900–1930). Cited in Cameron, K. (ed.) *National Identity*. Exeter: Intellect Books.

Cohen, A.P. (1986) *Symbolising Boundaries: Identity and Diversity in British Cultures.* Manchester: Manchester University Press.

Colley, L. (1992) Britishness and Otherness: An Argument. *The Journal of British Studies*, 31 (4), pp. 309–329.

Colls, R. (2002) *Identity of England.* New York: Oxford University Press.

Conway, D., Potter, R.B. and Bernard, G.S. (2008) Dual Citizenship or Dual Identity? Does "Transnationalism" Supplant "Nationalism" among Returning Trinidadians? *Global Networks*, 8 (4), pp. 373–397.

Cox, T.H. (1993) *Cultural Diversity in Organizations: Theory, Research and Practice.* San Francisco: Berret-Koehler.

Danziger, K. (1997) *Naming the Mind: How Psychology Found Its Language.* London: Sage.

Davies, P.G., Steele, C.M. and Markus, H.R. (2008) A Nation Challenged: The Impact of Foreign Threat on America's Tolerance for Diversity. *Journal of Personality and Social Psychology*, 95 (2), pp. 308–318.

Dicken, P. (2003) *Global Shift: Reshaping the Global Economic Map in the 21st Century.* London: Sage Publications Ltd.

Dijkink, G. (1996) *National Identity and Geopolitical Visions: Maps of Pride and Pain.* London: Routledge.

Eaton, L. (2002) South African National Identity: A Research Agenda for Social Psychologists. *South African Journal of Psychology*, 32 (1) pp. 45–53.

The Economist (2008) Billion Dollar Babies. *The Economist*, April 26, 2008.

Eisenstadt, S.N. and Giesen, B. (1995) The Construction of Collective Identity. *Archives Europeennes de Sociologie*, XXXVI, pp. 72–102.

Espino, C.M., Sundstrom, S.M., Frick, H.L. and Peters, M. (2002) International Business Travel: Impact on Families and Travellers. *Occupational and Environmental Medicine*, 59, pp. 309–322.

Fine, R. (2007) *Cosmopolitanism.* London: Routledge.

Finkielkraut, A. (1987) *La Defaite de la Pensee.* Paris: Gallimard. Cited in Peters, B. (2002) A New Look at "National Identity". *Archives Europeennes de Sociologie*, XLIII, pp. I3–32.

Freeland, C. (2007) The No-Nation Generation. *Financial Times*, October 27/28, 2007. The Economist (2008) Billion Dollar Babies. *The Economist*, April 26, 2008.

Gleason, P. (1983) Identifying Identity: A Semantic History. *Journal of American History*, 69, pp. 910–931.

Goffman, E. (1990) *Stigma: Notes on the Management of Spoiled Identity.* Harmondsworth. Cited in Wodak, R., De Cillia, R., Reisigl, M. and Liebhart, K. (1999) *The Discursive Construction of National Identity.* Edinburgh: Edinburgh University Press Ltd.

Green, P. (2008) Family and Nation: Brazilian National Ideology as Contested Transnational Practice in Japan. *Global Networks*, 8 (4), pp. 418–435.

Gross, R. (2001) *Psychology: The Science of Mind and Behaviour* (4th Ed). London: Hodder Headline plc.

The Guardian (2010) *Englishness: The Forbidden Identity.* Available at: www.guardian.co.uk/commentisfree/2010/feb/11/english-nationalism-fight.

Gustafson, P. (2009) More Cosmopolitan, No Less Local. *European Societies*, 11 (1), pp. 25–47.

Hall, S. (1996a) *The Question of Cultural Identity*. Cited in Hall, S., Held, D., Hubert, D. and Thompson, K. (eds.) *Modernity: An Introduction to Modern Societies*. Cambridge, MA. New Look at "National Identity". *Archives Europeennes de Sociologie*, XLIII, pp. I3–32.

Hall, S. (1996b) Introduction: Who Needs "Identity"? In Hall, S. and Du Gay, P. (eds.) *Questions of Cultural Identity*. London: Thousand Oaks and New Delhi.

Hannerz, U. (1996) *Transnational Connections: Culture, People, Places*. London: Routledge.

Hardy Leahey, T. (1996) *A History of Psychology. Main Currents in Psychological Thought* (4th Ed). New Jersey: Prentice-Hall, Inc.

Haste, H. (2004) Constructing the Citizen. *Political Psychology*, 25, pp. 413–439.

Hetherington, K. (1998) *Expressions of Identity: Space, Performance, Politics*. London: Sage Publications.

Holton, R. (2002) Cosmopolitanism or Cosmopolitanisms? The Universal Races Congress of 1911. *Global Networks*, 2 (2), pp. 153–170.

Holzinger, W. (1993) *Identitat als sozialwissenschaftliches Konstrukt*.

Hopkins, N. and Moore, C. (2001) Categorising the Neighbours: Identity, Distance, and Stereotyping. *Social Psychology Quarterly*, 64 (3), pp. 239–252.

James, W. (1890) *The Principles of Psychology*. New York: Henry Holt & Company. Cited in Gross, R. (2001) *Psychology: The Science of Mind and Behaviour*. London: Hodder Headline plc.

Kellner, D. (2002) Theorizing Globalisation. *Sociological Theory*, 20 (3), pp. 285–305.

Kennedy, P. (2005) Joining, Constructing and Benefiting from the Global Workplace: Transnational Professionals in the Building-Design Industry. *The Sociological Review*, 53 (1), pp. 172–197.

Kennedy, P. and Danks, C.J. (eds.) (2001) *Globalisation and National Identities: Crisis or Opportunity?* Basingstoke: Palgrave.

Kentor, J. and Jang, Y.S. (2004) Yes, There Is a (Growing) Transnational Business Community: A Study of Global Interlocking Directorates 1983–98. *International Sociology*, 19 (3), pp. 355–368.

Kentor, J. and Jang, Y.S. (2006) Different Questions, Different Answers: A Rejoinder to Carroll and Fennema. *International Sociology*, 21, pp. 602–606.

Kumar, K. (2003) *The Making of English National Identity*. Cambridge: Cambridge University.

Lonner, W.J. and Malpass, R.S. (1994) *Psychology and Culture*. London: Allyn and Bacon.

Mandler, P. (2006) What Is "National Identity"? Definitions and Applications in Modern British Historiography. *Modern Intellectual History*, 3 (2), pp. 271–297.

Mansbach, R. and Rhodes, E. (2007) The National State and Identity Politics: State Institutionalisation and "Markers" of National Identity. *Geopolitics*, 12 (3), pp. 426–458.

Martin, G.N., Carlson, N.R. and Buskist, W. (eds.) (2010) *Psychology* (4th Ed). Harlow: Pearson Education Limited.

Martin, D., Metzger, J-L. and Pierre, P. (2006) The Sociology of Globalisation: Theoretical and Methodological Reflections. *International Sociology*, 21, pp. 499–521.

Matsumoto, D. (2000) *Culture and Psychology. People around the World* London: Thomson Learning.

Mauss, M. (1997) *Sociologie et Anhtropologie*. Paris: PUF. (Orig. pub. 1950) Cited in Martin, D., Metzger, J-L. and Pierre, P. (2006) The Sociology of Globalisation: Theoretical and Methodological Reflections. *International Sociology*, 21, pp. 499–521.

Mayers, K. (2005) *North-East Passage to Muscovy: Stephen Borough and the First Tudor Explorations.* Stroud: Sutton.

McCrone, D. and Bechhofer, F. (2008) National Identity and Social Inclusion. *Ethnic and Racial Studies*, 31 (7), pp. 1245–1266.

Morgan, G. (2001) Transnational Communities and Business Systems. *Global Networks*, 1 (2), pp. 113–130.

Morris, J. (2005) The Empire Strikes Back: Projections of National Identity in Contemporary Russian Advertising. *The Russian Review*, 64, pp. 642–660.

Muldoon, O.T., Trew, K., Todd, J., Rougier, N. and McLaughlin, K. (2007) Religious and National Identity after the Belfast Good Friday Agreement. *Political Psychology*, 28 (1), pp. 889–103.

Munck, R. (2002) Globalisation and Democracy: A New "Great Transformation"? *ANNALS of the American Academy of Political and Social Sciences*, 581.

Oakes, P. (2002) Psychological Groups and Political Psychology: A Response to Huddy's "Critical Examination of Social Identity Theory". *Political Psychology*, 23 (4), pp. 809–824.

Papadopoulos, D. (2008) In the Ruins of Representation: Identity, Individuality, Subjectification. *British Journal of Social Psychology*, 47 (1), pp. 139–165.

Parekh, B.C. (2000) *The Future of Multi-Ethnic Britain: Report of the Commission on the Future of Multi-Ethnic Britain.* London: Profile Books.

Peters, B. (2002) A New Look at "National Identity". *Archives Europeennes de Sociologie*, XLIII, pp. I3–32. *Psychology Quarterly*, 63, pp. 284–297.

Popescu, C. (2006) Space, Time: Identity. *National Identities*, 8 (3), pp. 189–206.

Rauch, J.E. (2001) Business and Social Networks in International Trade. *Journal of Economic Literature*, 39 (4), pp. 1177–1203.

Reicher, S. and Hopkins, N. (2001) *Self and Nation.* London: Sage Publications Ltd.

Ricoeur, P. (1992) *Oneself as Another.* Chicago: University of Chicago Press.

Robbins, B. (1998) Actually Existing Cosmopolitanism. Cited in P. Cheah and B. Robbins (eds.) *Cosmopolitics: Thinking and Feeling Beyond the Nation.* Minneapolis: University of Minnesota Press.

Robertson, R. (1990) Mapping the Global Condition. Cited in Featherstone, M. *Global Culture.* Also published in *Theory, Culture and Society*, 7, pp. 15–30.

Robinson, W.I. and Harris, J. (2000) Towards a Global Ruling Class? Globalization and the Transnational Capitalist Class. *Science and Society*, 64 (1), pp. 11–54.

Rose, S. (2003) *Which People's War? National Identity and Citizenship in Wartime Britain 1939–1945.* Oxford: Oxford University Press.

Rothkopf, D. (2008) *The Superclass: The Global Power Elite and the World They Are Making.* London: Little, Brown.

Savage, M., Wright, D. and Gayo-Cal, M. (2010) Cosmopolitan Nationalism and the Cultural Reach of the White British. *Nations and Nationalism*, 16 (4), pp. 598–615.

Schlesinger, P. (2007) A Cosmopolitan Temptation. *European Journal of Communication*, 22, pp. 413–426.

Schnapper, D. (1991) *La France de l'integration: Sociologie de la Nation en 1990.* Paris: Editions Gallimard. Cited in Peters, B. (2002) A New Look at "National Identity". *Archives Europeennes de Sociologie*, XLIII, pp. I3–32.

Schnapper, D. (1995) The Idea of Nation. *Qualitative Sociology*, 18, pp. 177–187.

Scholte, J.A. (2005) *Globalisation (2nd Ed). A Critical Introduction.* Basingstoke: Palgrave.

Skey, M. (2010) 'A Sense of Where You Belong in the World': National Belonging, Ontological Security and the Status of the Ethnic Majority in England. *Nations and Nationalism*, 16 (4), pp. 715–733.

Sklair, L. (2001) *The Transnational Capitalist Class*. Oxford: Blackwell.

Smith, A.D. (1991) *National Identity*. London: Penguin Books.

Smith, A.D. (1995) *Nations and Nationalism in the Global Era*. Cambridge: Polity Press.

Smith, M. and Kollock, P. (eds.) (1999) *Communities in Cyberspace*. London: Routledge. *South African Journal of Psychology*, 32 (1), pp. 45–53.

Smith, R.E., Sarason, I.G. and Sarason, B.R. (1986) *Psychology. The Frontiers of Behaviour*. New York: Harper & Row Publishers.

Stone, D.L. and Stone-Romero, E.F. (2008) *The Influence of Culture on Human Resource Management Processes and Practices*. New York: Taylor and Francis Group, LLC.

Stone Sweet, A. (2006) The New *Lex Mercatoria* and Transnational Governance. *Journal of European Public Policy*, 1 (5), pp. 627–646.

Stone-Romero, E.F. and Stone, D.L. (2007) Cognitive, Affective and Cultural Influences on Stigmatization and Its Impact on Human Resource Management Processes and Practices. *Research in Personnel and Human Resource Management*, 26, pp. 117–167.

Stone-Romero, E.F., Stone, D.L. and Salas, E. (2003) The Influence of Culture on Role Conceptions and Role Behaviour in Organizations. *Applied Psychology: An International Review*, 52, pp. 328–362.

Stryker, S. and Burke, P.J. (2000) The Past, Present, and Future of an Identity Theory. *Social Psychology Quarterly*, 63, pp. 284–297.

Tajfel, H. (1982) *Social Identity and Intergroup Relations*. Cambridge: Cambridge University Press.

Theoretische Grundlagen und Forschungsfragen. Unpublished Manuscript. Cited in Wodak, R., De Cillia, R., Reisigl, M. and Liebhart, K. (1999) *The Discursive Construction of National Identity*. Edinburgh: Edinburgh University Press Ltd.

Therborne, G. (2000) Globalisation. *International Sociology*, 15 (2), pp. 151–179.

Velayutham, S. and Wise, A. (2005) Moral Economies of a Translocal Village: Obligation and Shame Among South Indian Transnational Migrants. *Global Networks*, 5 (1), pp. 27–47.

Wakslak, C.J., Nussbaum, S., Liberman, N. and Trope, Y. (2008) Presentations of the Self in the Near and Distant Future. *Journal of Personality and Social Psychology*, 95 (4), pp. 757–773.

Wallwork, J. and Dixon, J.A. (2004) Foxes, Green Fields and Britishness: On the Rhetorical Construction of Place and National Identity. *British Journal of Social Psychology*, 43, pp. 21–39.

Weight, R. (2003) *Patriots: National Identity in Britain 1940–2000*. London: Pan.

Welch, D.E., Welch, L.S. and Worm, V. (2007) The International Business Traveller: A Neglected but Strategic Human Resource. *The International Journal of Human Resource Management*, 18 (2), pp. 173–183.

Wodak, R., De Cillia, R., Reisigl, M. and Liebhart, K. (1999) *The Discursive Construction of National Identity*. Edinburgh: Edinburgh University Press Ltd.

Zhou, Y. and Tseng, Y-F. (2001) Regrounding the "Ungrounded Empires": Localisation as the Geographical Catalyst for Transnationalism. *Global Networks*, 1 (2), pp. 131–153.

3   The International Business Traveller

Part One
The International Business Traveller

The idea of national identity erosion that concerns this book presupposes a potential shift from nation-bounded thinking to a cosmopolitan understanding of self. The goal is to interrogate major transformations in the perception of one's national identity and to provide insights into the degree of shift (if confirmed) from association with the national to belonging to the global. Global business travellers represent the section of world society that perhaps is exposed to boundary-less living more than any other social group. Trotting the globe with business profits in mind, they are on a voyage into new realms of thought and experience. Leaving safe and secure attachments of the habitual and established behind, they embark on an exciting and exhilarating engagement with new experiences through exposing themselves to the post-modern world with its "new technologies, novel forms of culture and experience, and striking economic, social, and political transformations [that] constitute a decisive rupture with previous ways of life, bringing to an end the modern era" (Best and Kellner, 1997: viii).

Here, global business travellers are seen as highly mobile cosmopolitan people open to those "other" peoples, places and cultures that they encounter during their journeys (Szerszynski and Urry, 2002: 468–471). They are agents of a new type of social formation characterised by the increasingly disorganised order of capitalism, the fragmentation of class allegiances, the growth of a culture of consumerism, the development of lifestyle politics and the impact of globalisation on nation-states and national economies (Owen, 1997: 14–15). Zygmunt Bauman (1992) admits that this new social formation is hard to narrate. It is not easy to bring order into a semantically-loaded yet confused space, which means different things to different people. The post-modern world is a state of mind demolishing and destructive of the establishments and structures of modernity, yet constructive in its uncovering the truth and self-reflexive effort (Bauman, 1992: vii–xxviii).

It is through the lens of this world, with its "fullness of moral choice and responsibility" and, at the same time, with scarceness of self-confidence and spread of fear, that this book approaches the issue of national identity erosion among global business travellers. These people are seen as the agents of postmodernity, who Perry Glasser (1999: 46) perceives as "stateless and unbounded by anything as mundane as territory". Certainly some of them can be associated with those postmodern minds "who have the habit (or is it a compulsion?) to reflect upon themselves, to search their own contents and report what they found: the state of mind of philosophers, social thinkers, artists—all those people on whom we rely when we are in a pensive mood or just pause for a moment to find out whence we are moving or being moved" (Bauman, 1992: vii).

The existing body of research on the transnational business community and international business travellers has addressed the issue using both qualitative (Sklair, 2001; Welch *et al.*, 2007; Gustafson, 2009) and quantitative research traditions (Carroll and Fennema, 2002; Carroll and Fennema, 2004; Kentor and Jang, 2004; Kentor and Jang, 2006). This book aims to contribute to the knowledge already generated in the field and chooses to do so within the qualitative tradition. It seeks to explore *how* global business travellers understand their national identity, what changes are taking place in their sense of belonging to their nation state and whether the feelings of attachment are being weakened or, on the contrary, reinforced. Thus, this book is looking into the businesspeople's personal understanding of their own identity which is being constructed through their global business operations, social lives and lived experiences of problems and concerns that happen on a day-to-day basis. The book attempts to access these "embedded" processes by focusing on the context of people's everyday lives (Barbour, 2008: 13).

The focus of the book is on perception of self by the global business travellers, a much "hidden" internal vision of oneself. Personal insights do not provide any explanation of the social world and cannot be easily categorised. Thus, the value of the book is in contributing to our understanding of the social world through detailed descriptions and evaluation of the day-to-day reality of the international business travel by business travellers themselves.

In seeking to understand how the perception of national self of international businesspeople is evolving in the contemporary global environment, the book adopts a comparative approach based on two countries, Russia and Great Britain, in order to clarify whether one nation is more open to change than another. The common constant is the state structure in which the business travellers reside. Both Russia and the United Kingdom are multinational countries with one dominant nation whose language is adopted as a national language of the state. Both countries practice a system of devolved administration, e.g., Scotland in the UK and Tatarstan in Russia. Both are seen as influential players in the global political arena as demonstrated, for example, by their membership of the Security Council of the United National Organisation.

At the same time, these countries are significantly dissimilar regarding their cultural heritage, originating from Slavonic descent in case of Russia and Anglo-Saxon in case of Britain. These nations' official languages belong to different language groups. For the majority of the 20th century, Russia was governed by the Communist Party, advocating principles of communist economic development and ideology, whereas the United Kingdom operates according to the values of a free democracy, although it remains a Constitutional Monarchy.

The comparative design of the book fulfils a desire to understand better the international business traveller by comparing people from two distinct national backgrounds and to make generalisations about their degree of detachment from their national roots. Comparative analysis assists with understanding whether this process affects both Russian and British people in the same way and whether cultural differences leave a mark on people from divergent national backgrounds and therefore affect their advancement on the way of assimilation with the global.

By comparing Russian and British people's attitude towards their national identity and their views on the emergence of the transnational global nation, the book seeks to isolate certain factors that would indicate any patterns in the attitude towards the business travellers' original national belonging and to draw parallels between similarity and dissonance in identity construction and national attachment between the Russians and the British. Thus, through insight into these aspects of understanding the self, the book contributes to a broader picture of globalisation and assesses the power of its influence on the contemporary businessperson.

International business travellers who have contributed to this book through sharing their experiences occupy a range of positions: support and engineering staff, lower-level managers, middle-managers, higher-middle and senior professionals. The book is informed by 20 semi-structured interviews with business travellers who reside in the south of England, 20 in Russia and 20 in Scotland.

The International Business Traveller

Existing definitions of the international business traveller highlight the unique peculiarity of this social group centred on its members' professional activity and, in particular, travelling abroad with the purpose of conducting their business. The function of business travel defined by Aguilera (2008: 1109–1110) as "work-related travel to an irregular place of work (for example: to visit a client, participate in a conference or attend a meeting)" clearly explains the purpose of this business activity. Thus, those who travel with business profits in mind (i.e. international business travellers) are the "persons for whom a part—generally a major part—of their role involves international visits to foreign markets, units, projects and the like" (Welch *et al.*, 2007: 174). This definition closely echoes Beioley's (1991) understanding of the business traveller as an "overseas or domestic traveller who stays overnight away from home for the purpose of conducting business" (p. 1). Analysing characteristics of frequent business travellers,

Per Gustafson (2009) highlights over-representation of "male high-income earners, especially managers, professionals and entrepreneurs" (p. 42) in international work-related travel. The creation of the global traveller's portrait can be complemented by the range of skills expected to be seen in a transnational manager:

> . . . transnationally competent managers require a broader range of skills than traditional international managers. First, transnational managers must understand the worldwide business environment from a global perspective. Unlike expatriates of the past, transnational managers are not focused on a single country nor limited to managing relationships between headquarters and a single foreign subsidiary. Second, transnational managers must learn about many foreign cultures' perspectives, tastes, trends, technologies, and approaches to conducting business. Unlike their predecessors, they do not they do not focus on becoming an expert on one particular culture. Third, transnational managers must be skilful at working with people from many cultures simultaneously. They no longer have the luxury of dealing with each country's issues on a separate, and therefore sequential, basis. Fourth, similar to prior expatriates, transnational managers must be able to adapt to living in other cultures. Yet, unlike their predecessors, transnational managers need cross- cultural skills on a daily basis, throughout their career, not just during foreign assignments, but also on regular multicountry business trips and in daily interaction with foreign colleagues and clients worldwide. Fifth, transnational managers interact with foreign colleagues as equals, rather than from within clearly defined hierarchies of structural or cultural dominance and subordination.
>
> (Adler and Bartholomew, 1992a: 53)

The findings of the study that inform the book are a contribution to the image of the international business traveller presented above.

Age

Out of 60 people interviewed, four were in their twenties, nine people were in their thirties, 24 were in their forties, 17 were in their fifties, five were in their sixties and one was in his seventies.

It was observed that the majority (40 per cent) of the global travellers interviewed were in their forties. Neugarten *et al.* (1965) in their findings on age-related characteristics distinguish this age as the middle-age when most men/women hold their top jobs and when a man has the most responsibilities. At this age, a man/woman accomplishes most and is seen as at the prime of life (Neugarten *et al.*, 1965). This is the age of professional maturity when skills and knowledge obtained through education are further developed through practice and experience. Interviewees in this age group commented on gaining satisfaction from their professional activities and clearly stated that international business travel, and particularly the experience of living abroad, is an enjoyable experience which they found life-enriching and influencing their personal development:

> I lived abroad in various countries around the world for 1–2 years in each country: Kuwait, Libya, Norway, Azerbaijan, Dubai. All of them but Kuwait were great. I met great people, although sometimes I was misunderstood. I personally did not find it difficult living in foreign countries because if you treated people fairly and responsibly, you could always get along with people. Azerbaijan is still very much a blame culture and finger point but if you treat people nicely and with respect you can always get along with them.
>
> (E8)

The next largest age group was composed of those in their fifties, representing a smaller section (17 people or 28 per cent) of the total number of the respondents. International travel for some of them remained an enjoyable experience that had become ingrained in their life:

> If I had a contract to go and work in Spain for a year—I'd love it! Once you have had an experience of living in another country, you get a buzz from that experience, from that change. And travel is easy. You have got email, cameras. . . . It is a big world to explore.
>
> (E17)

Some others noticed a decline of the intensity of their international travel:

> I enjoy visiting my customers although now I do not do it as much as I used to.
>
> (E3)

Respondent S10 felt really relieved to have stopped travelling not long before the interview took place. Life without business travel had opened up an opportunity to focus on starting his own business and, more importantly, had influenced positively the state of his health:

> Having travelled for 12 years and intensively for the last 5 years, I am really relieved to have stopped travelling. Travelling does take a lot out of your life, you do not realise. . . . Since I stopped travelling I was so well, it is incredible.
>
> (S10)

The next group according to the number of interviewees (nine people) represented 15 per cent of the sample. These were people in their thirties. For two respondents from this group, it was always their ambition to work internationally:

> For me, for what I do now it was not necessarily structured and it was not something that I planned to get into. But in terms of working internationally it is something I always wanted to do. After I left school I spent first two years travelling around Europe. I went to France, I wanted to develop and learn and get to a fluent level. For me it was always a mindset of working, living, travelling outside the UK.
>
> (S13)

For two other respondents (E4 and R2), their education influenced their future career paths, with R2 being educated abroad and in the UK, and E4 studying for a degree in foreign languages at university. Three remaining people from this age group just happened to find themselves in their international roles.

The sixties age group (eight per cent of interviewees) was represented by five people, with three of them still being in full employment and two individuals who had retired but were still leading an active international lifestyle. International business travel for respondent E2 is a means to an end.

> [Name of the company]'s life is international travel, without it [the company] will cease to survive. In specific areas we have to have face-to-face meetings. In our currency operations we have to meet governors of Central Banks face to face. That is it. There is no shortcut, you can't send emails, you can't have conference calls on such issues as national currency. As far as sorter machines are concerned, you probably can, but as far as currency operations you can't.
>
> (E2)

Interviewee E20, having worked for more than 20 years in/with Russia and now recently retired, nevertheless continues to support very close links with the country through his regular visits and contacts with Russian friends.

There were four people (seven per cent of the sample) in the twenties age group. The relatively low number of interviewees in their twenties can be explained by people's general immaturity at that age and the fact that they are not professionally ready to act as global representatives for their company. A low number of respondents in this age group can also be a reflection on people's lack of international focus or ambition at that stage in their careers. A few respondents from other age groups commented on their early career stage, saying that upon their graduation from university and at the beginning of their career, they did not necessarily plan their international career path. Their international roles developed independently of them:

> . . . it was not because I wanted to work in a global community; it was my decision to go into human resources. I have worked in HR for

13 years and during that time I developed to an international role. Initially it was dealing with employees in Scotland and then it grew into managing employees in Netherlands, Germany and then I took a role supporting a sales organisation working with the whole of Europe and Middle East region. That's the type of role I do now. For the last couple of years I moved in European role, so it is kind of developed my career rather than a specific role.

(S11, age group 50s)

When I left University I did not know what I really wanted to do.

(E4, age group 30s)

However, three out of four respondents in their twenties admitted that they did want an international dimension in their careers. They were very eager to experience overseas business travel and living abroad. All people in the twenties age group were females, which reflects the findings by Collins and Tisdell (2002) who in their study on Gender and Differences in Travel Life Cycles, observed high numbers of females in their twenties travelling for employment purposes compared to any other female age groups. They explain this phenomenon by females' freedom of family commitments at this stage in their life cycle and also by a sense of adventure combined with the opportunities that business travel gives them in gaining new skills, experience and making contacts.

The fact that all four representatives of the twenties age group were Russian females, can be explained by the national characteristic of high expectations of women and, as a consequence, the way girls are brought up in the Russian environment. Culturally, Russian girls are under immense pressure to study well at school and to progress well in life. Girls are also disciplined in a much stronger way than boys. It would not surprise anyone in Russian society if a girl receives much more criticism and stricter disciplinary measures for misbehaving equally to a boy. Comments such as, "You are a girl! You cannot do that!" separate the society by gender expectations from a very early age. As a rule, girls in Russia grow up to be more responsible than boys and demonstrate a high desire to work (Ashwin and Bowers, 1996). One of the Russian male interviewees (R8), discussing peculiarities of Russian business, noted that if one wants to have something done in Russia, one should ask a (Russian) woman to do it. Another respondent reiterated this view by sharing his memories of delegating tasks with a high level of importance to Russian women rather than men (E20).

Out of 60 people interviewed, there was only one respondent in his seventies. For him, age was not an obstacle to continuing his career and being actively involved in collaboration with foreign colleagues and international business travel. At the time of the interview, he remained extremely active in his field and still travelled abroad when his business required him to do so.

Gender

The gender composition of the research sample showed a prevailing dominance of male respondents: 49 male businesspeople heavily outweighed only 11 female business travellers, representing an 82:18 per cent gender ratio. Among female interviewees, nine were Russian, one was Scottish and one was English. Four of them were in the twenties age group (all of them were Russian, non-married), three businesswomen were in their thirties (two Russian and one English, all married). Among three businesswomen in their forties one was Scottish (single) and two were Russian (one of them was married and another chose not to comment on her marital status). One Russian businesswoman was in her early fifties and was married.

The much lower representation of female interviewees compared to male respondents of this research sample directly reflects a "think manager—think male" global phenomenon (Schein *et al.*, 1996), which holds the view that the perception of middle-level managerial success is strongly associated with male characteristics, especially among males. This standpoint has not undergone significant changes since it was first debated in the 1970s (Schein, 1973, 1975) apart from the change of the attitude of females towards managerial positions. It was reported in 1989 that females no longer "sex-type" the managerial position, believing that females are as likely as males to have characteristics required for success in managerial positions (Schein *et al.*, 1989).

The family life cycle theory developed by Wells and Gubar (1966) appears to be highly appropriate for explaining the male—female ratio in international business travel. According to this theory based on the traditional and nuclear family, the family cycle can be divided into nine stages: bachelor, fully married, full nest I (preschool children), full nest II (school children), full nest III (older/dependent children), empty nest I (still working), empty nest II (retired), solitary survivor in labour force and solitary survivor retired. This categorisation broadly mirrors the following age groups:

- Younger than age 15—no defined stage
- 15 to 24—bachelor/newly married
- 25 to 34—newly married/full nest I
- 35 to 44—full nest I/full nest II
- 45 to 54—full nest III/empty nest I
- 55 to 64—empty nest I/empty nest II/solitary survivor (working)
- 65 and older—empty nest II/solitary survivor (retired)

As the data in this study show, the largest group of international business travellers were in their forties, which, according to family life cycle theory, coincides with full-nest stages. At this age, employment travel by men peaks, and female employment sharply declines, as the majority of women choose to fuel their time and energy into domestic duties, looking after their children. Even those women who prefer to return to work after giving birth have less time and energy for international business travel (Sinclair and Stabler, 1997).

As women progress through their family life cycle, getting married and settling down to rear children, their domestic arrangements appear to influence very strongly female career decisions. This was demonstrated by interviewee E4, who travelled extensively in the past and lived abroad for a while. Having married, her attitude to international business travel and to possibilities of relocating abroad with a job changed:

> I have got married and I have new responsibilities. So . . . no. I think I would find it quite difficult to do it now. But when I was younger I would have gone anywhere with work as long as the job was interesting.
>
> (E4)

This is not to say that male business travellers are less considerate regarding their families. Following the traditionally established pattern of family responsibilities, men remain the major breadwinners in the family and, if their job requires travelling internationally, they continue to do so in full nest family cycle. As some interviews demonstrated, some families where the husband was an international business traveller made conscious choices to return to their home country from living abroad as expatriates in order to give their children an opportunity to be educated and brought up in their national environment and an uninterrupted setup:

> I have friends who travelled when their kids grew up a bit older. In fact, there is something similar with the Army, where kids travel a lot and when eventually parents do settle, then the kids do not really settle, they keep travelling. Education . . . I have friends who travel, in every nation school is different and the kids are not that clever. You work for your kids. . . . I do not want my kids to be like nomads. As I said one was born in Norway, one was nearly born in America, one was born here. We brought them all here (UK, the interviewee's home country), so that they were not of different nationalities. If I had an opportunity to go to another country, I would have no hesitation doing it if it did not mess up my kids' education. Given an opportunity I would but I do not think it will happen now.
>
> (E8)

Reporting the dominant prevalence of male over female respondents in this research, it is necessary to acknowledge the relatively small research sample in this study and would be careful with drawing the conclusion that this is a general trend among all international business travellers. To prove the generality of the gender claims of this research, a much more extensive quantitative study would be necessary.

Religion

Religion did not come up as a theme in interviewees' discourse about themselves. Even when specifically asked to identify one's religious affiliation, some interviewees pointed out that religion did not play an important part in their lives and was irrelevant to their understanding of themselves. Those British respondents (both English and Scottish) who could identify their religious affiliation emphasised their connection with Christianity, and the majority of them pointed out that they were not practicing believers. The Russian interviewees identified themselves as having affiliations with the Russian Orthodox Church, although the majority of them also were not practicing their religion actively.

Education

All Russian interviewees were educated to university-degree level, and two of them had the higher academic qualification of "Kandidat Nauk" (Candidate of Sciences). Owing to a different academic system, this degree cannot be easily attributed to any British degree. Although the Oxford Russian Dictionary (Wheeler *et al.*, 2000) translates it as "doctor", i.e. someone with a PhD, it is a generally perceived as of somewhat lower qualification than a PhD.

All but three respondents in the English sample also possessed a university degree and post-graduate certification. The three people without a university degree had received their technical training in colleges and occupied technical positions in business, providing technical support for their companies. All but one respondent in the Scottish sample were educated to a degree level. The one person without a university degree acquired his professional skills through practical involvement in his business. Four interviewees in this group of respondents held a doctorate degree (PhD) in various disciplines.

Such a high proportion of people in the research sample holding higher educational qualifications was not surprising. There is world-wide consensus that improving levels of education is the path to raising living standards. "Across the industrialised world, and in many developing countries too, the thought is paramount that the way to economic growth is via skill formation to raise labour productivity and hence average living standards" (Ashton and Green, 1996: 1). Thus, taking into account the global occupational roles of the research participants, their high levels of education are not surprising and rather expected.

Proficiency in Foreign Languages

The importance of linguistic skills in international business was brought up by the majority of interviewees in their discourses on the international business environment. However, out of 40 British people interviewed, only twelve (20 per cent of the total British sample) could speak foreign languages fluently. Out of 20 Russian respondents, only three had limited foreign language ability, whereas the remaining 17 people had a good command of English.

This could be a reflection of the current general state of foreign language proficiency in the UK. As *The Linguist* (2010) reports, the British Government is concerned with the damage that has been done to language teaching in UK schools and continuing decline of language entries at GCSE (General Certificate of Secondary Education). For example, it has been recorded in the recent years that French dropped out of the top ten most popular subjects for the first time. In order to bridge the languages gap, the new "English Baccalaureate" is being introduced which "will be awarded to 16-year-olds with "good" GCSEs in a foreign language and four other named subjects, and will become the measure of success at Key Stage 4" (*The Linguist*, 2010: 6).

The most common foreign language among British interviewees was French. German and Russian were less commonly spoken languages, and only one British businessperson could speak Chinese. English was recognised as the language of international communication by almost all interviewees in whose discourse the theme of foreign languages was mentioned and discussed. For the Russian businesspeople, it was an essential skill for working in the international environment and, as the research results show, 17 out of 20 Russian interviewees spoke English. British businesspeople were proud of their mother tongue being the language of international communication, and a few of them pointed out that they usually adopted a slightly different manner of speaking when communicating with their foreign colleagues: speaking more slowly than they otherwise would and carefully choosing their vocabulary to avoid misunderstanding and misinterpreting. Their English was tailored to the people they were talking to.

This phenomenon was studied by Jennifer Jenkins (2000), who recognises the changing character of the use of the English language. English is becoming an international language rather than a foreign one. The difference lies in the context of the use of the language. In the case of English as a foreign language, people learn English in order to speak to native English speakers, where the non-native speakers' aim is to match their English skills as close as possible to the native standard. English as an international language is spoken by those whose objective is to communicate not only with the native speakers but also in many cases with speakers of other than English native languages. Thus, international English is commonly spoken during international business operations by both English and non-English native speakers.

British (native English speakers) often referred in their discourse to the widely known stereotype of British people being lazy with learning foreign languages. Those British people who did speak foreign languages regretfully mentioned that often they did not have a chance to practise their foreign language skills in their dealings with foreign counterparts, as their colleagues usually switched into English with the intention of practising their English with native English speakers:

> The problem I had was that I wanted to speak German and at all the meetings I went to I found people who were desperate to learn English. So, I was denied. I tried speaking German but they would speak English. So, I could use my language skills in the restaurants but that was as far as got. It is a regret. I was acting as an English teacher. . . . You really do not have much chance to develop your language.
>
> (S19)

However, in some countries (e.g., China and Russia), business is still conducted in the language of those countries. Even if English language proficiency is good enough for day-to-day discussions on running the business, when it comes to agreeing contracts and signing important documentation, the host country business partners will default to their native language and the use of interpreters becomes absolutely essential:

> In Russia we do have customers who speak fairly good English but again they default to their own language when it comes to the final points of contracts. We tend to have very detailed contracts and every contract is in two columns one is in English where there is what we are negotiating and then we have an independent translation to convert it into the local language. Then the Russian review it and all their comments are in Russian. Then we have to go back to our translators to get it translated into English. . . . So there are some things that we have to do that will allow us as an English-speaking company to do our business in such countries.
>
> (E1)

The development of communication technologies has made international business more continuous and more efficient, faster and cheaper (Rogers and Allbritton, 1995). Interaction with foreign counterparts outside face-to-face meetings nowadays happens via email and telephone:

> I am constantly in touch with my business partners over the phone. Primarily, these are people who left Russia and now represent interests of foreign companies. So, communication happens in Russian and in English.
>
> (R9)

> If we are not in the same room, [we communicate] by email. I am a big fan of email particularly if you are trying to say lots of people the same thing. Sometimes, when we have to make sure we are clear on

something, we have telephone conferences. 15 years ago it would have been written memos and centralised typing pools. So, contacts now are much easier with technology.

(E10)

Travel Abroad

Travel abroad for business purposes was a central criterion for choosing businesspeople for this study. Neither the level of their position on the career ladder, the industry they specialise in, nor the countries that they travel to, were critical for this study. It is the exposure to the international business environment through international travel and communication with foreign colleagues that was the focus of this research. It appeared in the course of the interviews that the degree of international business travel differed for different people, from spending on average just a week in their home country per month to travelling internationally once in two to three months in a year. For some interviewees international business trips were very short-term, lasting from a few days up to a week, while for others, it was a longer exposure to the foreign environment, from a couple of weeks to a few months. For some people, the frequency and destinations of business travel changed over the years of their career:

> It varies a lot. In the last two years it has been somewhat different role, which is very interesting. Well, it is always interesting. In the last seven–eight years I completely moved from manufacturing and engineering into executive management, so for the last five or so years I had responsibility for around ten manufacturing facilities globally. For the last two years I have been dismantling that business. I used to travel almost every week. In the last two years I have been travelling once in three–four weeks. Nowadays it is predominantly USA and Asia, prior to that I travelled to Eastern Europe as well. Usually short-term trips. I never stay away for more than ten days. Ten–fifteen years ago I spent from one month to three months away and that would be France and North America. Not as much cultural difference as some of the other countries I have been in the last five–six years.

(E15)

The geography of the interviewees' international business travel was extremely broad; some people had covered up to 30 countries, having been to almost every continent with their business: "Probably 25–30 [countries]. Something about that" (S17). Some tended to focus on particular countries with their company's operations positioned in a few certain locations: "Nowadays I typically travel to the Netherlands, Bulgaria, Switzerland and Germany. The teams I work with are located in these countries. In other roles I travelled in almost all of Europe" (S11).

The interviews also revealed that 30 businesspeople had experienced living abroad up to a few years at different stages in their lives and careers, and the recollections of their expatriate experiences added a slightly broader aspect to the study. They shed light on the advantages and disadvantages of long-term exposure to living in non-home countries. Discourses on expatriate living consequently brought up a theme of influences of such experiences on families and, vice versa, of families influencing international business movement decisions for certain individuals. Two respondents experienced expatriate living as children travelling with their parents to different countries. That was the case for interviewees S7 and S13 from the Scottish line of interviews. Two respondents were educated in foreign universities as in the case of R2 and S13; and five other interviewees spent a year abroad as students (E12, E4, E6, E19 and S3). It is worth pointing out that four out of those five people were language students.

Five out of 10 Russian interviewees had lived or were still living away from their homeland, namely in the UK (R1, R2, R3, R4, R6). Among Scottish respondents four people lived abroad for an extended period of time (more than a year) (S2, S5, S9 and S10) and nine interviewees from the English sample have experienced an expatriate way of living and working (among them E1, E2, E4, E6, E8, E10, E11, E16 and E17). The majority of interviewees at some point in their careers had an extended posting of up to a few months working in a foreign country.

Initial Ambition to Travel Abroad for Business

The interviewees' comments on whether it was always their ambition to travel internationally for work purposes demonstrated that for the majority of people, international business travel developed as a natural progression of their professional career as happened, for example, for respondent E1:

> It just happened. Before 1995 I was in a company for 10 years designing traffic control equipment. I was headhunted by a company that found the enclosures for speed cameras. My reason for that career move was my desire to become less internally focused and more externally customer focused. That was a good opportunity. But I never dreamt of it to evolve into a global role. So that was not planned, it just evolved and it was not just me, it was the whole industry generally. If BT previously were buying their equipment from the UK manufacturers, now they are buying it from China. You would not have dreamt about anything like this when I first started.
>
> (E1)

Similarly, an international role in the company was a result of a natural career development for respondent E5:

> There are very few people, purchasers or buyers, who start their lives thinking I want to be a buyer. . . . It tends to happen that you are

drifting into it through some other jobs or positions. So, it is not that I started out thinking I want to work for an international company as a buyer. I have been with [the name of the company] for over 25 years and I enjoy working for it. My international role is something that has developed as my position and role developed.

(E5)

As shown by interviewee S6 below, for some people, international travel was even an unwanted necessity:

No, it was not an ambition. It was a consequence. . . . I enjoy travelling but I never had an ambition to have travelling as part of my career. Quite the opposite. At some stage I was travelling an awful lot when our first son was born and I tried to reduce my travelling so that I could spend more time at home. And I changed role[s] specifically to do less travelling.

(S6)

However, for 13 respondents (R3, R18, R19, E3, E6, E12, E17, E19, S2, S7, S8, S13 and S15), international travel was a compulsory element in their career planning. For example, a language graduate (R3) always wanted to experience living in the UK, which became possible through obtaining work in this country:

I always wanted to come to Britain and I had very happy expectations when I was moving here. It has always been my favourite country and I always thought of it as my second homeland. England is something very special; only here can one find the best possible version of English.

(R3)

A language graduate from the English sample (E6) had an ambition to master his linguistic skills in the country of the language he studied at university:

I graduated and did some work in journalism and then I decided I wanted to be in a career that would involve my Russian and I wanted to be based in the USSR.

(E6)

For some respondents, the motivation to travel internationally was encouraged from an early age by their parents and was seen as a way of self-development through broadening one's horizons:

When I was about 17 I had a career choice: did I want to go into business or did I want to go into engineering? The reason why I chose business was because I wanted to travel. I wanted to see the world. From the very early age my parents told me that I had to travel to broaden my mind. I was encouraged to travel from a very young age.

(S2)

It is in my family. My father travelled with the RAF a lot, my brother travelled a lot with the Army. I also always wanted to travel. It is learning about different countries via travelling. It gives you more than best education in the world. By being there you can understand what is going on in the world. I have seen how different people live and how they do things. I probably have seen more than some highly positioned people because I have been there and lived there, worked with those people and understand what their culture is about. It is a mind-opening experience.

(E17)

Interviewee S7 grew up abroad travelling with her parents working overseas; for her international travel was "engrained" in her character:

Travelling abroad and experiencing foreign environment was kind of engrained and it was my upbringing. And I had a passion for travelling. So, when I first qualified and I qualified as an accountant I had a passion to find a job that had travelling in it. So, I had various roles where I travelled to different countries around the world. And that's how I spend most of my personal time and money: travelling as well.

(S7)

Danziger and Waldfogel (2000) stress the importance of family influence on social and educational well-being of children. Positive encouragement for learning and inquisitiveness (ideally combined with real opportunities for new experiences) result in maximising children's potential. So, as evident from the research findings, the international travel of some interviewees at early stages in their lives did affect their future career choice and to some extent did serve as a springboard to their professional success in adult life.

Integration/Assimilation

All interviewees highlighted their interest in learning more about the cultures and customs of the countries they went to on business. All interviewees in the English sample pointed out their desire to get as close as possible to the local life of the country they are visiting. They also spoke about the barriers on the way to integration. In many cases, the inability to speak the local language was seen as an obstacle, however not sufficient enough for not making an effort to immerse oneself into the local way of living:

> I do try to integrate. Like in China for the first time I would try to go to a local market and barter. You try to get through the language barriers. Do I learn languages? No. I am not really good at languages.
>
> (E10)

All interviewees, however, pointed out their learning of basic greetings and appreciation of common phrases and expressions in the language of the countries they cooperated with. That knowledge equipped them with the option of making the initial communication step, described by the respondents as "ice-breaking" initiations.

Integration brought satisfaction and enjoyment of learning about new cultures:

> I am not really an expat community person. I do try to experience the culture. As you know I met my wife in Poland. If there are other people within the company who are living in that country, then I will spend time with them outside of work. But more often than not I will be wanting to meet local people, so when I started in Poland, we were recruiting local people and some of them were really fun people and outside of work I would spend time with them. And that is one thing I really enjoy about my international travel. It is getting to know the cultures.
>
> (E1)

Interviewee E15 pointed out that the depth of integration can depend on the time people spend abroad and also on personal attitudes and openness towards international experiences of travelling businesspeople:

> It depends on where you are. And people are also different. Some people go native and I have seen people really integrating. It generally happens when you stay abroad for some time, you sometimes have to do it. But it is not me. I try to be respectful of culture and people but I am quite a British person. I think I am very patriotic about our heritage in terms of particularly manufacturing. . . . I have been to about thirty countries. I am always very appreciative of people, of culture, of food, of seeing things; it creates opportunity but if I compare myself to let's say Martin, we are a little bit different. And he is married not to a British person, as is Jason. I think this also gives you a different perspective on life and a different view. My wife is British of Irish descent.
>
> (E15)

The findings on businesspeople's integration differed significantly for English and Scottish interviewees. The majority of the respondents in the

English sample stressed their eagerness to integrate into new cultures and provided examples of their experiences of doing so. The majority of people interviewed in Scotland, having also indicated their interest in learning more about the places, cultures and customs on their business travel, however, pointed out their limited ability to do so due to work demands (e.g., having to work long hours) and also limited time available for exploring new places:

> Usually it is airport-hotel-airport. But when we were in Japan we had a few weekends, so we went to see all the sights and tried to understand Japanese history, value systems and their background. That becomes very valuable in business, it helps you understand how they think as they do not think the same as us. Particularly in Japan where the background is totally different. So, we spent a lot of time getting a cultural immersion, if you like: what to say and what not to say. Some of our colleagues who did not do that got themselves in trouble sometimes. So, yes, I tried every attempt to grab some of the local culture or customs.
>
> (S19)

> I do not think that we do very much. We generally stay in hotels, which is a bit separate. When I had a trip to Uganda on my own in February, I was hosted by the livestock ministry there and I managed to socialise more than I do when I am in my company's group. I played some golf and drinks when I was there. I went out in the night with one of the vets playing pool and out and about, I went to places where I would not have gone if I was the only white person there for example. It was a very authentic feeling, I suppose.
>
> (S15)

It was pointed out that the best integration happened through the initiative of local people, when the process becomes more natural for foreigners who get involved into the local way of doing things without much theoretical preparation and in the most effective way:

> It happens through invitation generally. You cannot really do it unless you are invited. You can be taken in Cameroon by Cameroon nationals to a restaurant and you would be very obviously European when everybody else is obviously African, that is a nice way to enter society through the locals.
>
> (S5)

Feeling Comfortable/Uncomfortable Abroad

Travelling abroad constituted a significant part of interviewees' professional lives. None of those interviewed expressed strong feelings of discomfort when on their travel in a foreign environment, mainly due to the fact that most people travel to well-developed countries where the local socio-economic environment did not threaten their safety and security:

> I do not remember going anywhere where I felt uncomfortable. I have not had to work in a country with a specific conflict, I have not worked in Iran or Afghanistan. . . . Most of the countries I have been to are reasonably well developed, so I would always be comfortable from that perspective. I have never had to work in Africa. I do not think I shall ever be uncomfortable travelling . . .
>
> (S13)

However, eight people pointed out that the degree of feeling comfortable depends on the country one is visiting. Several respondents stressed the importance of security concerns when travelling to places with unstable political order or poor economic conditions where Westerners were seen as a target. That, naturally, raised feelings of discomfort in one way or the other:

> It depends where I am and what the situation is. I think we, Europeans, are looked after like infants or toddlers when we visit Africa. Because of the mentality of our hosts or because of the recognition that we are out of our depth in some sense and also because of the basic security issues too because we are perceived by some as good targets for theft or whatever . . .
>
> (S15)

Feelings of comfort when in a foreign land, as was noted by four respondents, develop with experience. It is natural to feel slightly hesitant when one is facing an unfamiliar environment for the first time; however, this feeling goes away with acquiring more experience of business travel and more knowledge about the new place:

> I believe that all people when they first start travelling they all find the whole thing quite exciting and interesting and surprising. I do not ever remember feeling uncomfortable about it, I do not ever remember feeling different or out of place. Not understanding things that were happening around me—Yes. But that passed quite quickly. I covered a huge part of the world over the years and what I found is that there are common values that apply and if you stick to those you will not find much of a difference.
>
> (S12)

> For people going to a country for the first time it is a learning curve but after being there several times you tend to assimilate. And I think one needs to assimilate.
>
> (E2)

I think when you start travelling you feel a bit uncomfortable but as you do more travelling . . . again it varies. . . . If you go to Budapest, it is a very cosmopolitan city and a lot of people speak English. If you go to the factory up North [in Hungary], very few people speak English there. You are more aware of it then. You are trying to explain what you want to eat on the menu, sometimes they do not even have an English translation on the menu. So, you definitely feel like that then. But you become used to that and you become more comfortable with it as time passes.

(S8)

Feeling a Foreigner Whilst Abroad

Despite feeling comfortable in most of their business travel destinations, the majority of interviewees (54 people), nevertheless, felt foreign and quite different from the native population whilst abroad. Answering the question about their feelings whilst being abroad, they admitted feeling conscious of being different:

> . . . you are conscious of it because you are never quite attuned to the country to the extent that people who live there are. In the UK I always know what is going on here, and you are never quite sure when you are abroad.
>
> (E16)

> I do feel very different. But we tend to travel in such a way that we do not impact on the community. We rely a lot on local people and local knowledge and the good will of the local population. So, there is definitely a defining line between ourselves and the people of those countries we travel to.
>
> (S3)

One of the Russian respondents (R17) shared her recollections about recently working with 15 colleagues from other European countries in Britain:

> All these people were from European countries and I was the only one from Russia. So, they looked at me as if I was a dinosaur. They were all shocked to hear that I had travelled 17 hours by train to get to Moscow before my flight to London. They could not stop talking about it! They were asking me about my way of life, my work, my family and many other things that help people form their opinion about me and my country. And I felt very responsible for the image I was creating by giving the answers. I had to control my every answer (in a good way as I wanted to project a certain image). In that sense I of course stay Russian.
>
> (R17)

Noticing cultural differences challenged businesspeople to learn more about the new environments in order to facilitate a smooth flow of their business. Interviewee E1, for example, consciously recognising those differences, tried to embrace them:

> I do try to experience the culture. . . . And that is one thing I really enjoy about my international travel. It is getting to know the cultures. When people are interviewing me or when we are on a development programme and people ask what my strength are and what other people would think of me, it would be my ability to speak and be understood by many countries. I probably have the best understanding of Chinese culture amongst my colleagues and I can be best understood whereas my peers just can't understand the "loss of face" thing, for example. For them to go back after negotiations and change their mind or to admit they were wrong or to say "No" is something that cannot be understood in Chinese culture. You do not say "No", you just do not give an answer. Changing your mind is a real loss of face. It is difficult sometimes for Western people to understand Asian culture.
>
> (E1)

Several people pointed out that their feeling of being foreign whilst on overseas business travel depended on whether one travelled alone or was being accompanied by colleagues from the same company:

> It depends. There is a number of scenarios. Sometimes you are travelling alone and you feel very much a foreigner because you are on your own, you are eating on your own, you are going for a drink on your own. So, you feel it more. Other times there are some other people from other disciplines (Scotland is European headquarters): supply chain, materials, and programme management. So, these people will be travelling as well sometimes and there will be three or four of you staying in the same hotel, so you are not conscious of it.
>
> (S8)

For other people, the country where they did their business and its culture and people's previous experience of it were determining their feeling of being a foreigner. In some countries, people feel much more comfortable than in others:

> It depends on where you go and familiarity with places. Having travelled and lived in the US and Canada I feel as comfortable in Canada as anywhere in the UK. When I worked in Taiwan briefly I found that quite challenging. At that time in Taiwan (the early 1990s) there was virtually no English spoken. And there was no English Latin based signage, that was really quite challenging and therefore one feels very obviously a foreigner. If I worked there longer I would try to put an awful

lot of effort into trying to learn their local language. So, it depends on where one goes but I feel pretty comfortable in many foreign places.

(S6)

Six people out of 60 said they did not feel foreign at all when finding themselves abroad (E4, E17, S1, S12, S17 and S20). For S17, going on business trips abroad did not significantly alter the daily routine he usually practised in the UK: He went running every morning (which gave him an opportunity to experience the feel of the new place) and merely focused on work. Busy time schedules seemed to erase the significance of the place one was in. Working with their foreign colleagues, businesspeople also noticed the universal aspirations of people in other countries that guided their actions and made people from many different countries feel quite similar:

> . . . in my case I talk to businesspeople and I talk to students, you tend to find that there are very similar drivers and very similar pattern of behaviour. In our area people want to improve their business schools, do better their jobs, take more control over their lives, look after their families—they are kind of universal aspirations . . .
>
> (S1)

The spread of the English language (particularly in the business world) was also noted to influence people's appreciation of the environments they found themselves in whilst on international travel:

> It is no longer England, Russia, Spain . . . the world is so mixed now! It is changing so fast! I wonder what language people will speak in the future. I think we will all speak one language more and more. Over the last 10 years I have met so many people from different countries that speak English. It has made us so lazy! It is ridiculous! We are becoming all international.
>
> (E17)

For interviewee E4, the power of universal attributes, such as the sense of humour, was something that made all people appreciate their similarities rather than noticing differences:

> No . . . I do not think I feel foreign. Everyone thinks that the sense of humour is very important. I was never made to feel uncomfortable.
>
> (E4)

It was pointed out that exposure to the foreign environments did change people's perceptions of many things in life compared to what they were at the beginning of their international career:

> I have dear friends since I was a child but I have changed. My way of thinking has changed from my friends' who have a local job, go

home every day. Their lives have been the same for the last 20 years, whereas my life changes daily, weekly, monthly. I meet different people and I start having different ways of looking at life. I must admit, I have new friends now through travel. We can relate more as we have so much in common whereas with my friends I can't relate as much.

(E17)

Seeing different ways of doing the same thing broadens people's horizons and opens their minds: Interviewee E12 vividly remembers his French experience of using a thermometer to measure one's body temperature; respondent R2, who had always intended to marry only a Russian man, was now married to a British (English) person. International experiences influenced people's attitudes and perceptions, views and habits; sometimes, that caused frustration, as people saw better ways of doing things whilst being unable to adopt those changes in their home country:

I am not very attached to Britain now. I cannot see anything better here than it was 10–15 years ago. I have seen other countries that are accelerating in developing their facilities and accumulating wealth. Here we are stuck behind in everything like schools, healthcare, police, traffic, service, politeness, manners, violence. Everything is going down. If you compare this with life in Shanghai which is pretty unique (it is not really China). . . . I was feeling unwell on a Saturday night. In 20 minutes I was in a brand-new hospital, seeing an English-speaking doctor, prescribed medication, given medication and taxied back home again. That cost me about 10 pounds. Here you can't even get an ambulance: if you are feeling unwell you have to wait until the next day and wait for five hours in the doctor's practice. And it did not used to be like that.

(E11)

For interviewee E17, on the contrary, international business travel reaffirmed his attitude towards his country. This came through comparing England with other, much poorer countries.

I have always said that England is the best country in the world. English people do not realise how lucky they are. With our healthcare. . . . When they say "poor people" . . . there are not poor people. They have not seen poor people. It is safe. But the problem with that is that you have to pay for it. We expect so much now. Whereas other countries get on with what they have.

(E17)

Friendship with Foreigners

Close communication with business colleagues in many cases transformed into personal friendships. This often happened with those businesspeople who lived abroad for some time and established friendships with foreign nationals living in that country based on shared interests and attitude to life:

> I still have good friends in America, we still swap emails. Azerbaijan . . . not so much, the same in Dubai. American culture is not that different from the UK culture plus there is no language barrier there. Social income is also important. In some countries like Kuwait, Libya and Azerbaijan, the local income is so low . . . when you go out and enjoy eating and drinking . . . it is not so easy for your friend. So, in Azerbaijan if we were taking people out we were paying most of the time.
>
> (E8)

As evident from the quote above, people tend to sustain some friendly relationships even after moving on to another job. However, these relationships are often not very close, and, due to people's busy life-styles, they naturally weaken over time:

> It is very difficult to keep track of people once you have moved on. I have a couple of friends in Germany I still keep in touch with. A Japanese gentleman who unfortunately went back to Japan and I lost touch with him that way. Not a huge number of people but a few special people who I worked with very closely.
>
> (S19)

However, mutual personal interests facilitate people's communication even after they have moved on to other companies and industries. In such cases business is not the only binding force which forms the basis for long-lasting friendships:

> Friends . . . Several people. It is interesting how now, having left the company, I am still keeping in touch with them and I know I will continue keeping in touch with them outside of business.
>
> (S18)

Very often, business and personal relationships are tightly intertwined and, after a while, become inseparable:

> What happens is if 20 years ago I met someone when I was 20–25 years younger and these people were in their 30s. And as they moved up in the echelons of the bank, if I entertained them in their country or they come to this country, they probably brought their wives; I met their wives and their children. When their children are sent to the UK for their education, I would be asked to keep an eye on them while they are in the UK. That means that there is a mesh of a personal relationship as well as a professional one. . . . It is not only working relationship.

As one comes to the UK on holiday or travels via the UK, one will drop me an email and we make sure we catch up. But I do not go out of my way to keep in touch with them just for the sake of keeping in touch with them.

(E2)

Of course, personalities vary immensely. Some people rarely transformed their business relationships into personal ones, as in the case of respondent S14:

I've made work friends who live internationally. A couple of Americans. I do not keep up with a lot of people. I have a very small circle of friends. Some people have dozens, hundreds of people they keep up with. I keep up with about 15. Everybody else just passes through my life. But every person I keep up with. . . . Do I make friends easily? Or do I keep people in? Most of my friends I have known for 20+ years.

(S14)

Some people preferred to keep their close friendships outside work:

I would not say close friends. In a factory there I know a few people who I know quite well. And we would discuss how things are going and holidays I have just had. But it is not necessarily that I would visit them and they would visit me. It is mainly work and during these conversations some of the other personal stuff would be discussed.

(E5)

People's understanding of the concept of friendship varied among different respondents. For some, for example respondent E12, friendship was not a definitive notion. His comment "Not sure what a friend is" was linked to comments by some Russian interviewees on friendship and the different weight that this concept carried in different societies. For the Russians, friendship was a type of relationship that was embedded into people's common culture and equal mutual sharing of a similar mindset, the so-called "cultural baggage" (R2):

For some people the cultural baggage that people acquire from their childhood is very important. Cheburashka, Yozhik [Soviet Cartoon characters]. . . . For me it is very important. And to some extent, this Russian community is the manifestation of how important this cultural baggage for me is. All my friends are Russian. I had a period when I had foreign boyfriends and friends but all that was not strong enough to keep going. Here are all my new Russian friends and this circle is very strong.

(R2)

Friendship for the Russians is a "strong moral force" (Markowitz, 1991: 645). The analysis of the meaning of friendship, experienced by Soviet immigrants in the USA and Israel, is still equally applicable today. The Russian understanding of friendship is not a "result of urban dwellers' choices in selecting companions with similar interests and preferences" but rather "an emotion, an institution, a multifunctional connection between two or more nonrelated people" (p. 637). Russian friendships come from people's souls and therefore are emotionally extremely intense. Friendships for Russian people are those only arenas "where they can act out their individualism and express their own particular joys, needs, and grievances. These friendships may be best characterised as states of communitas, or "anti-structure", based on spontaneity and emotion. In the state of communitas, the total person, not one or another of one's social roles, interacts with others. Ordinary structure is suspended; social responsibility and accountability are disregarded, and people relate to each other without inhibition, with their feelings, not with their rational minds" (Markowitz, 1991: 639).

This point of view is firmly supported by Russian interviewee R9, who clearly differentiated the notion of Russian friendships and friendships among foreigners:

> I do not have the type of friends [abroad] like in Russia. This is because everybody seems to be friends but at the same time everybody is very isolated, particularly when it comes down to finances. You can be considered friends but if you are not buying any equipment, then difficulties arise. In Russia a friend is a friend in happy times and in difficulties. People support each other in any circumstances. I cannot say the same about foreigners. The notion of friendship is different. And you know it all very well that people only visit each other when they have permission. Therefore friends . . . People there have interests . . . That is all.
>
> (R9)

Other themes that came up in the course of interviews

Acquiring Foreign Habits

A curious feature of the data was some businesspeople's acknowledgement of acquiring foreign habits or forms of behaviour. This usually applied to those businesspeople who have spent a prolonged length of time abroad or studied foreign cultures and languages in depth. Interviewee E6, for example, even when outside Russia, followed the Russian superstitious habit of looking into a mirror and not talking to anyone if one had to return back home to pick up something that had been forgotten on the way out of the house.

A more common manifestation of adopting foreign cultural traits was developing an affinity with national cuisines and celebrating foreign holidays. This usually occurred after an extended expatriate experience or in mixed marriages, where cultural interconnectedness became interwoven into people's lives.

Attachment to Foreign Places

International travel and exposure to foreign cultures in some cases resulted in people developing particular attachments to foreign countries. Often, it is connected to living in those places and keeping close contacts with people from those countries even after moving on somewhere else. Interviewee E20, for example, having completed his overseas posting to Russia many years ago, still goes back there very regularly to visit his friends and to immerse himself into the culture he has become very fond of. Equally, interviewee R7 has developed a particular affinity with Finland, which he finds closely attuned to Russia in many ways and feels very comfortable there.

Enjoyment/Dissatisfaction with a Busy Lifestyle

Although some respondents did point out negative implications of international business travel on their physical health or causing stress on family relations, the vast majority of people interviewed loved their transnational lifestyle and could clearly see and appreciate the positive impact of their foreign exposure on their personal and professional development. This was particularly striking when they compared their experiences with the lives of those people they knew who had never moved from their local areas and had not gone through the transformations that international travel had influenced in business travellers.

The primary line of enquiry of this chapter originated from the need to portray the global business traveller. The product of the rise of global business civilisation, these people are constantly on the move pursuing their business objectives. Businesspeople, bankers, politicians . . . members of the TCC (Sklair, 2001). Who are they? And what do they think they are?

If Hahnel (1999) is right in saying that globalisation is the replacement of diverse modes of human intercourse with the single mindset and values of universal commercialism, does it mean that all TCC members, including the international business travellers interviewed, have "a single mindset" driven by the ideology of consumerism and pursuing their goals of personal economic advantages through their involvement in international business and travel? Is there a connecting force holding these people together and differentiating them from the others?

Following Adam Smith's (2010) theory of social classes based on the division of labour and "human propensity to truck, barter and exchange one thing for another" (p. 14), class division arises not from the nature of people but from their "habit, custom, and education" (p. 17). Thus, having analysed these and similar characteristics of the global business travellers, the following generalised image of this representative of the TCC emerges:

An upwardly striving manager, in a middle or senior-management position, more often a male than a female, in his/her forties, married, educated to a degree level or higher, not necessarily possessing foreign language skills in the case of a native English speaker and usually with a good command of business English in the case of any other mother tongue and with no strong religious affiliations. International travel is an integral part of his/her job, which emerged through his/her career progression. Sometimes tiring and unpredictable, it, nevertheless, is an enjoyable and enriching experience. The international business traveller might have had some expatriate experience and have developed a genuine curiosity for integrating into foreign environments when it appears possible. He/she operates with ease and feels comfortable in any part of the world, apart from dangerous places. However, the feeling of being a foreigner persistently stays with him/her regardless of the extent of foreign travel experience. An effective IT user, he or she eagerly and easily communicates with his/her foreign colleagues in person and often forms friendships with his/her overseas counterparts which are often sustained even when business relationship ceases, growing into personal relationships. Equipped with extensive overseas experience and knowledge of foreign cultures, he/she might have developed a certain affinity with foreign countries/places and acquired foreign habits. He/she fully appreciates the challenges that arise as a consequence of international business travel but, nevertheless, enjoys his/her busy lifestyle and its enriching experiences.

Generally applicable to all respondents that were interviewed for this book, can this portrait be equally suited to the interviewees from all three national groups? Is it possible to assume that the global business environment outweighs other influences shaping people's understanding of themselves? Do all international business travellers project the same image and perception of the world and themselves? Is it more strongly shaped by their global professional roles rather than by their attachments to their countries of origin? And, finally, to what extent are international business travellers truly global? Answering these questions will be approached through the lens of businesspeople's understanding of their national belonging.

References

Adler, N.J. and Bartholomew, S. (1992a) Managing Globally Competent People. *The Executive*, 6 (3), pp. 52–65.

Aguilera, A. (2008) Business Travel and Mobile Workers. *Transportation Research Part A: Policy and Practice*, 42 (8), pp. 1109–1116.

Ashton, D. and Green, F. (1996) *Education, Training and the Global Economy*. Cheltenham: Edward Elgar Publishing Limited.

Ashwin, S. and Bowers, E. (1996) Do Russian Women Want to Work? Cited in Buckley, M. (ed.) (1997) *Post-Soviet Women: From the Baltic to Central Asia*. Cambridge: Cambridge University Press.

Barbour, R. (2008) *Introducing Qualitative Research*. London: Sage Publications.

Bauman, Z. (1992) *Intimations of Postmodernity*. London: Routledge.

Beioley, S. (1991) The Business of Winning the Business Traveller. *Hotels*, 24 (9), pp. 19–20. Cited in Callan, R.J. and Kyndt, G. (2001) Business Travellers' Perception of Service Quality: A Prefatory Study of Two European City Centre Hotels. *International Journal of Tourism Research*, 3, pp. 313–323.

Best, S. and Kellner, D. (1997) *The Postmodern Turn*. London: The Guilford Press.

Carroll, W.K. and Fennema, M. (2002) Is There a Transnational Business Community? *International Sociology*, 17, pp. 393–419.

Carroll, W.K. and Fennema, M. (2004) Problems in the Study of the Transnational Business Community: A Reply to Kentor and Jang. *International Sociology*, 19, pp. 369–378.

Collins, D. and Tisdell, C. (2002) Gender and Differences in Travel Life Cycle. *Journal of Travel Research*, 41, pp. 133–143.

Danziger, S. and Waldfogel, J. (eds.) (2000) *Securing the Future: Investing in Children from Birth to College*. New York: Russell Sage Foundation.

Glasser, P. (1999) Virtual View: Global Citizen. *North American Review*, 284 (6), pp. 46–47.

Gustafson, P. (2009) More Cosmopolitan, No Less Local. *European Societies*, 11 (1), pp. 25–47.

Hahnel, R. (1999) Fighting Globalization. *ZNet Daily Commentary* (www.zmag.org), September 22, 1999. Cited in Cromwell, D. (2001) *Private Planet: Corporate Plunder and the Fight Back*. Charlbury: Jon Carpenter.

Jenkins, J. (2000) *The Phonology of English as an International Language*. Oxford: University Press.

Kentor, J. and Jang, Y.S. (2004) Yes, There Is a (Growing) Transnational Business Community: A Study of Global Interlocking Directorates 1983–98. *International Sociology*, 19 (3), pp. 355–368.

Kentor, J. and Jang, Y.S. (2006) Different Questions, Different Answers: A Rejoinder to Carroll and Fennema. *International Sociology*, 21, pp. 602–606.

The Linguist (2010) Back Up Plan? New "English Baccalaureate" Will "Bridge the Language Gap", Says Gove. *The Linguist*, 49 (5), p. 6.

Markowitz, F. (1991) Russkaya Druzhba: Russian Friendship in American and Israeli Contexts. *Slavic Review*, 50 (3), pp. 637–645.

Neugarten, B.L., Moore, J.W. and Lowe, J.C. (1965) Age Norms, Age Constraints, and Adult Socialization. *The American Journal of Sociology*, 70 (6), pp. 710–717.

Owen, D. (1997) *Sociology After Postmodernism*. London: Sage Publications.

Rogers, E.M. and Allbritton, M.M. (1995) Interactive Communication Technologies in Business Organisations. *The Journal of Business Communication*, 32, pp. 177–195.

Schein, V.E. (1973) The Relationship Between Sex Roles Stereotypes and Requisite Management Characteristics. *Journal of Applied Psychology*, 57, pp. 95–100. Cited in Schein, V.E., Mueller, R., Lituchy, T. and Liu, J. (1996) Think Manager—Think Male: A Global Phenomenon? *Journal of Organizational Behaviour*, 17 (1), pp. 33–41.

Schein, V.E. (1975) The Relationship Between Sex Role Stereotypes and Requisite Management Characteristics Among Female Managers. *Journal of Applied Psychology*, 60, pp. 340–344. Cited in Schein, V.E., Mueller, R., Lituchy, T. and Liu, J. (1996) Think Manager—Think Male: A Global Phenomenon? *Journal of Organizational Behaviour*, 17 (1), pp. 33–41.

Schein, V.E., Mueller, R. and Jacobson, C. (1989) The Relationship Between Sex Role Stereotypes and Requisite Management Characteristics Among College Students. *Sex Roles*, 20, pp. 103–110. Cited in Schein, V.E., Mueller, R., Lituchy, T. and Liu, J. (1996) Think Manager—Think Male: A Global Phenomenon? *Journal of Organizational Behaviour*, 17 (1), pp. 33–41.

Schein, V.E., Mueller, R., Lituchy, T. and Liu, J. (1996) Think Manager—Think Male: A Global Phenomenon? *Journal of Organizational Behaviour*, 17 (1), pp. 33–41.

Sinclair, M.T. and Stabler, M. (1997) *The Economics of Tourism*. London: Routledge. Cited in Collins, D. and Tisdell, C. (2002) Gender and Differences in Travel Life Cycle. *Journal of Travel Research*, 41, pp. 133–143.

Sklair, L. (2001) *The Transnational Capitalist Class*. Oxford: Blackwell.

Smith, A. (2010) *The Invisible Hand*. London: Penguin Books. Part of The Wealth of Nations, first published in 1776.

Szerszynski, B. and Urry, J. (2002) Cultures of Cosmopolitanism. *The Sociological Review*, 50, pp. 461–481.

Welch, D.E., Welch, L.S. and Worm, V. (2007) The International Business Traveller: A Neglected but Strategic Human Resource. *The International Journal of Human Resource Management*, 18 (2), pp. 173–183.

Wells, W.D. and Gubar, G. (1966) The Life Cycle Concept in Marketing Research. *Journal of Marketing Research*, 3 (4), pp. 355–363.

Wheeler, M., Unbegaun, B. and Falla, P. (eds.) (2000) *The Oxford Russian Dictionary* (3rd Ed). Oxford: Oxford University Press.

Part Two
National Identity Construction by English International Business Travellers

This part addresses the construction of national identity by British business travellers interviewed in England. It focuses on how national identities are being understood, interpreted and articulated by international business travellers and explores the personal and deeply internal understanding of national attachment, taken outside any particular context. It aims to uncover what elements of people's lives constitute their national identity and whether the national explanation of self occupies an important role in their day-to-day activities or remains insignificant and distant from factual reality.

This section is the first part of the analysis of the British research sample. The total number of 40 British business travellers interviewed is equally represented by two groups of 20 English and 20 Scottish interviews. The enquiry into the constructs of national identity by respondents in England and Scotland seeks to establish differences and similarities in perceptions of national belonging by people living in these two parts of the United Kingdom.

Of course, all four political and territorial elements of the UK (England, Wales, Scotland and Northern Ireland) equally represent the state formed by the historical evolution of their political relationship. Having been firmly established by 1066 as a unified state with a common law and administration, a common coinage, and, increasingly after the 14th century, a common language (Wood, 1991), England [and it was England, not Britain (Easthope, 1999) at that stage], following unsuccessful attempts to advance into continental Europe in 16th and early 17th centuries, turned north and west to colonise the Scots, the Welsh and the Irish. It took almost three centuries for it to become Britain: In 1536, Wales united with England in matters of law; in 1707, Scotland and England signed the Act of Union; and, finally, Ireland agreed to the union with England in 1801 (Easthope, 1999).

Britain historically has been shaped as an empire based on a unity of diversities (Lee, 2004). Lee (2004) supports his statement with reference to Lucas's "Introduction to a Historical Geography of the British Colonies" published in 1887, where Britain was described as a diverse nation composed of the "English, Saxons, Jutes, Danes, Northmen, Flemings" as well as "the Welsh, the Irish, the Manx, and the Northern Scotch . . . of the Celtic stock" (Lucas, 1887: 92). Thus, in talking about the four nations of the United Kingdom, it would be wrong not to acknowledge the heterogeneous multinational composition of contemporary Britain.

However, the book focuses particularly on England and Scotland as possessing distinct territorial and ethnic features. It is centred on cultural and territorial influences of social conditions on people's understanding of their national belonging and, in order to demonstrate this, further addresses Pittock's (1999) claim that it is cultural self-definition that plays a key role "in the attempts of Celticism and Celtic identities to gain recognition for themselves within the British Isles" (p. 127). In this light, the Scots not only represent the territory of the United Kingdom with a devolved administration, but they are also part of the Celtic population as opposed to Anglo-Saxon English.

What Is National Identity? The Importance of National Identity to the English

The English research sample revealed a significant span of opinions on national identity. Different degrees of engagement with the issue were easily noticeable. Some respondents demonstrated a remarkably weak connection, perceiving it simply as a fact of life which did not bear any significance. They acknowledged that they did not tend to think about their national identity; it was not important and therefore did not present any particular relevance in their day-to-day life:

> It is just a fact. I am English. That is it. I am English. I see everyone as an individual rather than being part of a nation.
>
> (E4)

The sparseness of some of the English people's discourses on national identity demonstrated that although English people were firmly aware of their national affiliation, they often found it challenging to interpret the meaning they attached to it. However, that was not the case for all English interviews. Like their Scottish counterparts, a few people in the English research sample were prepared to share their views outside the 30-minute timeframe allocated for each interview.

The quote from interviewee E4 above illustrates Susan Condor's (2010) findings on the lack of political engagement of English people in their consideration of their national identity. Condor explains it firstly by English political apathy, which she describes as "a moral or motivational failure, often seen to be the product of arrogance, complacency or lethargy" (p. 527) and secondly by "a supposed cognitive deficiency of the English public" (p. 527). The author suggests that "people in England have somehow failed to recognise their identity, and hence their distinctive interests, as English" (p. 527).

Thus, affiliation with the English is not so much a political entitlement but a subjective sense of self arising from a psychological condition. Debating different explanations of the English political apathy, often based on the stereotypical judgements of the English character, Condor proposes another approach to understanding this phenomenon. She suggests that English people might regard "political action based on appeals to (majority national) identity as incompatible with the objective neutrality and public reason normatively required of citizens in diverse liberal democracies" (p. 541). This proposition, however, is also related to a widely available stereotypical perception of English people's commitment to fair play, thus providing a certain degree of credibility to a broad set of national characteristics attributed to English people.

Such national traits as "fairness, discretion, honesty" (E16), "being polite and rational, not flustered, the stiff upper lip and not being over emotional about things" (E3) were frequently mentioned by many respondents when asked to define their national identity. Often, this aspect of the national identity discourse was accompanied by a warm smile on respondents' faces as if they signified something very personal. And indeed, national identity for the majority of respondents constituted an inseparable part of themselves. It was neither consciously in question or in need of defence, nor was it merely absent. It was there, it was their life, it was what they were:

> I am English. Absolutely. I do not think about my English identity on purpose but it is important to me. I have my English mug with me [laughs]. I like the things we stood for, I like our history and I am proud of our history. It is interesting and "proud" is not always the right word. I can understand our history and I would like to be associated with the traditional stereotypical values of the English person.
>
> (E16)

The implicitness of the English national identity is recognised by Frank Bechhofer and David McCrone (2008), who see national identity as different from other forms of social identity as it is connected in some ways to citizenship or belonging to some nation. At the same time, they acknowledge the intimate and personal character of national identification (Bechhofer and McCrone, 2008) which is not "set in stone" and is not "the plaything of the privatised individual". In times of stability and security, be it national or personal, identity is not in question. Until something threatens it, it is merely there. "Identity only becomes an issue when it is in crisis, when something assumed to be fixed, coherent and stable is displaced by the experience of doubt and uncertainty" (Mercer, 1990). Otherwise, identity is an inseparable part of one's life that is connected to the place where one was born; it develops in the cause of time, absorbing traits and features specific to one's surrounding experiences.

For many, the sense of self and place is formed through routine practices and is defined in national terms (Billig, 1995). "Taken-for-granted" national identity provides a reliable framework for making sense of the world and presents a psychological stability and status understood by Michael Skey (2010) as "ontological security" (p. 716). Skey (2010) underpins his argument by Anthony Giddens's (1990) suggestion that the key sense of self and belonging lie in "the confidence that most human beings have in the continuity of their self-identity and in the constancy of their surrounding social and material environments of action" (Giddens, 1990: 92).

It appeared through some of the interviews that the above-mentioned ontological security arises from the firmly grounded national self-definition of the respondents. For many of them, the knowledge of being English acted as a token of stability and emotional security. Their sense of national belonging was filled with assurance, familiarity and continuity:

> I am English. It just happens to be where I was born. This is where I was brought up. This is what I know, this is what I am familiar with. Everybody is a result of the way they have lived most of their life. So, I shall always be, does not matter where I live, I shall always be English, British, I think.
>
> (E13)

The interchange in use of English/British identity was not an uncommon feature. The confusion of "England" and "Britain" often occurs not only in everyday conversations but also in journalistic writing and scholarly use (Kumar, 2003). A few instances were recorded when people described themselves interchangeably as English or British, once again supporting the stereotypical claim that some people in England did not know the difference between Englishness and Britishness (McCrone, 2002; Condor, 2006; Condor *et al.*, 2006; A.D. Smith, 2006). David McCrone (2002) asserts that the interchangeable use of "British" and "English" has almost made the two identities synonymous to the extent that if an English person in Scotland claimed to be British, he/she would not necessarily get acceptance north of the border (p. 309).

Anthony Barnett's (1997) observation appears to have a similar perception of intermix of British and English identities; however, he specifically stresses the confusion of the two national signifiers by English people:

> What is the difference between being English and being British? If you ask a Scot or a Welsh person about their Britishness, the question makes sense to them. They might say that they feel Scots first and British second. Or that they enjoy a dual identity as Welsh-British, with both parts being equal. Or they might say "I'm definitely British first". What they have in common is an understanding that there is a space between their nation and Britain, and they can assess the relationship between the two. The English, however, are more often baffled when asked how

they relate their Englishness and Britishness to each other. They often fail to understand how the two can be contrasted at all. It seems like one of those puzzles that others can undo but you can't; Englishness and Britishness seem inseparable. They might prefer to be called one thing rather than the other—and today young people increasingly prefer English to British—but, like two sides of a coin, neither term has an independent existence from the other.

(Barnett, 1997: 292–293)

Murray Pittock (1999) offers an historical explanation to such a common intermix of Englishness and Britishness, claiming that the roots of English ideas of Britishness lie in England's long history of partial absorption of its neighbours. That process has a much longer history than that of Britain (Pittock, 1999). In the case of British and English identities, their confusion and intermix largely take place when national identity is not in question but is a matter of taken-for-granted practice exercised by native English people in their everyday lives. For them, national identity as a set of cultural markers comes as a norm, accepted and not causing debate over surrounding social matters, and is not a subject of sentiment.

On the contrary, for a non-ethnic British person living in England, one's national identity is a highly important aspect of one's life which shaped the person's character and is central to one's behaviour and vision of oneself:

I take national identity seriously. I would buy and die for the British against everyone else in the world. Because that is the country of nationality I have picked.

(E18)

Similarly, for a businessperson who was born in India, brought up in Britain since the age of three and considered himself half-Indian and half-British, his national identity was a cause of personal displacement. A British citizen according to his passport and an international traveller with extensive overseas experience, he did not feel that he belonged anywhere. His attitude to the issue of national identity was therefore extremely sensitive as he tried to find solutions to how to adapt to the insecurity of not belonging anywhere and learning to live with it. The nomadic lifestyle, with its excitement of interacting with new cultures and a high quality of life, did not provide him with the sense of confidence in consistency and continuity of the social environment. Not having roots anywhere was a primary concern for respondent E8 when he considered the well-being of his children. It was important for him that they had a home, some roots and a sense of belonging. For this reason, interviewee E8 had to make a conscious decision to come back to Britain after living as an expatriate in various countries and settle here:

I think it [the issue of national identity] bothers me. I think if I stayed in India I'd have . . . not to say much better life but . . . I do not actually belong anywhere. I think it is the trouble when you travel. . . . I spent half of my life travelling. So, I do not have strong roots here, I do not have strong roots anywhere. That's part of the reason why I want to come home. I miss things. I do not want my children to be like nomads. I want them to have a home.

(E8)

For such respondents as E8 and E18, national identity was negotiated rather than simply accepted and, as noted by Susan Condor *et al.* (2006), raised concerns regarding their social integration. For them, ethnic equality was not "dependent upon being, becoming, feeling, calling oneself, or being recognised by others, as English". Rather, national identity was a matter of social inclusiveness based on "freedom from racist harassment, the ability and will to accommodate when necessary to the majority culture, and the opportunity and inclination to engage in meaningful interpersonal contact with people from a variety of different backgrounds" (Condor *et al.*, 2006: 152). In contrast to ethnic English people whose ontological security remained unquestioned for those living in England, respondents E8 and E18 were lacking the continuity of their self-identity in their chosen place of living.

Their search for constancy in their surrounding social and material environments brought to the fore the issue of national identity as a major identifier of their ontological security. Thus, the respondents interviewed in England demonstrated different perceptions of involvement with the issue of national identity. For the ethnic English living in England, national identity was not a matter of concern or of particular significance. It was merely there; it was a fact and was, therefore, often taken for granted. At the same time, for those of other ethnic backgrounds who "picked" their British identity by consciously choosing to become a British citizen and live in England, the issue of national identity was highly topical and important.

The research data showed that, attempting to define their national identity, the respondents employed a broad spectrum of national characteristics that could be divided into several groupings: English (seven respondents); British (five respondents); and those who firmly recognised their association with a state, thus claiming to be British but at the same time being strongly aware of their English ethnic roots (four respondents). Three respondents perceived themselves not only as English/British but also as European or even global. Nevertheless, they acknowledged that their background had been formed within certain national boundaries. There was one respondent in the sample who felt he did not belong anywhere.

The analysis of the interviews has identified several categories in the respondents' national identity discourse.

History

Respondents in the English research sample most commonly referred to the history of their country (nine respondents). History as an important reference point offered them links with the country's past and provided a sense of belonging to something common and shared, of which everybody was part. Often the interplay of English and British history came to the fore, marked, for example, by the Union of England and Scotland in 1707 as presented by respondent E6, an ethnic Scot who described his national identity as British:

> We have been united for 300 years. Not just several generations but 300 years. And we [Scotland] have not actually been an independent country. The same for England, England has not been an independent country for 300 years. So, it is more of a British identity than anything else.
>
> (E6)

Some of the respondents referred to history in a geographically narrower approach, limiting it to their association with England rather than Britain:

> Well, we have a fantastic history. It goes back hundreds and hundreds of years. So, I am always proud as a national English person, respect our heritage, our culture . . .
>
> (E7)

For others, the history of their country was inseparable from the history of their family. They did not simply know or understand the history of their country; their families were seen as playing an important role in making it. Thus, respondents had a personal feeling of being associated with their country's past:

> I am very patriotic about our heritage particularly in terms of manufacturing. I come from manufacturing background, I come from a manufacturing family and I can probably trace back all the way through my family generations. Fundamentally I think of myself as English. . . . It is an interesting point about how I feel, because where I am from. Not only do I see England as our heritage in terms of industrial heritage but where I am from was the centre of that within England, so first and foremost I guess that's where really my roots are. I am English not for any strong reason other than that I feel it.
>
> (E15)

Often in their discourses, interviewees referred to British history and its colonial past, feeling proud of Britain's achievements and success. It is worth remembering that it is exactly at the time of the British expansion as an empire that the English identity also became significantly vaster. Robert Young (2008) asserts that during the course of the 19th century, Englishness was translated from the national identity of the English living in England into a diasporic identity beyond any geographical boundaries which included all the English who had now immigrated all over the globe. "England" was no longer attached to a particular place, but rather to imaginative identifications such as the countryside, Shakespeare or sport—an England that could always be recreated elsewhere. The word "England" itself became a synonym that could be used equally to describe the country England, Great Britain and Greater Britain (so even today, England and English are often used instead of Britain and British) (p. 231).

Young (2008) states that by the end of the 19th century, Englishness was transformed from the set of defined cultural characteristics attached to a particular place into a transportable collection of "values which could be transplanted, translated and recreated anywhere on the globe, embodying the institutions and social values of Anglo-Saxon culture: language, literature, law, liberty, justice, order, morality and protestant Anglican religion" (p. 232). Thus, Englishness became a general category. It was no longer a single ethnicity but "an amalgamation of many; it became a cosmopolitan ethnicity" (p. 232–233).

The explanation of the "emptiness of Englishness" particularly noted by academics and politicians at the end of the 20th and beginning of the 21st century lies in its historical dislocation. Englishness "was never really there, it was always there, delocalised, somewhere else; by the end of the 19th century, England had been etherised, so that England and the English were spread across the boundless space of the globe, held together by the filiations of a vaguely defined Anglo-Saxon ethnicity, institutions and values. Even within England itself, identity in terms of origins and attachments top place had long since been dissolved, so that the situation was no different for those who had never gone abroad. Millions of English and Irish people were migrants, without ever having left the British Isles" (Young, 2008: 236).

Young (2008) offers a very clear explanation of the detachment of the English from their national identification caused by the historically developed migratory lifestyle of the nation. However, it does not explain why interpretation of national identity by some of the English respondents was seen through their attachments to places where they were born and grew up. This articulation of national belonging appeared the second most commonly used marker of national identity and mentioned by seven people in their national identity discourse.

A place where one was born and grew up

> What does it mean to me to be English? Not particularly that much really, because of the fact that I do travel a lot. I was born in England, so I class myself as an Englishman rather than British because Britain is England, Scotland, Wales, Ireland. So, I will always class myself as an Englishman.

> (E17)

Being born in England by default provided a link with the English nation. The meaning of this identity was not important; it was a fact that did not require much consideration. Being born in England assured one's unquestionable belonging with the English nation and being accepted as a native here.

Raymond Williams commented in 1983 that being native is of critical importance for individuals, far more important than artificial associations with the nation-state: "Nation as a term is radically connected with "native". We are **born** [author's emphasis] into relationships which are typically settled in place. This form of primary and "placeable" bonding is of quite fundamental human and natural importance. Yet the jump from that to anything like the modern nation-state is entirely artificial" (Williams, 1983: 180, cited in Easthope, 1999).

This might be the reason for E17's feeling of disengagement with the meaning of national identity. For him, English national identity did not bear much significance and was seen as something artificially constructed. What did matter was the place where one's life was taking place, where the surroundings were familiar and the relationships were meaningful. National identity was simply a fantasy that was being endowed with some meaning but did not relate to people's everyday flow of life.

It appears plausible to draw some links between the lack of meaning that the native English business travellers recognised whilst discussing their national identity, with the results of the Freedom's Children report published by Demos in 1995. Demos is the think-tank that investigated attitudes to work, relationships and politics among England's 18–34 year olds in 1995 (Wilkinson and Mulgan, 1995). The publications in the press detailing the research findings commented on a diminishing attachment to any national identity among the young people in England (Easthope, 1999). Considering that the average age of the businesspeople interviewed for this book was in their forties, it is logical to say that the current research respondents represent the opinions of those who were the subjects of the Demos investigation. The continuity of their fading attachment to their national identity suggests that English people find more meaning in their territorial identity given to them by birth and relationships that are settled within it, rather than in their national identity. They recognise their allegiance with the nation and the state, but this is not implicitly supported by meaningful commitment to Englishness.

It appears that association with the place where one was born provides people with a sense of belonging, another category of national identity established in the course of the interviews and highlighted by seven respondents. As it has been demonstrated earlier, this category was particularly strongly articulated by respondent E8, whose international experience and travel from a very early age had prevented him from putting down roots in any particular place, resulting in the feeling of insecurity, of not belonging anywhere and, in a way, regret at not being a natural part of any particular community.

Contrary to that view, interviewee E12 questioned the idea of people belonging to a certain ethnic grouping, whether it be English, Scottish, Welsh or Irish. He stated that:

> we are all mongrels. I can tell you with some accuracy about my parents, my great parents, my great-great parents on the male line. . . . I have a good understanding of where they came from. On the female line I have no idea whether they were of Welsh, Irish or Scottish origin.
>
> (E12)

Seeing the concept of national identity as a very recent one, E12 believed that people chose to belong to a certain national group because they "like to be a part of something and have an identity, a team to follow, a tribe to be part of. But if you actually analyse it . . . who knows". However, the recognition of the importance of feeling of belonging demonstrated people's need to be associated with a wider group of people, and often it was an affiliation with the nation in which one happened to be born that gave people that much needed feeling of identity and, therefore, security.

Feelings of belonging appeared to be closely associated with the concept of "home":

> I suppose it is that feeling of belonging. It is not MY country but at the moment it is my . . . home. I see it as being my identity. What that is, is difficult to explain.
>
> (E5)

Issues of home and belonging as attributes of national affiliation are deeply personal, highly sensitive and tightly intertwined and hard to articulate. Absolutely intangible, identity seems to be felt rather than observed, experienced rather than tested. It is constantly in flux, easily malleable, influenced by external environment and people's cognitive and emotional flows in the course of their lives. It appeared that other constructs of national identity that were employed by interviewees in their discourses were similarly fluid, as, for example, the notion of culture which was depicted in varied interpretations but fundamentally was used as an expression of people's collective mindset.

Culture

It was a curious discovery to observe that the term "culture" as a national identity construct was referred to by only three respondents. Additionally, culture's different manifestations, e.g., national stereotypes, the language, behaviour and hobbies (e.g., sport) were mentioned by five interviewees, bringing the total number of this category's occurrence to eight:

> What does Englishness mean to me? It probably just means the culture in which I was brought up, particular nature; most countries have their

own ethos and particular characteristics. Britain has its own . . . even within Britain England, Wales, Scotland differ from each other. I grew up in a big city. I am probably quite different from someone who grew up in a rural village. So, what does it mean? I do not think it means other than culture in which one was brought up. I do not mean artistic culture, I mean culture in a sense of growing up.

(E9)

Five business travellers in their national identity discourse emphasised fairly stereotypical traits of the English character:

English people do generally tend to be more reserved, a bit more . . . you can see . . . controlled, cynical, pessimistic [laughs], but reasonable.

(E11)

Another interviewee identified the following features as characteristic for his nation:

Honesty, discretion, fairness; we stand up for small people, fight against bullies, that sort of thing.

(E16)

This view was closely mirrored by his travelling colleague:

From a national identity perspective I'd like to view us as honest, fair, appreciative of other people, intelligent, creative . . .

(E15)

Association with national sport also emphasised the sense of belonging and unity with the nation. However, not the whole English research group referred to sport as a national identity signifier. To some extent, this finding contradicts Crolley and Hand (2006), who state that sport and national identity have been tightly intertwined since the introduction of international competition at the end of the 19th century. Fast forwarding a hundred years on, nearly half of the world's population watches the World Cup final on television every four years (Crolley and Hand, 2006). Thus, football becomes not only a sporting arena but also a field where "ideologies linking country, culture and national identities are produced, reproduced, and contested" (Vincent *et al.*, 2010: 200). Consistent with the research findings on Patriotic Sentiment and English National Football Support by Abell *et al.* (2007), no parallels were drawn by the respondents of the current study to consider national sport as a symbol of exemplified nationalism. Here, sport was rather presented as a subject of national pride and as a mechanism to capture notions of Englishness during important sporting competitions such as at football games when "at internationals, the team embodies the modern nation, often literally wrapping itself in the national flag" (Giulianotti, 1999: 23).

The small number of references to national sports in the English research sample, perhaps, reflects the traditionally modest attitude towards public displays of their Englishness by the English. And although it has somewhat changed in the last decade, owing to identity anxiety springing from the devolution within the United Kingdom, the manifestation of English national identity expressed through sport was not actively replicated by the English interviewees. The majority of my interviewees chose to articulate their national identity through the use of other signifiers rather than sport. They, for example, did not comment on joining the hordes of English fans that "invaded" Germany during the World Cup in 2006 (Vincent *et al.*, 2010). This tactic distanced the research participants from mass expressions of English patriotism potentially reflecting a slightly different nature of values and norms of self-expression of the social class and age group that they represent.

The English language was claimed to be another prominent feature of the common culture. One of the respondents pointed out the importance of the English language as the most distinctive characteristic of the nation:

> It [international business travel] has certainly made me realise that there is nothing to us Brits without the language.
>
> (E7)

This is not surprising as throughout its historical development, language has gone through "varying, conflictual and power-laden set of relations concerned with the intertwining of language and race, language and nationality, language and colonisation, language and institutions and so on" (Crowley, 1991: 7). Tightly enmeshed into the social reality, language does occupy an important role in the construction of different forms of social identities (Crowley, 1991).

The quote above, although exhibiting the value attributed to the respondent's national language, also expressed the concern about the nation: the main and the only feature of which to be proud was its language. This feeling was reiterated by many other respondents who seemed to be very conscious of the decline of British/English identity associated with disintegration of cultural norms in the country and big changes which had been challenging Britain in its recent history:

> Countries do go through cycles, through periods of strength and weakness. A few hundred years ago Britain had the biggest navy in the world and was the strongest navy power. All that has changed and other powers grew up.
>
> (E9)

> I think English culture now is getting out of hand. I think . . . people lack respect for law. You know it is a runaway culture now. . . . There is

just no control. And we have got big drink problem with young generations. It is nothing to be proud of. Well, I am proud to be English but
I see what goes on inside England and outside England. It's not nice, it's
not nice I think.

(E17)

These concerns are echoed by Krishan Kumar (2003) who puts the future of
the English nation in question: "for the first time ever . . . the English have
been forced to consider themselves as a nation, as a people with a particular
history, character and destiny" (p. x). According to Kumar, the question of
the future of England and its nation became particularly topical after the
disappearance of Britain's industrial supremacy and global power and in
the political climate "when the longest-lasting and most significant creation,
Great Britain itself, threatens to dissolve and disintegrate" (p. x).

This concern was addressed in David Cameron's (2011) speech at the
Munich Security Conference where, focusing primarily on terrorism, he
also highlighted the importance of building "stronger societies and stronger
identities" in Britain where collective identity has weakened under the doc-
trine of state multiculturalism. As a result, Britain today is a society where
different cultures "live separate lives, apart from each other and apart from
the mainstream" (Cameron, 2011). The importance of achieving social
solidarity and a minimum sense of "being in this together" is crucial for
multicultural Britain in order to resist global pressures (Goodhart, 2008).
"The paradox of Britain is that although it was substantially made by the
English they did not—unlike the other British nations—define their role in
it. England dissolved itself into Britain, and so to this day has only minimal
political/institutional identity. There is indeed no formal English political
community, one of the reasons why sport has become such a rallying point
for expressions of English identity" (Goodhart, 2008).

Indeed, Jeremy Clarkson (2007) states with bitter disappointment that
the English have been robbed of their Englishness. Perhaps a revival of the
attitudes towards English identity will change the role of Englishness in our
society? According to the Guardian (2010), research conducted by the Insti-
tute for Public Policy Research in 2010 has revealed that "an attachment to
Englishness has become a more significant feature within the social culture
of England than many of our politicians have realised". The research points
to a new sense of Englishness, characterised by a revival of English musical
traditions, literature and art and the absence of any single political or social
agenda. In the era of powerful global influences on the political and social
world order, England remains one of the most tolerant developed countries
in the world (The Guardian, 2010).

The Archbishop of York strongly believes that what England needs is a
sense of purpose and a common vision that has been lost with the passing of
the British Empire where England played a defining role. However, England
is hopeful in her identity and certainly does have something to celebrate

(www.Archbishopofcanterbury.org). According to the data gathered for the current research, the English can certainly be proud of their people and their highly valued qualities of honesty, fairness and appreciation of others.

Characteristics of People

Honesty, fairness and appreciation of others were perceived by interviewees as the most pronounced peculiarities of the traditional character. They were the object of people's pride and were consciously reflected in the businesspeople's professional behaviour which recognisably distinguished them from the business tactics of their colleagues from other countries. This was pointed out by eight respondents:

> I think we are quite proud of our ability of fair play and being straightforward with our customers and clients. What are the English traits? I think the primary one is being fair-minded and equitable in the way we deal. It is a lacking trait possibly because we do not push hard enough for the benefits of our company. Maybe our German competitors are rather better at closing a deal than we are. Because we tend to be fairly backward in coming forward whereas they are much more aggressive, they would sit there and say: OK, let's try to sign the contract today. And the English will turn around and be rather laid back and say: well, let us know when you would like to sign the contract. That is it.
>
> (E2)

> A traditional English person would be somebody who is mildly mannered and, polite. I am trying to be a good example of my country. And from the company point of view I suppose I am a diplomat for the company as well.
>
> (E3)

It appeared that, working in the international environment, some businesspeople undertook the additional role of a representative of their country. The interviews showed that this particularly applied to people working for a company that originated in the same country as them. A country's cultural traits were being transmitted through the company's own culture which was supported, carried and advocated by its employees. This was particularly evident in the course of interviews within De La Rue, a proudly British company with a global span of operations.

Four respondents commented on feeling proud of their country and finding themselves promoting their homeland while abroad:

> Wherever I go, whether it is the States, Eastern Europe, Europe, I shall let people know where I am from. I am quite proud of my country, I am

very proud of being English. I believe we are the most civilised country in the world.

(E7)

Respondent E17 experienced a slightly different vision of his country and, although also feeling proud of his belonging to its multicultural nation, he expressed his pride of belonging to a country of strong people:

it is such a multinational country, there are people from all parts of the world. We let them into our country. And apart from small isolated situations it works, it works, so . . . I am proud that we are what we are, you know. We are strong people. We are strong people and I am proud of that.

(E17)

This view goes against Raphael Samuel's statement (1989) that being seen as English has more palpable disadvantages than advantages, that the sense of personal worth of an English person has been eroded. For example, for respondent E2, his pride of living in this country was inseparable from his pride of the English way of doing business. Having worked in international business for more than 30 years and now occupying one of the most senior positions in his company, his business was inextricably a dominant part of his life and his identity:

I am very proud of living in this country. . . . I think in business we are quite proud of our ability of fair play. And level playing fields and things like that.

(E2)

Perhaps, the international business environment shapes international business travellers' understanding and appreciation of their national belonging through the exposure to other cultures and peoples. Representing their business in the international arena brings more emphasis on national differences and similarities: this influences business travellers' understanding of their national strengths.

Nature and the English Countryside

The country's nature and the country itself in general were mentioned among other constructs of national identity. However, the English countryside was discussed by only two businesspeople. Reminders of homeland and its boundaries might seem innocuous, but they act as indicators of materiality of the homeland. As Wallwork and Dixon (2004) have argued, landscapes are powerful signifiers of national identity. They represent the material grounding of nationalism and "reification of "the nation" arises through a ceaseless discourse on place and identity" (Wallwork and Dixon, 2004: 36). The appreciation of their country's natural beauty expressed by only two people is, perhaps, a reflection of the majority of respondents' urban lifestyle in the South East of England, one of Britain's mostly developed and populated areas (Office for National Statistics, 2009).

Wallwork and Dixon (2004) particularly emphasise the spatiality of society and the significance of places for personal and social identities in their investigation of the relationship between constructions of Britishness and constructions of the English countryside as one type of material environment. Drawing on earlier academic enquiries into the subject of national identity, they note Lowenthal's (1991) observation of a long history of the relationship between British national identity and the "quintessential national virtues" (p. 213) of the English countryside. They also refer to Rose's (1995) perception of the English countryside as a "rural idyll" that often acts as a privileged site for the expression of national identity and is often associated with "values such as harmony, social cohesion and continuity—the sedimentation of an organic relationship between people and place that has purportedly acquired a near mystical balance over the centuries" (Wallwork and Dixon, 2004: 24).

Thus, the analysis of the national identity accounts by English businesspeople orientate explicitly to the dilemmas of constructing their national identification through belonging to the place where they were born and not placing much attention on the meaning of landscape in the process of their national self-identification. It could be argued that the failure to appreciate the important role of the countryside in national identity claims is influenced by the respondents' broader environment comprising their urbanised lifestyle, which is further exacerbated by the cosmopolitan nature of their extensive international travel. Thus, the "space" of the international business travellers in the English research sample appears to be shaped by the cosmopolitan and urbanised conditions of their social environment. Therefore, for this group of business travellers, the essence of the relationship between nation and landscapes is being diminished, giving more power to other signifiers of national identity.

Other Observations

"Class" as an attribute of English national identity was mentioned by only one interviewee and thus did not imply that the respondents attributed much weight to this characteristic of the English nation. This is contrary to Kate Fox's (2004) opinion that class pervades all aspects of English life and culture and that England is a highly class-conscious country. She stresses that the way the English judge social class is very subtle and complex: Precisely how you arrange, furnish and decorate your terraced house not just the make of car you drive, but whether you wash it yourself on Sundays, take it to a car wash or rely on the English climate to sluice off the worst of the dirt for you. Similar fine distinctions are applied to exactly what, where, when, how and with whom you eat and drink; the words you use and how you pronounce them; where and how you shop; the clothes you wear; the pets you keep; how you spend your time; the chat-up lines you use; and so on (p. 15). Fox states that every English person "is aware of and highly sensitive to all of the delicate divisions and calibrations involved in such judgements" (p. 16). The issue is whether people openly admit it or not.

In the course of the interviews none of the respondents apart from one openly mentioned the class system. Generally representing England's middle class, the interviewees, according to Robert Colls (2002), present the national average with the characteristic qualities of balance, reason, composure, equanimity and compromise. They can be seen as "moderate in all things, avoiding a 'scene', trimming extremes, sidling carefully between their own passions" (p. 80). The English businesspeople, however, did make some indirect references to class status. Mentioning of such aspects as a certain background and education, the importance of private education for the future of their children and hobbies did imply middle-class commonalities. Nevertheless, the class issue, which quite possibly affects the shaping of the respondents' vision of the world and understanding of themselves as belonging to a particular nation, did not transpire as a valid signifier of national identity categorisation.

This can be explained by Fox's (2004) supposition that class differences are not accentuated, discussed or analysed by the native people who carry those class signifiers with them. Foreigners can be much better at noticing, analysing and categorising those things that native English take for granted (p. 18). For example, George Mikes' *How to be an Alien* (2007) has proved that point by masterfully depicting characteristic English traits and exclusively English ways of conduct, such as talking about the weather, introducing people to each other or particularities of speaking English, that seem to be profoundly obvious to foreigners and routinely practiced by the natives.

The discussions of national identity have demonstrated that national identity as a concept is seen by the respondents of the English sample as an inseparable part of their everyday lived experiences. The majority of ethnic English people interviewed did not consider it a highly topical issue, simply perceiving their national identity as a fact of life. However, for respondents with other ethnic backgrounds (e.g., Indian), the issue of national identity represents a notion of high importance, and thinking about it might at times cause the feeling of displacement underpinned by insecurity of absence of strong social attachments.

The discourses on their national identity allowed identification of the following constructs of this social phenomenon. Firstly, the respondents firmly associated themselves with the history of their country and showed great pride in its past victories and achievements. Secondly, national identity for the people interviewed was related to the national culture that the respondents described while talking about the English language, sport and certain human qualities that were seen as particularly specific for the English person. Thirdly, characteristics of the English businessperson, among which were honesty, fairness and appreciation of others, appeared a prominent feature of the English character. This was heavily supported by the feeling of pride in the English way of doing business and the feeling of responsibility of projecting this image abroad and acting as diplomats for their country. Fourthly, the place of birth and growing up, where the foundations of one's character and personal qualities were installed and developed, presented another category of constructing national identity. And finally, English nature and countryside that were employed only by a very small number of respondents. The low number of interviewees mentioning this category suggests that it does not have strong emphasis on the national identity construction by people in this research sample. It was observed that the issue of class did not appear directly as a category of national identity, while indirect references to class were noted in the interviewees' discourses.

Overall, the international business travellers interviewed in the south of England, in the majority of cases demonstrated the adoption of the ethnic approach to understanding their national identity. In their discourses, they commonly referred to such attributes of national identity as English culture, characteristics of the English people and place of birth (and the feeling of belonging associated with it). In contrast to that, only a few comments were directed towards the civic understanding of national identity in occasional displays of national pride in the achievements of the British Empire.

References

Abell, J., Condor, S., Lowe, R.D., Gibson, S. and Stevenson, C. (2007) Who Ate All the Pride? Patriotic Sentiment and English National Football Support. *Nations and Nationalism*, 13 (1), pp. 97–116.

Barnett, A. (1997) *This Time: Our Constitutional Revolution*. London: Vintage Books.

Bechhofer, F. and McCrone, D. (2008) Talking the Talk: National Identity in England and Scotland. In Park, A. et al. (eds.) *British Social Attitudes: the 24th Report*. Aldershot: Sage.

Bechhofer, F. and McCrone, D. (2010) Choosing National Identity. *Sociological Research Online*, 15 (3), p. 3. Available at http://socresonline.org.uk/15/3/3.html.

Billig, M. (1995) *Banal Nationalism*. London: Sage.

Cameron, D. (2011) *MP's Speech at Munich Security Conference*. Available at: www.number10.gov.uk/news/speeches-and-transcripts/2011/02/pms-peech-at-munich-security-conference-60293.

Clarkson, J. (2007) *We've Been Robbed of Our Englishness*. Available at: www.timesonline.co.uk/tol/comment/columnists/jeremy_clarkson/article293 5442.ece.

Colls, R. (2002) *Identity of England*. New York: Oxford University Press.

Condor, S. (2006) Temporality and Collectivity: Diversity, History and the Rhetorical Construction of National Entitativity. *British Journal of Social Psychology*, 45, pp. 657–682.

Condor, S. (2010) Devolution and National Identity: The Rules of the English (Dis) Engagement. *Nations and Nationalism*, 16 (3), pp. 525–543.

Condor, S., Gibson, S. and Avell, J. (2006) English Identity and Ethnic Diversity in the Context of the UK. *Ethnicities*, 6 (2), pp. 123–158.

Crolley, L. and Hand, D. (2006) *Football and European Identity: Historical Narratives Through the Press*. London: Routledge.

Crowley, T. (1991) *Proper English? Readings in Language, History and Cultural Identity*. London: Routledge.

Easthope, A. (1999) *Englishness and National Culture*. London: Routledge.

Fox, K. (2004) *Watching the English: The Hidden Rules of English Behaviour*. London: Hodder and Stoughton Ltd.

Giddens, A. (1990) *The Consequences of Modernity*. Cambridge: Polity Press.

Giulianotti, R. (1999) *Football: A Sociology of the Game*. Cambridge: Polity Press.

Goodhart, D. (2008) *A Mild Awakening, England's Turn?* Available at: www.open democracy.net/article/ourkingdom-theme/post-post-nationalism   englands-turn.

The Guardian (2010) *Englishness: The Forbidden Identity*. Available at: www.guardian.co.uk/commentisfree/2010/feb/11/english-nationalism-fight.

Kumar, K. (2003) *The Making of English National Identity*. Cambridge: Cambridge University Press.

Lee, M. (2004) The Story of Greater Britain: What Lessons Does It Teach? *National Identities*, 6 (2), pp. 123–142.

Lowenthal, D. (1991) British National Identity and the English Landscape. *Rural History*, 2, pp. 205–230.

Lucas, C.P. (1887) *Introduction to a Historical Geography of the British Colonies*. London: Oxford University Press. Cited in Lee, M. (2004) The Story of Greater Britain: What Lessons Does It Teach? *National Identities*, 6 (2), pp. 123–142.

McCrone, D. (2002) Who Do You Say You Are? Making Sense of National Identities in Modern Britain. *Ethnicities*, 2 (3), pp. 301–320.

Mercer, K. (1990) Welcome to the Jungle: Identity and Diversity in Post-Modern Politics. In Rutherford, J. (ed.) *Identity: Community, Culture and Difference*. London: Lawrence and Wishart.

Mikes, G. (2007) *How to Be an Alien* (Russian Ed). Б.С.Г.—Пресс.

Office for National Statistics (2009) *Key Population and Vital Statistics 2007*. Available at: www.statistics.gov.uk/downloads/theme_population/KPVS342007/KPVS2007.pdf.

Pittock, M.G.H. (1999) *Celtic Identity and the British Image*. Manchester: Manchester University Press.

Rose, G. (1995) Place and Identity: A Sense of Place. In Massey, D. and Jess, P. (eds.) *A Place in the World?* Oxford: Oxford University Press.

Samuel, R. (1989) *Patriotism: The Making and Unmaking of British National Identity. Volume I. History and Politics*. London: Routledge.

Skey, M. (2010) 'A Sense of Where You Belong in the World': National Belonging, Ontological Security and the Status of the Ethnic Majority in England. *Nations and Nationalism*, 16 (4), pp. 715–733.

Smith, A.D. (2006) "Set in the Silver Sea": English National Identity and European Integration. *Nations and Nationalism*, 12 (3), pp. 433–452.

Vincent, J., Kian, E.M., Pedersen, P.M., Kuntz, A. and Hill, J.S. (2010) England Expects: English Newspapers' Narratives About the English Football Team in the

2006 World Cup. *International Review for the Sociology of Sport*, 45 (2), pp. 199–223.

Wallwork, J. and Dixon, J.A. (2004) Foxes, Green Fields and Britishness: On the Rhetorical Construction of Place and National Identity. *British Journal of Social Psychology*, 43, pp. 21–39.

Wilkinson, H. and Mulgan, G. (1995) *Freedom's Children*. London: Demos. Cited in Easthope, A. (1999) *Englishness and National Culture*. London: Routledge.

Wood, E.M. (1991) *The Pristine Culture of Capitalism*. London: Verso. Cited in Easthope, A. (1999) *Englishness and National Culture*. London: Routledge.

www.Archbishopofcanterbury.org. (2011) *Archbishop's Speech on 'Englishness'*. Available at: www.arcgbishopofcanterbury.org/2369.

Young, R.J.C. (2008) *The Idea of English Identity*. Oxford: Blackwell Publishing.

Part Three
National Identity Construction by Scottish International Business Travellers

This part analyses the findings of the research conducted in Scotland. It firstly comments on the composition of the research sample. This is followed by a discussion of the role of the Scottish businesspeople's national identity in their daily life in order to establish how important national identity is for these people. Secondly, it addresses those national identity constructs that appeared most prominently in the business travellers' discourses: Scottish people's attitudes, values and behaviour; sense of belonging; Scottish countryside; Scottish culture; and people's business characteristics. At the end it summarises the research findings and concludes that the Scottish national identity in this research is constructed on ethnic rather than civic terms.

All 20 business travellers who contributed to this book were citizens of the United Kingdom of Great Britain and Northern Ireland. Following their own categorisation, 15 respondents believed they were of Scottish origin; two respondents defined themselves as English; and three persons were of mixed background (two were of English/Scottish and one English/Irish descent). The main focus of this section is, however, on national identity construction by Scottish businesspeople. Therefore, the stress first and foremost is on Scots and people with mixed background.

What Is National Identity? The Importance of National Identity to the Scottish Business Travellers

Similar to the English respondents, the Scottish interviewees' discourses demonstrated that the concept of national identity, especially when it is taken out of any particular context, is not something they deliberately ponder. However, the majority of my Scottish respondents commented on paying significant attention to cultural and national differences that became transparent during their international business travel and interaction with foreign colleagues. Observed behaviours and traits of overseas colleagues and experiences that businesspeople encounter in culturally different environments emphasise the differences in self-conduct, influenced and firmly established by national and cultural surroundings, values and norms of behaviour. These observations encourage people to look deeper into their own expressions of themselves and tend to direct their thinking towards positioning themselves against "the other" in order to understand the self better:

> I think it *[international business travel]* makes you understand and appreciate what your national identity is more than when you are in your country. When I go to European countries I see that people do speak two-three languages. So, it feels like people are more developed in terms of their capabilities. That makes me feel that I should make more effort to learn a foreign language. And you also feel you ought to know more about your own country when people ask you about Scotland. What is it like? What is the weather like? What do people do? Through that you think about your own identity a bit more. I'd say that when I go to other countries I am interested to learn more about what those countries are like. And maybe understand what is different in those countries. Maybe that is another way of appreciating what you are like.
>
> (S11)

Scottish businesspeople's extensive and open discourses about their national identity support findings of earlier qualitative studies stating that the Scottish people, those living in both Scotland and in England, have more willing and explicit attitudes to discussing their national belonging than English people (McCrone and Bechhofer, 2008). This was certainly observed in Scotland when often interviews intended to last 30 minutes went well over 45 minutes or even an hour. This was despite my interviewees' busy work schedules and because of their genuine personal interest in the subject matter and willingness to express their views on it. This is not to say that English people were totally indifferent to questions of national identity; as demonstrated earlier, they simply exhibited different approaches to talking about it (Condor *et al.*, 2006).

It was observed in this study that international business travel provides Scottish businesspeople not only with an opportunity to discover more about other nation, their culture and national peculiarities, but also to form more effective and collaborative relationships which help further their business:

> In Canada, for example, I feel very much at home. There is similar attitude, similar culture and same sort of ethnic backgrounds to a large extent as well. China felt very alien. Singapore felt less alien. Nepal . . . I was there for quite a long time. . . . We got engaged with the Nepalese, they are absolutely wonderful people. I grew to absolutely hate young Israelis who were rude, arrogant, self-opinionated and entirely pompous. There were some absolutely delightful French people I met and

absolutely delightful German people I met. It made me very conscious of how important it is to develop a proper relationship with the people who are your hosts.

(S16)

Overseas experiences encouraged businesspeople to learn more about their own cultural and national traits. Having found themselves in a foreign territory or in the company of foreign colleagues, they saw themselves more obviously and vividly through the lens of their overseas observations. A well-balanced application of these observations to the process of their national self-identification emphasised both positive and negative aspects of their national self-categorisation. Sometimes openly admitting certain disappointing factors, my interviewees nevertheless tended to feel proud of the nation they belong to and accentuated the positive aspects of their national background:

> It is interesting when one travels and meets people from different cultures. Some people are very proud of their nationality and others have less interest in it. Personally, I am quite proud being British (and we have done some poor things over the years, we have made some mistakes) but we do our best to make the world right. I am pretty proud of where I come from.
>
> (S6)

It was mentioned several times that understanding who one is and what is unique about one's own culture and national background can become a valuable advantage in business. Recognition of this inner knowledge about oneself, which, when skilfully used, might contribute to one's business objectives, became of significant importance and deep appreciation. This certainly is appropriate to respondent S13:

> As a Scot you are constantly thinking about it. Because being Scottish is actually a great door opener. Most people in most countries know at least something about Scotland, whether it is whisky or whether it is golf. . . . Particularly in business it will be one of these things. A businessperson is likely to play golf and enjoy whisky. It is a great icebreaker. It is something to talk about.
>
> (S13)

The analysis of the Scottish data has revealed the five most commonly used constructs of the Scottish identity: Scottish people's attitudes, values and behaviour; the sense of belonging; Scottish countryside; Scottish culture, and people's business characteristics. The overview of these categories of the Scottish national identity is presented below.

Scottish People's Attitudes, Values and Behaviour

The respondents' discourses on their national identity often led to their appreciation of the nation's social peculiarities and Scottish people's attitudes, values and behaviour. References to sport and hobbies, and also to the outgoing character of Scottish people, were very commonly present in the respondents' understanding of their national self. Interviewee S11, talking about what he would say to other people about his national identity, adopted a comparative approach relating the behaviour of Scottish people to what he had observed while working in Switzerland:

> I'd talk to people about what type of sport and activities that we are interested in. I'd talk about family values that are important as part of our identity. I'd talk about what people are like: outgoing, friendly, what kind of people there are and I'd compare that to what I see in some of the countries that I visit. Like in Switzerland people are very helpful but very conservative. So, they would ask you something but they would not dream of interrupting you; whereas in Scotland people will just come and approach you. So, that's what people would talk about: values in the family, interests that you do.
>
> (S11)

Like the English respondents who also used the comparison with "the other", the Scottish interviewees in their discourses positioned themselves against people from other countries who they had come across in their international business interactions. The comparative approach acted as a tool for identifying their own national characteristics when opposed to the ones claimed by members of other national communities.

Interviewee S13 also approached the issue of his national identity reflecting on people's social behaviour and attitudes to life. Like interviewee S11, he adopted an international perspective in his discourse; however, he was not relating the Scottish people to any other nation. His international experience allowed him to see the difference between how Scottish people were perceived abroad and how they saw themselves in their home country:

> Being a Scot in Scotland is different from being a Scot abroad. There are different perceptions of what a Scot is abroad. Perhaps you are expected to be more outgoing, friendly, outwardly, enjoying life, etc. But being a Scot in Scotland. . . . People talk about something that I hate because it is self-perpetuating. . . . The idea of a Scottish cringe. . . . It is pretty self-deprecating, putting yourself down: "Scotland will never qualify for the World Cup" or "Scotland will never get there again" or "it is so cold up here, why would anyone want to come here to Scotland?" or "we have such a terrible diet, we all are going to be fat and old and

die young". That is a stereotypical perception of Scots. . . . But I do not think that's the way we are generally. I do not think that externally and internationally that is what people see in Scots.

(S13)

References to Scottish people as a friendly nation came up several times, with a very touching example from interviewee S14 illustrating his standpoint:

If there is a little boy who is lost, people will be incredibly generous with him. Bringing him in. . . . Somebody will go and find where he has come from. There is incredible warmth . . .

(S14)

Perhaps such friendliness is rooted historically in people's close connections in Scotland that stem from strong family values and ties with friends that firmly hold the Scottish nation together. Sally Tuckett (2009) asserts that in the 18th century, for example, the role of family was integral in political life. Particular importance back then was given to influence, interest and patronage that shaped the role of women, giving them reasons for becoming more involved and having stronger impact on the closely intertwined social and political arenas.

The role of family in the Scottish culture continues to be important today. Nick Hopkins and Christopher Moore (2001) found that "loyalty to family ties" is one of the five most commonly used characteristics employed for describing the Scottish. The other four adjectives most frequently selected for the Scots were "Warm, Tradition-Loving, Passionate and Kind" (p. 243).

In the 21st century, the role of family is still seen as central and heavily influencing people's sense of belonging which is commonly associated with the place where one's family come from. Interviews with Scottish businesspeople suggested that people who had left their country to work abroad for extended periods still found themselves seeking connections with their homeland through establishing links with nationals of the same country of origin. Family values and relations were still of great value and importance. In seeking such connections, they joined national clubs that temporarily became their substitute broader family, as described by interviewee S14:

I will *always [respondent's emphasis]* feel I am from Scotland wherever I am in the world. I worked in Barbados for six months and I always felt Scottish there. I joined the St Andrews club. There is a St. Andrews Society where you walk in and people ask you where you are from, your family. . . . It is very important to me. It is fantastic! Most of the time I do not really care about my front bar *[meaning external image]*, but I suppose my corner is my family . . . and being Scottish.

(S14)

It was noted that there was no mention of the Scottish clan in the respondents' accounts of their national identity. Following the work of T.M. Devine (2006), this research observation should not be surprising, as the disintegration of the Scottish clan started as early as in the late 17th century. The Scottish clan was originally a grouping of people based on a social contract between the ruling families and the commons of the clans. The ruling families were expected to act as a guarantee for secure possession of land and its protectors in exchange for the clans' people's allegiance, military service, tribute and rental of the land. However, with the development of markets and commerce, the elites' ancient social responsibilities for their people gave way to the commercial interests of profit increase. This, combined with the Union's government's intention to eliminate clanship as a cause of rebellion and disaffection, were the critical influences that killed clanship (Devine, 2006).

Additionally, the traditional Highland way of life was destroyed by material, cultural and demographic forces that were particularly accelerated by the impact of market processes and transformation of clan chiefs into commercial landlords in the 1760s–1770s. In that period, a new order emerged based on significantly different values, principles and relationships. The transition of clan chiefs and gentry into landed gentlemen, reinforced by the Highland elites' education in southern schools and universities and extensive travel, resulted in the injecting of different, non-Gaelic values into traditional society and in "the relentless violation of the values of clanship" (Devine, 2006: 182) and "enormous collective disorientation throughout the Gaelic world" (Devine, 2006: 182). As a result, landlordism took triumph over the tribalism of the traditional clan.

As the interviews have demonstrated, contemporary Scottish society was not considered through the prism of Scottish clanship by those who permanently reside in Scotland. However, the idea of the Highland clan is somewhat idealised by those ancestral Scots living elsewhere throughout the world as a result of their ancestors' migrations. For these diasporic Scots, the notion of the Highland clan is used as a "particularly resonant resource to draw upon in the construction of their own indigenous identity" (Basu, 2005: 125). It helps the members of the "unsettled settler society" (Basu, 2005: 123) to re-root in their ancestral homeland in their attempts to find their unproblematic territorial belonging which has become impossible for them in their diasporic home countries.

To the native Scots, whose belonging to their country is certain and never in question, the concept of the Scottish clan bears no significance in their perception of their national self and belonging. The Highland clan for the contemporary native Scots is no more than just another unique feature of the Scottish cultural heritage. The psychological influence and importance of the idea of the Highland clan is weakened by my respondents' firm awareness of their belonging and affiliation with Scotland.

It appears that it is the emotional connection that holds Scottish people firmly attached to their motherland. Going on an extended overseas work assignment (as in the case of interviewee S2) can be a fantastic experience, but new social relationships with people from other countries do not provide a familiar degree of depth and intimacy in communication which is so highly valued by the Scots. Hence the psychological need to keep attachments with the social environment where these needs are satisfied, i.e. at home in Scotland:

> We lived in Australia, we lived in California and we came back home to Scotland once or twice a year. It was important to us, our family ties and our friendships here. So, national identity is quite strong, I think. Although I am a citizen of the world, there must be quite a lot of emotional ties back here in Scotland. It is things like familiarity. If you go along to a party in California, you can have a good time. But parties would generally be: you have a barbeque, you have one or two beers and the same conversation. Usually it is all superficial things: your Scottish background, talk about kids, school, weather, all fairly neutral topics. It was very pleasant, people were extremely friendly . . . but there did not seem to be a great deal of depth in these social interactions. But when you come back here in Scotland, it is almost . . . all these niceties . . . everybody can understand the culture and people can read and interpret each other a lot faster. And you seem to get more intimate relationships a lot faster.
>
> (S2)

Echoing interviewee S2, interviewee S3 referred to the communal nature of his nation and its social inclination. He talked of the Scots as passionate people and deep thinking. Confirmation of a passionate love for their country was easily recognisable in respondents' discourse through the use of superlatives in expressing their views about their nation [emphases in bold are mine]:

> It is a lot of pride of where I come from, of what Scottish people have taken to the world, what a great country it is. It is the sense of fierce nationalism and great pride. Doing this job is great because what I do every day is selling Scotland which becomes quite easy to do when you believe in the product. It is a huge and beautiful country. Having travelled around the world, it is one of the most beautiful countries I have been to. A lot of countries have beautiful places but other than some bits of Glasgow and a few places in Dundee, Scotland is probably the most beautiful. It is fantastic. So, that's what it means to me.
>
> (S17)

Every sentence in this abstract serves to express very strong feelings of pride for Scotland and its achievements, and also of its beauty. According to respondent S17, the country is a fantastic place to live in; it is "probably the most beautiful" of all he has been to. Such emotional expression of one's feelings for one's country is a sign of a passionate, "feisty and fiery" (S6) character, able to experience deeply emotional feelings towards what they hold true:

> I would see myself as pretty fiercely Scot. We are very proud to be Scottish. I try and use it when I am overseas.
>
> (S16)

In a similar way to respondent S16, three more interviewees pointed out the unique identification of Scottish people that they know they will always possess. These people acknowledged the recognisable difference between their Scottish identity and English identity. Respondent S14, who works in London, is always seen as Scottish in the British capital:

> I will always be known as Scottish in London and when I moved down there I did not think that. . . . When I pick up the phone and people say: Hi *[name omitted]*, it is only you here who has a Scottish accent. In London they perceive me as Scottish.
>
> (S14)

Interviewee S2 recalled being subjected to national demarcation during his working in London in the 1970s–1980s, and even experienced a feeling of discrimination towards the Scottish people:

> Going back to the late 1970s—1980s, I was training with *[the name of the company omitted]*, a large accounting firm. And a lot of training was in London, so every time I went to London I felt discrimination against Scottish people. Scottish people would be called "Jock", you'd be teased in a way and Scottish people would be quite self- conscious. . . . It was not great and most Scottish people had a chip on their shoulder. So, to me it was being a foreigner, a minority in a group of people, not in a good way.
>
> (S2)

Although according to S2, this has changed by now, and being a Scotsman is seen as an advantage and "a very positive thing", the memories of such division and distinction within the same nation-state have not been eroded fully. However, despite the differences that might be identified between English and Scottish people, some Scottish interviewees, among other qualities of their national character, emphasised their honesty and a principle of fair play, also highlighted by the English respondents.

Humour was another trait discussed by both Scottish and English businesspeople. It is something that is equally enjoyed in the South and in the North of the Union and helps bridge different people and make them feel more comfortable wherever they are:

> Scottish people like their humour. I like laughing with them. It helps building rapport and you feel much more comfortable.
>
> (S5)

Belonging

The sense of belonging was mentioned by eight respondents, and this was the second most commonly employed category of national identity construction by my Scottish interviewees:

> It is a lot of pride of where I come from, of what Scottish people have taken to the world, what a great country it is. And it is also that sense of belonging. Most people like to belong somewhere; you do meet people who do not like to belong but most want to belong somewhere. I could support Scotland in any sport in the world, even in something I am not remotely interested. I'd still support a Scottish team because it is a Scottish team. I come from a very mixed background and a lot of people in the UK do. I am very definitely Scottish. I was born in Scotland, brought up in Scotland and have not known anything else. . . . I would always say I am Scottish. Full stop.
>
> (S17)

The sense of belonging provided an eagerly sought feeling of emotional safety and stability to people. Firmly identifying themselves with Scotland, they were secure in the knowledge that after their international business travel, they could always come back to their country, to the familiar. It was a feeling of having roots in the place where they had grown up and developed through learning and interaction with family, friends and environment; it was their "corner" (S14).

Similar findings were reported by David McCrone and Frank Bechhofer (2008, 2010) in their studies on national identity claims by English and Scottish people. Even though they openly recognise Susan Condor's (2006) belief that surveys and the use of pre-determined questions are not good instruments for investigating national identity, they nevertheless used a quantitative approach to their study. Their quantitative analysis, in support of earlier qualitative research, claims that national identity, in contrast to citizenship, "involves cultural markers, of birth, ancestry, language as well as residence, and operates through complex progress of social interaction" (McCrone and Bechhofer, 2010: 941).

Sport—one of manifestations of social interactions—was often referred to by the respondents in my research. As shown by interviewee S14:

> It is just growing up in Scotland; growing up there, playing rugby, watching rugby with your kilt on.

(S14)

Fiona Gill (2005) comments that rugby is the sport most analysed in relation to differing British national identities. It should not be surprising that respondent S14 positioned playing rugby very closely to his place of birth in his explanation of his national identity. To a certain extent, rugby can be perceived as a contemporary signifier of the successful promotion of the game in Britain's colonies during the process of establishing British values on a foreign land (Gill, 2005). This view mirrors Vincent's (1998) claim that rugby was a tool for encouraging a "British identity" in Britain's colonies and to strengthen links between Britain and her dominions (p. 124).

Rugby, seen as a British game, has its long history in both England and Scotland. Gill (2005), with references to a number of publications on the development of the game, gives an insight into its history which dates from the 14th century. As an extension of the "folk-football", the regulated versions of this game began to be developed primarily in public and grammar schools in the 19th century. The first written copy of the rules was produced by the students of Rugby School and dates from 1845. Admittedly, this was not the only form of the game in existence. In Scotland, the rugby game had been played in public schools since 1824. It is quite indicative that rugby does have its own "national weight" if this game was mentioned by a few Scottish respondents in their national identity discourse. Quoting Cronin (1999), "the success of the national sports team is a way of measuring success and prestige of the nation which produced it. Consequently, sport acts as a means of 'articulating national belonging' that stands closely to another very prominent national identity characteristic, the place of one's birth" (p. 51).

The research on national identity by McCrone and Bechhofer (2008, 2010) that analysed the results of the Scottish Social Attitudes Survey 2005 reinforced the previously claimed findings (Kiely *et al.*, 2005a, 2005b, 2006) that place of birth is the main marker of national identity leading to its acceptance by those to whom this claim is made. However, in everyday social situations, when place of birth is often not known, individuals' claims for national identity are assessed on the grounds of such indicators as accent and place of residence. Often in Scotland, having Scottish parents can be seen as another attributor to the Scottish identity, leading to its acceptance (McCrone and Bechhofer, 2008).

Indeed, Lindsay Paterson and Richard Wyn Jones (1999) state in their analysis of attitudes to definitions of Scottish identity that to have Scottish parents or grandparents is the second most popular category in national identity construction claimed by people in Scotland. This is preceded by "Scotland being a place of birth" as the most commonly used signifier of national identity; and followed by the condition of "living in Scotland" (p. 187). There is also a belief that someone, originally an outsider, but with a residence in Scotland over an extensive length of time and with an expressed commitment to Scotland, can be considered Scottish, to become an "adopted Scot" (McCrone and Bechhofer, 2008: 1261).

Scottish Countryside

Images of the Scottish countryside and Scotland as a country were mentioned by seven respondents as a place of their strong affinity and admiration. For some of these people the best memories of their life were associated with the Scottish landscape and the beauty of the countryside:

> When I think about the happiest moments in my life, it is standing somewhere on a golf course in Scotland or on the top of a mountain. Scottish is something I like being perceived as. I like the romance of the Highlands, whisky, burns, and the cloud in the water. Peaty water. Americans ask me what peat is. . . . And you now, you can have a bath which is dark brown. And they go: Yuck! But actually it is probably the cleanest water you will ever bath in, although it looks like mud . . .
> (S14)

For respondent S3, being Scottish is akin to a very personal relationship with the Scottish environment. It is the Highlands and the mountains and the lochs that have captured his heart from his childhood. But Scotland is much more than simply a place where he grew up; it is a place where he belongs. This is a place which he knows very well and has a unique personal understanding of. Other Scottish people, from S3's point of view, might have a different vision of Scotland and their Scottishness, perhaps, could be expressed through some other images or associations or in some other ways. Nevertheless, for this respondent, it is the Scottish landscape that brings up the deepest feelings of sharing, understanding and belonging:

> My vision of what Scottishness is might be completely different from someone else's. I grew up in the Highlands of Scotland and I feel an affinity with the Highlands and the mountains and the lochs. For some people it might be shortbread. But that is the Scotland I belong to, which might not be the same to the rest of population. I love being Scottish.
> (S3)

The Scottish countryside is famously known for its scenery and much loved by those who appreciate and care about its beauty. For many people today, Scotland is considered a wild and "untamed" land, the majority of which is still untouched by human population. It is often used as a retreat for those who seek to "get away from it all" (Wickham-Jones, 2001). For the native Scottish people I have interviewed, the Scottish countryside was not just a subject of great pride: It was also their motherland. The interviews demonstrated that for them the Scottish landscape was not a blind idealisation of the country they belonged to. The Scottish respondents openly recognised the unpredictable nature of the Scottish weather. However, for them, Scotland was the most attractive place on this planet. According to interviewee S5, the weather did not make his country any less attractive or feelings about it any different. It was still the place where he belonged:

> When I am away on business I really look forward to coming back to where I come from. Even if the weather is bad here, it is still where I belong.
>
> (S5)

For interviewee S15, who admittedly did not feel any particular national attachment to any place and saw himself as European rather than Scottish or British, the affinity with the Scottish countryside where he grew up, nevertheless, remained recognisably robust:

> I grew up on the farms [in Scotland] with no particular identity or tie to any particular village or town or city. I feel an affinity with the countryside and the landscape. But beyond that I feel more . . . I do not know what. . . . European perhaps rather than Scottish or British per se.
>
> (S15)

It is notable that the Scottish countryside acted as a symbolic depicter of the sense of national community in personal interpretations of Scottishness by my respondents. The reflection of a similar perception of Scotland can be found in the literary works of Sir Walter Scott (1771–1832), a Scottish writer and a political figure of his times. Scott's novels reflected his political stance supporting simultaneously unionism of the United Kingdom and distinctive cultural nationalism of Scotland. His writings are characteristically famous for their unique sense of community placed in the context of the specifically Scottish experience. In his novels, Scott not only promotes his political position, he also attributes specific characteristics to Scotland. For example, in his well-known Waverly novels, the qualities of Scotland are narrated through its landscape and weather that are "dramatic enough to figure as actors in their own right" (Harvie, 1989: 183).

In a similar vein, in the Scottish interviewees' discourse, the beauty of their country was closely associated with the beauty of the human character of people who were born and bred there. This is evident from the discourse of respondent S7 which is full of excitement, admiration, love and pride for her country and her people:

> Just look outside: it is a gorgeous day, it is crisp and clear, you probably have to step 5 minutes out and you are looking at the hills. It is a stunning country and people are friendly. I have a pride and a sense of: I am Scottish!
>
> (S7)

Culture

Six respondents mentioned how proud they were of being Scottish. Respondent S8, for example, was proud of his country's inventors and economists who made Scotland known for their achievements:

> We are a fiercely proud nation. We are small but we have got some of the world's greatest inventors and economists and we tend to be protectively proud of that.
>
> (S8)

Similarly, respondent S16 was proud of his nation and pointed out its education system and its people's characteristics, such as their outward-looking nature, integrity and respect in the world. He clearly separated Scottish identity from the English identity but did it in a non-confrontational manner. He just saw himself and his fellow citizens as having a distinctive national character expressed through unique dress code and easily recognisable music:

> . . . most people know what it is to be Scots. A Scot is canny. A Scot has got a reputation for integrity. A Scot is someone who values education. A Scot is someone who goes out into the world, Scots do not stay at home, they go out. They'd been to Canada, they'd been to Australia, they go out. . . . It is the outward looking nature of the Scot that I think is very positive and we have a distinctive form of dress. We have a distinctive form of music, which some people absolutely hate, and some people absolutely love. It is nice to be Scots. The Scots are pretty well respected throughout the world and it is probably an advantage to say that you are not English. We can stand up and say: we are not English, we are Scottish and that is OK, no problems with the Scots there. Entirely harmless.
>
> (S16)

The quote above mentions a few of the cultural components of national identity employed by the Scottish international travellers in their national identity discourse, such as distinctive national music and unique form of dress. It also points out the value the Scottish people give to their system of education. Four people in the Scottish research sample referred to the Scottish system of education as an object of national pride that gives its citizens opportunities for personal development and growth, identifies their strengths and encourages maximising their potential. These opportunities are not taken for granted by Scotsmen. On the contrary, they are deeply appreciated and valued. As an example, for respondent S17, doing his business is his way of paying back to the country that gave him an opportunity to grow personally and professionally:

> I have had great opportunities given to me in Scotland and in a way it is a bit of a payback me selling Scotland worldwide.
>
> (S17)

Language as another cultural element of the national identity construction received its recognition by four Scottish respondents. Although the official language in Scotland is English, the Scottish accent is easily recognisable. It attracts by the complexity of its dialects that can appear very different and sometimes hard to understand even for fluent English speakers of foreign origin and, in some cases, even by native English speakers [personal observation]. Interviewee S16, originally from Aberdeen, described his original Aberdonian dialect (now he speaks with an Edinburgh accent, having lived in the city for 40 years) as the one "nobody can understand":

> When I am speaking like this *[with reference to him speaking with an Aberdonian dialect]* you can't really understand what I am saying, can you? Their words are different.
>
> (S16)

Interviewee S15 also referred to specifically Scottish words that he grew up with as part of his national identity. Such words as "wee" (small drink), "dram" (small drink), "burn" (stream), "bairn" (baby), "loch" (lake) and "glen" (valley) differentiate those who employ them in their vocabulary from other people in the United Kingdom. The habit of inserting such words into one's speech can be seen as a manifestation of one's difference from "the other" on the one hand, and belonging with the nation that shares the same linguistic unit, on the other. Equally, respondent S7 loved the Scottish accent as much as she loved being Scottish and expressed it in a very excited manner. Every note of her voice throughout the interview was demonstrating her love and passion towards her country, her people and her language.

Language can be categorised as a national identity construct and as a tool for creating one's national affiliation. That is clearly shown in the example of interviewee S9's 12-year-old son who lives in England and speaks Geordie (Newcastle English) most of the time. On occasions when he comes up to Scotland to visit his dad, he adopts the Scottish accent and starts supporting

Scottish sports teams. He very skilfully utilises his ability to switch between the two identities (English and Scottish), which his dad sees as significantly different:

> My youngest boy is twelve and he speaks with a Newcastle accent but when he comes to Scotland, he immediately picks up the Scottish way of talking and he would support Scottish teams. In that sense he is very Scottish even though he lives in England.
>
> (S9)

The Scottish kilt, whisky, shortbread and the Scottish humour were mentioned by interviewees as stereotypically common themes characterising the Scottish identity around the world. They have rightly become the national symbols of Scotland at home and abroad. National clichés are often the topic of conversation that bring international business travellers together on their business stays abroad. Every nation has its own set of clichés, and their recognition and discussion help people to get closer while seeing themselves through the lens of the other:

> I used to have a joke with my colleague in the Netherlands when we were collecting national clichés. We'd pick a country and discuss all the pre-conceptions, whether they are true or not. . . . That's sort of a game we used to play. What we found was that very often most of these clichés are actually true. Normally they do not come for no reason at all. Does not affect which country it is. So, I define myself by looking at others, comparing with other people.
>
> (S18)

Stereotypes are understood as "stored knowledge structures whose meaning is defined before activation" (Hilton and von Hippel, 1996). It became transparent through the interviews that for some Scottish businesspeople, stereotypical views of their country, although true, were, nevertheless, almost derogatory. Perhaps due to their profound understanding of their people and national traits, Scottish businesspeople could see much deeper than what was on the surface. They discussed the issue of their national identity with deeper precision and greater knowledge than common references to "kilts, bagpipes, green hills, and thick Scottish brogues that appear in films such as *Braveheart* (with the occasional Highland cow thrown in for good measure)" (March, 2002: 1).

> The Scots are seen as being honest (that's before the RBS). We do jobs well, we do jobs thoroughly. We are good at technical matters. We've got a reputation for engineering. That's a part of our culture. I am not going to talk about the kilts and bagpipes and haggis. The Scottish educational system gives you that particular flavour. We play rugby,

you know. All Scots are more pure than most English. Being Scottish is important but it is overwhelming.

(S19)

Looking deeper into what being Scottish means and proudly exhibiting their appreciation of belonging to the Scottish nation, the Scottish respondents nevertheless did recognise their national stereotypes and use the world-wide admiration of distinctively Scottish attributes to their advantage. As an example, they capitalise on the attraction of the kilt (officially recognised as a Scottish National Dress from 1822 (Tuckett, 2009)) as a "passport to talk to people" (S14) when it is necessary or convenient, in a way supporting the image of a "canny Scot" (S16). However, extensive international business travel provides opportunities to meet more people and to learn more about different nations and their cultures. Exposure to "the other" opens up new perceptions of themselves and other people and provides better understanding beyond national stereotypes:

> Even Robert Burns about a hundred years ago said that the more you travel the more you realise that you have to see people as individuals, not as people from different countries. The more you see people the more you have to see them beyond the national stereotypes. Everybody is different.

(S3)

Business Characteristics

Despite the recognition that everybody is a unique individual, the Scottish businesspeople nonetheless identified certain qualities shared by many Scottish businesspeople and that they regarded as specifically Scottish. In a similar manner to the English business travellers' perception, "fair play" occupied an important place in understanding of self by the Scottish business travellers. However, this notion of fair play was reinforced by the solid nature of the Scottish businessman who would pursue his business endeavours very seriously and would not allow his business decisions to be influenced contrary to his own opinion. The image of the solid character of a hard-working businessperson was shared and cherished by several Scottish businesspeople:

> In the international market Scottish people seem to be seen as friendly, outgoing, entrepreneurial, innovative, robust, reliable . . . all good characteristics. Those are the ones that are broadly recognised. Scotland is a small country but it has got a huge diaspora. And Scottish people do travel a lot, business associated people. So, that recognition of the Scots' identity has become quite universal. A Scot would take matters seriously; he would not be persuaded that a thing is good if it is not.

In a business sense this is seen as quite useful. Because one of the big problems in business today, and this is one of the problems which globalisation has brought, is that everybody seems to think that in business everybody has to be optimistic, you always have to be right, never wrong and in fact there is a lot of cases where what causes problems is that optimism. And solution here, I'd propose, you should know that this is not the right solution. It is much better to say: thanks, but I am not going to do this business because I know this is not the right solution. So, an image of a "dour Scotsman" is of someone who would be honest about that and walk away from business that others would pursue because they want the business, whether or not it is the right piece of business. So, there are interesting complexities in that, I guess. Small countries (and I am not suggesting that Scotland is unique because it isn't) have their advantage because small countries tend to work a bit harder to get their identity known. And that usually means that it is solid part of their identity that people have to know and recognise.

(S12)

It appears from the quote above that being Scottish, and particularly being a Scottish businessperson, was not only a big honour but also a big responsibility. The reputation that Scottish people were so proud of was the result of the hard work and commitment of many generations of travelling Scotsmen.

T.M. Devine's (2006) account of Scottish history 1700–2007 discusses historical influences on high levels of emigration by Scottish people. He observes that the Scots had always been a very mobile nation and always looked for advancement, opportunities and employment overseas and in England. The Scottish diaspora did not start with the opening of North America and Australia. The Scots migrated in thousands to Poland, Scandinavia, Ireland and England as mercenary soldiers, peddlers, small merchants and tenant farmers and labourers. Even at the times when the general emigration numbers fell in the UK, the Scottish exodus continued at high levels. In the 1920s, for example, Scotland topped the league table of emigrant nations (Devine, 2006).

The explanation for such an advanced emigration tradition can be found not so much in deprived economic conditions as in the lure of opportunity abroad and internally within the UK. It is worth noting that in the second half of the 19th century, Scotland was one of the most successful industrial countries in the world. It also acquired a global reputation for excellence in shipbuilding, engineering, iron and steel and agriculture. However, the differential between opportunities at home and overseas was significant enough for Scottish people to explore opportunities abroad. Emigration was also heavily influenced by the development of the transportation links and communications of the 19th century. Emigrants now did not see leaving Scotland as a permanent exile; they had an option of working overseas on a temporary basis. Thus, the numbers of "returned migrants" from those who had no intention of settling permanently abroad grew significantly. An illustration of this could be the seasonal migration of several hundred granite workers who moved to America each spring only to return back to Aberdeen for winter (Devine, 2006: 475–485).

In the contemporary world, as demonstrated through the interviews, Scottish people are still looking for business opportunities abroad and are willing to travel internationally for the benefits of their economic objectives. Their attitude towards doing business and the Scottish character have become a "good global brand" (S2), and the Scottish businesspeople I have interviewed were committed to preserve it and were keen to contribute to the further improvement and solidification of the image of themselves and their nation as "straightforward and hardworking" (S4) people that they presented around the world. Thus, being involved in international business implied much more than simply representing one's company in order to achieve its economic objectives. A businessperson voluntarily becomes an ambassador for his/her nation and aims to create the best possible impression of it:

> When you are in a foreign land you are an ambassador for your own nation. It emphasises how important it is to create a good impression.
>
> (S16)

The findings from the data collected in Scotland demonstrate that the Scottish businesspeople were very willing to talk about their national identity and provided open and explicit accounts of their understanding of their national belonging. National identity for them was not something they consciously pondered about. However, when exposed to other national and cultural environments, the Scottish business travellers, noticing differences, appreciated more strongly the significance of their own national belonging.

Five major characteristics of national identity were highlighted by the Scottish businesspeople in their passionate discourses on their national affiliation. The powerful feeling of pride for the country they come from underlined a vast majority of interviews, where love for Scotland was feeding through respondents' excited voices, intonation, choice of vocabulary and their body language. Firstly, Scottish national identity was strongly associated with the Scottish people, being seen as friendly, outgoing, warm, generous, emotional and very sociable. For them, strong family connections were critically important, as well as solid friendships that were often built on emotional connections and shared personal experiences.

A strong sense of belonging with the Scottish people/nation was also among the most common descriptors in the Scottish businesspeople's discourse on their national identity. It was presented as the feeling of security and familiarity with the place where one was born and bred, and harmony with the surrounding social life. National identity for my Scottish respondents was also associated with the Scottish countryside and its landscape and pride in its unique beauty. There was a sense of unbreakable affinity with the environment in which they grew up, an affinity that stayed with people forever, even if they had to move away from their motherland.

Speaking about their understanding of their national identity, the Scottish respondents proudly mentioned such elements of the national culture as the Scottish education system, the unique and easily recognised Scottish accent and regional dialects. These manifestations of the Scottish culture were complemented by recognition of specific Scottish humour and famous Scottish stereotypical images of kilts, whisky, shortbread and haggis, although the latter were taken lightly, simply as famously known symbolic signs of their national attachment.

Discourse on the characteristics of a Scottish businessperson, such as a straightforward and hardworking "dour Scotsman", signified the importance of the specific nature of their job in their self-identification. Being Scottish was recognised as an advantage in business operations. The Scottish identity, therefore, acted as a "good global brand", that also added extra responsibility while representing one's country in international business activities, thus bridging people's perception of their professional identity with their national understanding of themselves.

Overall, the data provided by the Scottish respondents in their discussions of what constitutes their national identity demonstrated that the majority of interviewees adopted the ethnic approach to understanding their national characteristics. Such constructs as national culture, characteristics of the Scottish people, affinity with the Scottish countryside and feeling of belonging, dominated over the civic vision of one's national identity expressed, for example, through associations with state structures (e.g., the system of education) and the impact it made on people's personal and professional development.

References

Basu, P. (2005) Macpherson Country: Genealogical Identities, Spatial Histories and the Scottish Diasporic Clanscape. *Cultural Geographies*, 12, pp. 123–150.

Condor, S. (2006) Temporality and Collectivity: Diversity, History and the Rhetorical Construction of National Entitativity. *British Journal of Social Psychology*, 45, pp. 657–682.

Condor, S., Gibson, S. and Avell, J. (2006) English Identity and Ethnic Diversity in the Context of the UK. *Ethnicities*, 6 (2), pp. 123–158.

Devine, T.M. (2006) *The Scottish Nation 1700–2007*. London: Penguin Books Ltd.

Gill, F. (2005) Public and Private: National Identities in a Scottish Borders Community. *Nations and Nationalism*, 11 (1), pp. 83–102.

Harvie, C. (1989) Scott and the Image of Scotland. Cited in Samuel, R. (ed.) *Patriotism: The Making and Unmaking of British National Identity. Vol.II. Minorities and Outsiders*. London: Routledge.

Hilton, J.L. and von Hippel, W. (1996) Stereotypes. *Annual Review of Psychology*, 47, pp. 237–271.

Hopkins, N. and Moore, C. (2001) Categorising the Neighbours: Identity, Distance, and Stereotyping. *Social Psychology Quarterly*, 64 (3), pp. 239–252.

Kiely, R., McCrone, D. and Bechhofer, F. (2005a) Whither Britishness? English and Scottish People in Scotland. *Nations and Nationalism*, 11 (1), pp. 65–82.

Kiely, R., McCrone, D. and Bechhofer, F. (2005b) Birth, Blood and Belonging: Identity Claims in Post-Devolution Scotland. *The Sociological Review*, 53 (1), pp. 150–172.

Kiely, R., McCrone, D. and Bechhofer, F. (2006) Reading Between the Lines: National Identity and Attitudes to the Media in Scotland. *Nations and Nationalism*, 12 (3), pp. 473–492.

March, C.L. (2002) *Rewriting Scotland: Welsh, McLean, Banks, Galloway, and Kennedy*. Manchester: Manchester University Press.

McCrone, D. and Bechhofer, F. (2008) National Identity and Social Inclusion. *Ethnic and Racial Studies*, 31 (7), pp. 1245–1266.

McCrone, D. and Bechhofer, F. (2010) Claiming National Identity. *Ethnic and Racial Studies*, 33(6), pp. 921–948.

Paterson, L. and Jones, R. W. (1999) Does Civil Society Drive Constitutional Change? The Case of Wales and Scotland. In Taylor, B. and Thomson, K. (eds.) *Scotland and Wales: Nations Again?* Cardiff: University of Wales Press.

Tuckett, S. (2009) National Dress, Gender and Scotland: 1745–1822. *Textile History*, 40 (2), pp. 140–151.

Vincent, G.T. (1998) Practical Imperialism: the Anglo-Welsh Rugby Tour of New Zealand, 1908. *International Journal of the History of Sport*, 15, pp. 123–140. Cited in Gill, F. (2005) Public and Private: National Identities in a Scottish Borders Community. *Nations and Nationalism*, 11(1), pp. 83–102.

Wickham-Jones, C.R. (2001) *The Landscape of Scotland: A Hidden History*. Stroud: Tempus Publishing Ltd.

Part Four
National Identity Construction by Russian International Business Travellers

This part is devoted to the understanding of the concept of national identity by Russian international business travellers. It firstly assesses the composition of the Russian research sample and examines the degree of depth to which the Russian respondents addressed the issue of national identity. The analysis of the data demonstrated that place of birth and growing up, national culture, the characteristics of people, national history and countryside were the most commonly occurring categories in their understanding of national belonging. This analysis is followed by a discussion of further observations, such as national pride, the feeling that accompanied the vast majority of Russian interviews. The chapter highlights the complex nature of national identity where its different manifestations are closely linked and tightly intertwined.

The composition of this research sample reflects the multi-ethnic and multinational character of the Russian state with its population of 146.5 million people (Federal State Statistics Service, 2017). Among my interviewees there was one Tartar, on half-Russian and half- Ukrainian, one half-Jewish and half-Tartar, one half-Azerbaijani and half-Russian, one Belorussian and one Karelian. All the research participants were nationals of the Russian Federation and native Russian speakers. Four people were also in possession of other citizenships: three British and one American.

What Is National Identity? The Importance of National Identity to the Russians

The interviews with the Russian businesspeople uncovered the general tendency of Russians to think about their national identity and to examine the concept in fine detail, often approaching it from a deeply personal perspective. This trend was also observed by Yale Richmond in his book *From Nyet to Da* (2003) where he addresses the impossible challenge (even for the Russians) to explain the Russian character in response to Grand Duke Aleksandr Mihailovitch's statement that he has "never met anyone who understood Russians". Richmond (2003) notices that "Russians and other citizens of the Soviet Union are very much aware of their nationality. Proud of their ethnicity, they are also curious about the national origins of persons they encounter. They will be pleased to tell foreign visitors about their own nationality, and visitors should not hesitate to ask" (p. 26).

The findings of the interviews with the Russian businesspeople display a very similar observation. The majority of my respondents were very interested in the subject of the interview and extremely eager to talk about their national identity. Many of them also exhibited a powerful desire to debate the meaning of Russianness as a topic of their personal concern:

> This is a very important issue for me because I love Russian history; I collect books about Russian history and the Civil War. I have been thinking about this issue for a very long time, since the early 1990s. It was a very turbulent time and the search for the Russian identity had always had place in Russia since the times of Lomonosov and the Decembrists. It is the desire to understand ourselves. I believe this issue is crucially important for the Russian people like for nobody else.
>
> (R7)

For interviewee R7, the issue of national identity was closely linked to his personal life journey. Thus, national identity was not simply an association with a place where one lived and worked; it was also a search for oneself in this world. R7 was fully aware that he was not alone in this search and to some extent sought no instant resolution. He enjoyed pondering about Russian history over a glass of beer with his friends. Finding the meaning of his national identity was a lengthy process, a curious journey of many years. R7 stated that the search of the Russians for their Russianness had been a national characteristic for decades and even centuries and was, perhaps, another factor distinguishing a Russian person from anybody else. It united people in their thinking of themselves as a nation and made it a particularly Russian feature, where gaining a better understanding of oneself seemed possible through finding sense in national belonging and through the understanding of the Russian national character.

Recognising without a shadow of a doubt his belonging to the Russian nation, R7, nevertheless, sought clarity in understanding what it actually meant to be Russian and in his approach positioned the issue of national belonging alongside such eternal issues as the ideas of good and bad:

> It is something that will never get resolved and I shall never stop thinking about it. It is similar to the idea of good and bad; or God. . . . But deep inside I am truly Russian. I love Russian birches, vodka and shashlyk, singing and dancing . . .
>
> (R7)

The deeply philosophical approach with which interviewee R7 evaluated the meaning of his national affinity was mirrored by interviewee R6, for whom

> these thoughts *[on national identity]* are absolutely natural. This is the state of my soul. They are automatic. I do not think about it deliberately at all. Simply in any situation I feel and perceive myself as a Russian person with our culture, with our attitude to life, with our attitude to children. I am constantly comparing and looking for the confirmation of bad and good things. I always analyse: this is better than at home, this is worse . . .
>
> (R6)

Some interviewees linked their thinking on national identity to the influences of their education (all were educated to at least degree level) and saw themselves as part of the Russian intelligentsia, "an educated, culturally productive, politically engaged segment of the population" (Knight, 2006: 738).

> Of course I do think about it *[national identity]* simply because every intelligent person thinks about it sometimes.
>
> (R20)

So, how do Russian businesspeople working in the international environment perceive their national identity?

Place of Birth and Upbringing

Thirteen out of 20 respondents produced accounts in which they expressed their recognition of the influences of individuals' place of birth and upbringing on their sense of national identity. For example, interviewee R5 associated all his life with living in the city of Saratov, where he was born, grew up and received his education; he still lived in Saratov at the time of the interview. Attempting to explain his national identity, he immediately referred to the place where he had lived all his life:

> I cannot explain it. Having been abroad and having seen all that beauty, I am still very much drawn back home to my country. Maybe it is because I never left Saratov for more than a month. I cannot live without Saratov, Saratov is everything for me. My parents lived here and everything is very familiar, this is where I belong. Everything abroad seems very artificial. Everything is very beautiful, very practical but also very artificial.
>
> (R5)

Familiarity with the known and the experienced gives people a sense of security and confidence that translates into a feeling of belonging. One can only belong if one feels a strong attachment, a solid bond and a sense of complete affinity with a place and its people which often develop through time (Barrington *et al.*, 2003). Ashley Carruthers (2002) refers to national belonging as a form of cultural capital that is accumulated through lived experiences and shared affinities. In a similar vein, interviewee R2 called it "cultural baggage", and her personal dilemma of living between two countries was intensified by the contrasting feelings of strong cultural affiliation with Russia, where she grew up, with her mother and her roots on the one hand, and ever-increasing influences of the foreign (British) environment in which she had lived for a number of years on the other. The prospect of losing some links with Russia due to her mother moving to live permanently in Switzerland was diminishing the sense of security attached to belonging to Russia:

> What determines me as a Russian? It is difficult to pin it down. I like Russian birches, Russian landscape. Perhaps this is because I grew up there . . . this is what I grew up with. . . . My native/original home is in Russia. Russia is something that has always been there, it is truly yours, it belongs to you, it is your roots. And now, when my mum is getting married to a Swiss person, the idea that what is associated with my mum will be removed from Russia is bothering me, frankly.
>
> (R2)

Reiterating this view, interviewee R1 defined his national belonging in association with the concept of motherland as the place where one grew up and developed as an individual, where a strong connection with that place was supported through family links and friendships:

> Russia is my motherland. In any situation you come back to your motherland and it is always the place where you spent your childhood and your youth, it is the place where your relatives and friends are. Yes, it happened that we now live abroad but our motherland cannot be taken away from us. . . . Like starlings that fly away for wintering to Africa but then they come back to their original nest. It is very important for me.
>
> (R1)

It appears that early memories of one's engagement with one's country have the potential to become a permanent platform for identity-building through the creation of the anchoring power of belonging as a guarantee of one's security and personal and emotional stability. That feeling is in many cases associated with people's early recollections of their parents, mothers in particular:

> From the age of three–four I went to the nursery. It was the time of the Great Patriotic War and we were taught to sing songs: Бей гранатой,

Бей прикладом Гадину ползучую [*Fight with grenade, fight with a butt creeping rats*]. So, what type of person could I grow up as? Of course I am a patriot of Russia. From a very early age I knew what a war was and what suffering it could bring. My mum used to come back home with newspaper cuttings about our [*Russian*] partisans and we all were reading these articles in the evenings.

(R10)

Culture and Language

Association with Russia as a nation-state was tightly intertwined with the Russian respondents' perception and degree of understanding of their culture. Discussing their national identity, the Russian interviewees often referred to Russian music, singing, folklore, classical literature and cinematography. To some of my respondents, a Russian person's connection with his/her nation transpired through close association with Russian and Soviet literature and the masterpieces of the national cinematographic industry that are known to almost every Russian from their childhood years:

> . . . it is the fact that I was brought up in a Russian-speaking family and in the Russian culture. And I grew up within the Russian system. I was a pioneer when the USSR collapsed. So, it is crucially important what books we read when we were growing up and what films we watched. All our jokes originate from a dozen Russian comedies of Gaigai and others. Yes, we all read Robinson Crusoe and other foreign books but here the books are very different.

(R2)

Indeed, children's reading in the USSR was managed so that children read the right books and in appropriate ways, with the view that child readers turned into "people who consume books in a rationalistic, self-conscious, exegetic manner" (Kelly, 2005: 751). As a result, children's sets of values, appreciations and beliefs rose to the level of national dogma through the management of children's reading under Soviet power (Kelly, 2005).

Russian and Soviet literature, rich in the beauty of its magnificent language, was an important cultural ingredient in the interviewees' construction of their national belonging. References to Russian and Soviet writers and a masterful use of the language also acted as useful instruments, skilfully employed in respondents' discourses. Interviewee R9 generously sprinkled his speech with Russian proverbs demonstrating the fascinatingly empowering wisdom of Russian folklore: Язык до Киева доведет [One's tongue can lead to Kiev]; Лучше синица в руке, чем журавль в небе [A bird in the hand is better than a crane in the sky]; Кто у власти—тот у сласти [One who has authority, has privileges]; Там дерутся, а здесь щепки летят [The fight is over there but the splinters are here]; Свой среди чужих, чужой среди своих [one's own among foreigners and a foreigner among one's own]; На каждый роток не накинешь платок [One can't put a headscarf over somebody's mouth] . . .". A skilful application of national proverbs was more than a sign of high-level intellect, education and awareness of the richness of the Russian language and literature. It was also a manifestation of deep understanding, love, following and implementation of this traditional knowledge in everyday life.

The spectrum of the respondents' literary and linguistic references varied significantly in the course of the interviews from Russian folklore to Russian classical literature; from the ideological writings of the Soviet leaders to Soviet dissidents. Interviewee R20, pondering about the meaning of his national identity, resorted to the view of his favourite writer Sergei Dovlatov:

> I love to quote my favourite Sergei Dovlatov who said: "the person, who speaks and writes in Russian, expresses his feeling of love and swears in Russian, can call himself Russian". I absolutely agree that expressing your deepest thoughts such as love and hatred, and also conducting your written and oral communication in a particular language defines your national identity.
>
> (R20)

Familiarity with the literary work of a Soviet dissident writer (Dovlatov was excluded from the Union of Journalists for his oppositional ideas and intentions to publish them and eventually immigrated to the USA) was not only a demonstration of an intellectual and open mind but also a symbol of people's personal affiliation with the messages conveyed in the published work of Russian writers. Dovlatov's quote, moreover, exposed R20's vision of a Russian person as someone expressing oneself through the Russian language and a certain pattern of behaviour. Thus, the national language was reaffirmed as a constructing force of one's national identification.

Characteristics of the Russian People and Their Mentality

The third most popular approach to identifying one's national belonging was focused on being part of the Russian nation and its people with their character and forms of conduct that were distinctive from any other nation. Ten interviewees applied this category, which could be illustrated through the rhetoric of respondent R11, for whom being Russian implied having a particular mentality, formed and enriched through close association with Russian people and their achievements. Such interconnectedness with the Russian nation developed through sharing the same values, supporting and following the same traditions, subconsciously adopting and consciously recognising the nation's peculiarities. Being Russian was being part of what was happening in Russia and being involved in social, economic and other processes concerning its development.

> I am Russian. Being Russian is about our values, traditions, peculiarities. It is our people, our achievements. I do associate myself with them. If Russia is now on the path of economic growth, I associate myself with it. If Russia is going through a devaluation of the national currency—it is also a part of my life.
>
> (R11)

It appeared that the Russian mentality, in the respondents' eyes, was a product of collective knowledge of Russian history and those ingredients that constituted the Russian culture. The concept of Russian mentality was also heavily rooted at its source, people's upbringing, where historical and cultural affiliations developed in first place under the influences of family, school, environment and friendships. It was observed in the course of the interviews that the term "Russian mentality" determined a common contour of people's consciousness characterising a particular national mindset. "Formed since childhood" (R12), the Russian mentality is different from any other (R10) and is characterised by a heightened sense of nationalism as a dominant value in the Russian consciousness (Laruelle, 2009).

As noted by Mikhail Gorshkov (2010) in his sociological study of contemporary Russia, Russian society after a few years of radical reforms continues to ensure "a relatively hopeful transmission of basic values in life, motives, and ways of perceiving reality" (p. 33). Among different characteristics of the Russian national identity that were conditioned by many circumstances, Gorshkov (2010) identifies historical experiences, the consequences of the reform years, people's individual sense of their status in society, their material conditions and a whole range of other factors. All these factors can be reduced to one general overall indicator, satisfaction with life as a whole (p. 36).

The Russian respondents' involvement in international engagements in their work environment presupposed a relatively advanced level of their professional development and opened avenues for further learning, growth and advancement that influenced the businesspeople's position in society, another important indicator of people's sense of social well-being. The satisfactory level of my respondents' social status might, of course, reflect the tendencies in their national identity construction specific for this particular social group. Therefore, it is important to bear in mind the limitations of the research sample, which by no means can be extrapolated to the entire Russian population.

Some respondents noticed that, representing their country in the international business environment, they experienced a degree of reinforcement of their national consciousness. That became particularly apparent when, during international meetings, they were faced with questions about Russian business and Russian people. Aiming to achieve positive business results, they focused on projecting Russia's positive image as a good business partner and on developing their business potential through making new business links and attracting potential business colleagues:

> . . . every trip is a fight for business clients. That is why I am trying to make the best possible impression. I get extremely tired as I spend a lot of energy to create the right impression and to be attentive and polite and patient. From that point of view I represent Russia and I see myself as Russian. There is no mergence *[with other cultures]*. I am Russian.
>
> (R17)

It was pointed out that knowledge of Russia and the Russians in the international business world was often limited and, consequently, the country and its people appeared unknown and therefore different and unique. Thus, the need to facilitate their business interactions and engage potential foreign partners necessitated the promotion of better understanding of "mysterious" Russia in the international business arena. This resulted in Russian businesspeople's deeper consideration of their national traits that reinforced their appreciation of their national identity during their international business interactions.

Such heightened national awareness, however, weakened outside the business world. For example, the same respondent (R17) admitted that her perception of her national identity changed while on holidays abroad. When not concerned with promoting the positive image of the Russian business climate, her distinction between herself as a Russian businesswoman and "the other" became far less pronounced. Indeed, while on holiday, her personal identity changed and in that circumstance she was simply a tourist and her international skills acquired through professional activities contributed to her feeling very comfortable abroad, well integrated and rather international. This feeling was reiterated by several other respondents who equally felt very comfortable abroad (especially in English-speaking countries) and not different from other people when they did not have to represent Russia and Russian business.

History

History was another feature commonly used by the respondents in their construction of national identity. Eight out of 20 people, when talking about their affiliation with Russia and the Russian nation, referred to Russian collective memories, historic events and the nation's past, highlighting the importance of preserving their cultural and historic heritage, as claimed by respondent R3:

> . . . it is very important to me to preserve my culture and remember my history and past.
>
> (R3)

However, it is not only the understanding of the country's history that reinforced affiliation with the Russian nation; it was also the possibility of sharing common memories that was critically important for sustaining the knowledge about the country and the feeling of unity with its people:

> I like Russian history. Who would I speak to about Russian history here *[in Britain]*? Perhaps just a few people . . . but to talk about the history of the WWI or the Great Patriotic War over a pint of beer in the pub is unlikely . . .
>
> (R7)

Shared memories of past experiences of the nation and mutual cultural values appeared to be important constructs of Russian national identity. Several respondents addressed the issue of their national identity through the lens of memories of their country's Soviet past, where one's base values were established through the system of Soviet education and highly politicised upbringing. This generally applied to the older generation of my Russian research subjects who grew up in the USSR and lived the bigger part of their lives and built their careers within the Soviet system. One could hear the notes of immense pride in certain elements of the respondents' pre-1991 country. The passionate recollections of the Soviet education system and great military achievements in the Great Patriotic War acted as a prime example. Some feelings of nostalgia accompanied the respondents' memories about living in a vast multinational state where everyone was equally a Soviet citizen regardless their ethnic origin. That nostalgic sentiment was sometimes mixed with the feeling of disappointment for the Russian population of the former USSR:

> When I was a little boy, I did not know any difference between Russian and non-Russian. Marriages between different nationalities did not raise any issues. And when everyone became very nationalistic, everyone started being proud of their nationality, the Russian nation became blamed for everything.
>
> (R10)

Countryside

The Russian countryside, its nature and landscape, can be categorised as another national identity marker, supporting Rosalinde Sartorti's (2010) claim that Russian scenery can be seen as a symbol of a national uniqueness (p. 394). Respondent R4 referred to the vastness of the Russian landscape, a topic raised by five other respondents too. The vastness of the Russian territory and severe variations in its climates reflect the breadth of the Russian character with its warm-hearted hospitality towards friends and family, and suspicion and hostility towards outsiders. Russian birches appeared in the interviewees' discourse several times as the symbol of Russia, the image that was captured and glorified by many Russian poets and artists. The snowed image of a birch from Sergei Yesenin's "The Birch Tree" is remembered by most Russians from the school curriculum on Russian literature. This image of purity, elegance and strength associated with Russian nature, once firmly established in a young person's mind as a symbol of Russia, appears to accompany one's affinity with Russia throughout life.

Other Observations

It is important to acknowledge a popular instrument that was observed in articulating national identity: Several people, in explaining their national affiliation (in other words, what they were), referred to establishing what they were not. R12, for example, claimed:

> I was born Russian and always will be Russian. I am not anything else as I am not German, for example . . .
>
> (R12)

R12, in order to define her national identity, positioned herself against people from other national backgrounds. Such certain confidence of R12 in being Russian and "not anything else" was particularly interesting because this respondent was the only person in the group of Russian interviewees who was very vocal about her desire to live abroad and had no patriotic sentiments towards her motherland. Nevertheless, she recognised that she would always remain Russian despite her hard criticism of certain aspects of the Russian reality that she despised, such as inefficiency, bureaucracy and attitude. R12 openly admitted that when on her business trips, usually lasting from ten to fourteen days, she never missed her country, never wanted to go back to Russia and felt that she understood foreigners and the foreign (Western) way of living extremely well. Nevertheless, she was and always would be Russian.

Positioning oneself against "the other" appeared a useful tool in the Russian interviewees' explanations of their national attachments. It is through the discussions of fundamental differences with other nations that a clearer picture of the Russian identity emerged:

> It is a particular culture there *[in Britain]* which we, Russians, cannot accept. If you pop out at nine pm in a small town, there is no one in the streets. The impression is that everybody is dead. You might find a small group in a local pub but that would be it. I come from a large city. I lived all my life in St. Petersburg (now I live in Moscow) and I find it very hard to understand a village mentality. I need to be involved in some activities; I need something to be happening around me. . . . I need to be able to go to a restaurant at any time of day spontaneously and if a friend has come to visit me, there is always an option of going to a

night club. When it is all close and accessible, it is part of your life but when it is quite far away and to get to a place you need to take a train . . . then you would not even want to do it. So, having seen all this, my desire to leave Russia lessened more and more. Now I do not want to leave Russia at all.

(R8)

Similarly, interviewee R3 built her discourse on a contrast between her Russian and British lived experiences:

I very often feel that I am lacking some adrenalin. Everything is so established and works according to some certain programme and everything is so easy. . . . In Russia to achieve something you need to get through fire and water. . . . Of course there are issues here *[in Britain]* as well and things that do not work. I often tell my friends that Russia is about 500 years behind you but we are young and we shall achieve everything.

(R3)

Thus, the contrasting approach clearly helped her to understand what she is by identifying what she is not.

Another observation focused on understanding the concept of national identification that stemmed from rather differing angles for different people. For example, for respondent R16 national identity was a deeply personal construct equated to the state of one's inner contentment. Answering the question what it meant to be Russian, the respondent commented: "it is a Russian soul in the first place, openness and hospitality" (R16). For some other respondents, national identification was a cognitive choice of associating oneself with a set of political institutions and the rule of law of a certain nation-state that arose not so much from personal psychological values but rather from economic and practical considerations, as in case of respondent R13 (who has an American passport):

Very often I am asked how I identify myself. . . . I feel myself an American perhaps because among all the models, countries and possibilities, I have become truly supportive of the American model. This model is very simple: any waitress from a tiny Polish village and any Olympic champion, having come to America, both have equal chances for naturalisation and equal chances to start their lives afresh. Both can equally become a teacher, a doctor, an engineer . . . and once they have gone through some period of five–ten years, they are no different from those people who were born in the States.

Also, as for the business side in America, I must say that America is the most tax-attractive place for people and different sizes of businesses and corporations. The European countries I have lived in do not give one a feeling of equality with those who were born there. Having lived for nine months in Europe, I still heard: these are Russians . . . nothing to do with the reputation, good or bad. . . . I do not know how many years one has to live in Greece to become Greek and in France to become French. I do not know. That is why I choose America. Everyone there is American. Everyone.

(R13)

The option of choosing one's national identity added a certain degree of complexity to people's understanding of themselves and their national affiliation. Not available to all my interviewees, it is a privilege of those who have the right to live in a country other than their country of origin. The option of being able to choose to associate oneself with more than one nation might seem an attractive advantage: an American citizenship, as in the case of respondent R13, has given the respondent some broader career opportunities and life experiences. However, the social and economic advantages of being a citizen of more than one country might complicate psychological matters when ethnic identity collides with the newly acquired civic one. One ethnic Russian businesswoman stated that, being Russian and living in the UK, she did not feel particularly at home anywhere. The most comfortable place for her was on the airplane flying between Russia and Britain.

Acquisition of a new civic identity did not presuppose the loss of the original ethnic one. Having consciously chosen to be American, interviewee R13 had not lost those cultural and social values and norms that had already been embedded in her character through growing up in the USSR. Seeing herself as American now, she, at the same time, remained Russian and supported Russian sport teams and felt extremely comfortable working in Russia after a very extensive period of living and working in the USA and other countries. A clear reasoning of associating oneself with this or that nationality (i.e. choosing between civic or ethnic national identification) can explain such mixed feelings as, for example, why people feel Russian when preferring to express themselves in their native language and American when considering advantages and disadvantages of the national healthcare system. When people do not possess the freedom to choose their national identity, the question of "who am I?" presupposes a much more straightforward answer. According to Vera Tolz (1998), many Russians prefer nation building to take place around their ethnic identification, such as culture and language (p. 1018).

The differing underlying assumptions of what it meant to be Russian employed by the Russian businesspeople in their national identity discourse that I have explored above, supported Stephen Lovell's (2006) approach to define Russia. Lovell points to a number of ways, each of which could be equally employed for this purpose. Firstly, Russia can be seen as a great power, a successor state to the USSR; secondly, it is feasible to define Russia in ethnic terms as the state of all Russians; thirdly, Russia can be approached in civic terms with considerations of its political institutions and the rule of law; fourthly, Russia can be contrasted with other nations and defined it in terms of what it is not: in other words, to play the anti-Western card. Of course, these approaches to defining national identity are not mutually exclusive: On the contrary, some overlap between them is natural and expected, as appeared in the interview with respondent R13, who defined herself as American considering her national identity in civic terms and also Russian when drawing national identity associations from the point of view of her ethnicity.

Patriotism

One of the most striking research findings was the passionate feeling about Russia by the majority of Russian businesspeople and especially those with extensive experience of living abroad. Patriotism for these respondents did not mean ethnic or cultural homogeneity: None of those who called themselves patriots expressed nationalistic feelings in order to promote the dominance and interests of the Russians in their country or globally. Rather, their discourse was aimed at expressing their devotion to Russia and Russian ways of life. Thus, no conflation of patriotism and nationalism was observed in the course of the interviews. Moreover, patriotism was expressed as the respondents' love for the Russian unity, the Russian nation, strongly supporting Maurizio Viroli's (1997) claim that patriotism is possible without nationalism.

Some of the respondents called themselves patriots of their motherland with excitement and enthusiasm, which could be heard in every note of interviewee R1's statement:

> I am a patriot! I support Russian sports teams and attend Russian meetings and gatherings. If there was a football match Russia—Scotland, I would still support Russia. I sort of feel 50/50, but anyway Russia is more like 51 per cent.
>
> (R1)

This comment was particularly interesting in its demonstration of people's enduring attachment to their motherland. Interviewee R1 had lived abroad for 15 years and during that time developed a strong attachment with Scotland, his current country of residence. However, despite the length of time and geographical distance that separated him from his home country and despite him openly admitting that he felt "50/50" [*50 per cent Russian and 50 per cent Scottish], he nevertheless was a Russian patriot. The country he grew up in and where his family still lived outweighed the adopted and acquired when he attempted to establish his national identification.

A highly-politicised perspective on citizenship was demonstrated by interviewee R10. For him, being a citizen of one's country was almost synonymous with being a patriot of that country; it was something natural or even ingrained in one's character and mentality:

> My belief is that every citizen of his country remains a patriot of his own country. For me Russia is Russia. Of course after a week *[abroad]* I start missing my home country.
>
> (R10)

R9's emotional connection with Russia was accompanied by a strong feeling of devotion to the country where he was born and lived. Russia was his motherland, and he was her devoted patriot. His view of Russia was quite realistic: He recognised that not everything was perfect in his country; nevertheless, it was his motherland, and he accepted and loved it for what it was.

> I do not want to go into philosophical discussions here . . . it is the country where a person was born and lives. Motherland can usually be only one place. Sometimes people acquire another one when they have moved to another country for different reasons: religious, financial, etc. My motherland is Russia and I am a patriot of my country. "Хоть она уродина, но она мне нравится, хоть и не красавица" [abstract from a song "even if it is ugly, I still like it, even if it is not a beauty"].
>
> (R9)

The reference to the lyrics of the song "Motherland" performed by DDT, a non-conformist, originally underground rock group, was not accidental. DDT is one of the most famous Russian rock bands that was formed in the year 1980 and for 30 years has been examining different aspects of life in the USSR and Russia. In his music, Yuri Shevchuk, the founder of the group, addresses not only the strengths but also the weaknesses of the Russian government, a stance that could not have been popular among the Soviet government and censoring officials. Although Shevchuk never considered himself as a political activist, his music, nevertheless, "continues to voice concerns and frustrations of the Russian people . . . today just as he did in the band's infancy" (Hudson, 2010). Association of one's own thoughts with ideas conveyed through music by DDT was symbolic of an active and searching mind of a person concerned with understanding his place on this planet.

The feeling of belonging with the Russian nation, the sense of being deeply rooted in Russian culture through its multiple manifestations, and the confidence in the invisible but powerful bond with Russia, was firmly supported by the interviewees' pride in their fellow citizens:

> Our intellect, our culture and education are very well respected all over the world. Maybe this is because many of our Russian people have

realised themselves very well abroad. That is why I am very proud to be Russian

(R6)

A heightened sense of pride in being Russian was a common feature throughout the majority of the interviews. According to R19, this feeling often accompanied people in their personal and professional interactions and did not stay in the background. Although none of the people interviewed expressed any Russian nationalist ideas and, on the contrary, saw themselves as very open-minded towards international and intercultural interaction, the pride of being Russian could be the influence of Russia's nationalist movement. This movement, following M. Brudny (2000), is capable of imposing its "profoundly nondemocratic views concerning the identity and boundaries of the nation-state on the political elite" and becoming "a major obstacle in the process of the consolidation of democracy" (p. 265).

Thus, nationalist ideas, able to influence the political climate in Russia, can be assumed to be effectively shaping the mentality of its citizens, especially when it concerns an issue that ever-troubles the Russian soul, namely Russian national identity. Such a politicised approach to developing national patriotism might be working, as the feeling of pride in belonging to the Russian nation has been observed as an underlying feature in many interviewees' national identity discourses. However, their feeling of pride in being Russian was associated with the nation and people, culture and nature rather than with state institutions, policies and ideology:

> First of all I am proud to be Russian. It means to represent a rich culture in its best manifestations. There is also much negative talk about Russian culture and people often remember Stalin and the Russian revolution, something that has a very negative connotation. But nevertheless it is the best of Russian culture, welcoming and friendly people, interesting cuisine and traditions, a vast country.

(R4)

The phenomenon of generic national pride could also be explained by the origin of Russian nationalism, unique in its character due to a mix of both popular and statist nationalist tendencies that evolved under specific Russian political, social, economic and cultural conditions. As Simon Cosgrove (2004) explains, Russian authoritarian political culture strengthened the ethnic nationalist discourse that reached Russia at the beginning of the 19th century. Liberal and civic ideas were rejected in favour of authoritarianism and collectivism. The Russian Empire, a multinational state populated by many ethnic groups rather than Russian, was nevertheless regarded by popular nationalists as a homogeneous realm, "Rus" (Russia) or "Svyataya Rus" (Holy Russia).

Statist Russian nationalism, following Cosgrove (2004), views the imperial, powerful, authoritarian and absolutely non-democratic Russian state
as the embodiment and fulfilment of the Russian nation. It had an inward-
looking character that promoted "anti-Western, xenophobic, anti-Semitic
and racist tendencies . . . interwoven with an endemic proclivity to conspir-
acy theory" (p. 4). Both nationalists in Russia, popular and statist, adopted
a firm anti-Western position to promote a Russian identity, distinctly non-
Western and filled with envy and hatred towards the West (Cosgrove, 2004).
Thus, one might suggest that the roots of the strong Russian identity have
been reinforced by the development of the Russian nationalistic tendencies
in the course of Russian history.

This chapter has explored how the Russian participants constructed their
national identity and what helped them to make sense of who they are. The
research findings suggest that for the majority of those interviewed the issue
of national identity was a topical area of their cognitive process. Although
some interviewees acknowledged that they "never consciously tried to define
it [the concept of national identity]" (R14), they, nevertheless, considered
the issue quite often and were eagerly prepared to share their thoughts on
the subject of the research. This suggests that for a Russian person, the need
to understand their national identity is a topic of high importance, which is
seen as an evolutionary process tightly intertwined with people's personal
life experiences and the social, cultural, economic and political development
of their country and heavily influenced by the collective memories of their
nation. To some, understanding their national identity is the path to a better
knowledge of themselves.

The analysis of the interviews with the Russian respondents, having
addressed "the values from below", i.e. personal considerations of individuals (Cassels, 1996: 8), identified the complex and interconnected way in
which Russian national identity was claimed. Five major themes in Russian
national identity construction were distinguished. Firstly, to be born in Russia seemed to signify belonging to the Russian nation by default. The fact
of birth on the Russian land was further strengthened via the development
of cultural norms and values by the means of Russian upbringing and personal individual and professional development. Secondly, Russian culture
was identified as one of the most influential constructs of national identity,
with its complexity of expression through the respondents' affinity with the
Russian language, art, cinematography and literature.

Thirdly, association with the Russian people and an overarching notion
of Russian mentality was commonly used as a national identity attribute. It
indicated a unique programming of the collective mind, difficult for other
nations to understand and depicted in one of Winston Churchill's *bons mots*
as "a riddle wrapped in a mystery inside an enigma" (in Lovell, 2006).
Fourthly, Russian national identity was perceived as a pool of collective
memories associated with the history of the Russian state. And, finally,
Russia as a country of unique natural beauty and great variety spreading

throughout its vast territory, was claimed to signify belonging to the Russian nation. These differing constructs of Russian national identity in many Russian discourses were closely intertwined and often were displayed and discussed simultaneously.

In their attempts to explain their national belonging, the Russian businesspeople employed different approaches. Some of them assessed the issue from a deeply personal angle and thus saw it as a condition of one's internal state, a soul. For others, national identity was a subject of personal cognitive choice, although there were only a few of those who adopted that approach.

It is significant to highlight that the businesspeople's appreciation of their Russian national identity was reinforced when they were exposed to interactions with their foreign business counterparts. Russia has not fully integrated into the international community, and Russian business culture is not clearly understood in the West and therefore appears "mysterious" and unknown. The aspiration to establish and further develop business operations with their foreign colleagues breeds the need for Russian businesspeople to present a positive image of Russia and the Russians, reinforcing their own understanding of Russian national peculiarities of not only the Russian contemporary business environment but also of the social and cultural traits of the nation. This, in its turn, might explain the prevailing focus on positive aspects of Russian life and the underlying feeling of pride in being Russian that fed through many interviews.

The recognition of one's national attachment with the Russian nation was amplified through experiences of living and working abroad. Exposure to the foreign environment for an extended period of time (e.g., expatriate living) allowed more opportunities for comparing and contrasting in further depth the norms and values of the host nation with the ones that one has already reaffirmed in oneself by growing up and living in the native country. In this respect the adoption of the contrasting approach to understanding national identity acted as a useful tool in identifying the meaning of national belonging.

The heightened sense of Russianness, however, weakened outside the international business environment. Sharing hobbies, social experiences and skills with representatives of other nations outside work brought Russian businesspeople closer to the broader international community. The majority of my respondents commented on feeling very comfortable abroad, and particularly in the English-speaking countries as almost all of the interviewees could speak English and communicate freely with other people due to their linguistic ability. Some respondents also noted that they felt very international in large cosmopolitan cities like New York and London, where they felt part of some international society, blending in and enjoying mutual experiences.

Nevertheless, they stressed that a Russian core would always remain in their consciousness. Being Russian was a fact and did not preclude feeling European or international at the same time. Thus, the evidence from the interviews supports A.D. Smith's (1991) claim that national identity is both "a flexible and persistent force in modern life and politics" (p. 15). However, it appears that in the case of Russian businesspeople, the flexibility of their national identity gave way to its persistency. Even when some of them acknowledged that they felt quite international, they nevertheless were firmly aware of their Russian origin, Russian mentality and their so-called Russian core. Such strong affinity with the Russian nation might find its explanation in the origins of specific Russian nationalism, unique in its complex combination of popular and statist tendencies resulting in a distinct non-Western attitude.

The feeling of Russian patriotism accompanied the rhetoric of the majority of the interviews and displayed the immense emotional involvement of the respondents with their nation. It is important to stress, however, that Russian patriotism was seen as a positive manifestation of solidarity with the Russian state and its people, which by no means supports an unhealthy state of exaggerated nationalism. It appears that, currently, Russian patriotism is the product of historically developed traditions of Russian popular and statist nationalism, the government's attempts to unite Russia under the auspices of some national projects, and traditional anti-Western tendencies stemming from the widespread belief in the uniqueness of the Russian national character.

Characteristically for the respondents with some lived memories of the Soviet experience, national identity was perceived through the lens of the Soviet reality, which in many ways shaped the formation of their core life values. The findings demonstrated that both ethnic and civic bases for national identity formation were employed by the interviewees in their national identity discourse, although not on an equal basis. Understanding national identity from the ethnic perspective was much more common for the Russian respondents than employing civic foundations in national identity construction.

References

Barrington, L.W., Herron, E.S. and Silver, B.D. (2003) The Motherland Is Calling: Views of Homeland Among Russians in the near Abroad. *World Politics*, 55 (2), pp. 290–313.

Brudny, Y.M. (2000) *Reinventing Russia: Russian Nationalism and the Soviet State, 1953–1991*. London: Harvard University Press.

Carruthers, A. (2002) The Accumulation of National Belonging in Transnational Fields: Ways of Being at Home in Vietnam. *Identities: Global Studies in Culture and Power*, 9, pp. 423–444.

Cassels, A. (1996) *Ideology and International Relations in the Modern World*. London: Routledge.

Cosgrove, S. (2004) *Russian Nationalism and the Politics of Soviet Literature: The Case of Nash Sovremennik 1981–91*. Basingstoke: Palgrave Macmillan.

Federal State Statistics Service (2017) *Resident Population*. Available at: www.gks. ru/wps/wcm/connect/rosstat_main/rosstat/en/figures/population/

Gorshkov, M.K. (2010) The Sociological Measurement of the Russian Mentality. *Russian Social Science Review*, 51 (2), pp. 32–57.

Hudson, T. (2010) *DDT History*. Available atttp://english.ddt.ru/history/

Kelly, C. (2005) "Thank You for the Wonderful Book": Soviet Child Readers and the Management of Children's Reading, 1950–75. *Kritika: Explorations in Russian and Eurasian History*, 6 (4), pp. 717–753.

Knight, N. (2006) Was the Intelligentsia Part of the Nation? Visions of Society in Post- Emancipation Russia. *Kritika: Explorations in Russian and European History*, 7 (4), pp. 733–758.

Laruelle, M. (ed.) (2009) *Russian Nationalism and the National Reassertion of Russia*. London: Routledge.

Lovell, S. (2006) *Destination in Doubt: Russia Since 1989*. London: Zed Books.

Richmond, Y. (2003) *From Nyet to Da* (3rd Ed). London: Nicholas Brealey Publishing.

Sartorti, R. (2010) Pictures at an Exhibition: Russian Land in a Global World. *Studies in East European Thought*, 62, pp. 377–399.

Smith, A.D. (1991) *National Identity*. London: Penguin Books.

Tolz, V. (1998) Forging the Nation: National Identity and Nation Building in Post-Communist Russia. *Europe-Asia Studies*, 50 (6), pp. 993–1022.

Viroli, M. (1997) *For Love of Country*. Oxford: Oxford University Press. Electronic resource available at: www.oxfordscholarship.com/oso/public/content/political science/9780198293583/toc.html.

4 Identity Claims in a Cross-Cultural Perspective

Part One
The Significance of National Identity from International Business Travellers' Perspectives

The previous chapter focused on the construction of national identity by English, Scottish and Russian businesspeople. By deliberately not placing national identity in any particular context and not conditioning the ways in which it was constructed, it aimed to explore how international business travellers understood the concept and constructed their own national identity. It was also sought to establish whether national identity was an important issue for the respondents in their everyday lives and whether it occupied a significant position in their cognitive thinking.

This chapter summarises the research findings of all three national groups of international business travellers and undertakes a cross-cultural comparative analysis of those findings. This will lead to a better understanding of how each group constructed their national identity and what precise categories dominated in that process. The cross-cultural comparison will explain the similarities and differences in the respondents' articulation of their national identity and so provide a further insight into how national identities are created and manifested by people of different national and ethnic origins.

The chapter starts with discussion of the significance that English, Scottish and Russian businesspeople attach to their national identity in their everyday lives and the degree of thought that they devote to considering their national belonging. This will be followed by consideration of "the other", a commonly used tool in national categorisation (Hopkins and Moore, 2001; Gill, 2005; McCrone and Bechhofer, 2008; Skey, 2010). The feeling of pride as an "underlying fabric" of national identity will continue the discussion of the interview data and will be further developed by an examination of the overlapping (or multiple) national identities that have been displayed by a few respondents in this research.

Having considered overall observations surrounding national identity construction by English, Russian and Scottish businesspeople, this chapter will summarise the national identity attributes that were most commonly employed by the interviewees in their discourses. Further on, the major identity constructs identified in this research will be tested against A.D. Smith's national identity theory in order to examine potential theoretical developments and recognise the evolution of new alternatives in the way national identity is lived, understood, performed and theorised. The conclusions of this chapter will suggest what more needs to be done in order to answer the question whether the erosion of national identity is taking place in the global business environment.

The Significance of National Identity in English, Russian and Scottish Businesspeople's Lives

By examining the international businesspeople's own identification of their national belonging and their discourse on their understanding of it, different approaches to national identity construction became transparent. The Russian businesspeople seemed to think and analytically process the meaning of their national identity more often and with deeper consideration than the British people in general. To the Russians, it was something natural, occurring quite commonly in people's minds. According to one of the interviewees, in Russia this trend was particularly relevant to educated people, to the "thinking" ones. Indeed, all Russian interviewees were educated to degree level at least, and some of them had post-graduate degrees, including PhDs.

The interviews revealed that the subject of national identity for the Russians is something stirring, needing personal clarification: It was part of their enduring quest to understand themselves. Finding the sense of purpose often required people to discover the role of their social environment and how it influenced the shaping of their personality, values and norms of behaviour. Thus, for the Russian respondents, conversations about the meaning and place of their national identity were not unnatural. The Russian interviewees were very elaborate in their discourses and in majority of cases appeared very open, willing to discuss and explicit in sharing their thoughts. Those with some extensive experience of living abroad were particularly advanced in their thinking about national identity, obviously influenced by their immersion into other cultures, and benefited from extensive observations of similarities and differences between people from varying national backgrounds, in other words by being opposed to "the other".

In contrast to the Russian businesspeople, the majority of interviewees in the English research sample did not consider national identity as an issue of high importance and therefore did not spend much time deliberately pondering about its place and meaning. For them, their national identity was a fact of life. Secure in the knowledge that they were English, they did not seek to unfold the components of their Englishness in order to understand what constituted it. It was simply there; it was merely present; it had been with them since their birth; it was an integral part of their personality which did not require explanation. Thus, while clearly recognised and firmly acknowledged, national identity was not at the forefront of their daily concerns. This might explain the difficulty which the majority of the English respondents encountered attempting to describe the meaning of their national affiliation.

Declaring without any doubt their belonging with the English nation (in some cases intermixed with the British), they often found it challenging to describe their identity or explain what it meant to them.

However, this did not apply to all the people interviewed in England. Two interviewees, who represented the second generation of immigrants in the UK, demonstrated through their discourse that their national identity had a heavy influence on various aspects of their professional, social and personal reality. With their backgrounds differing significantly from the majority of their surrounding population, they strove to be socially accepted through proving their allegiance with the state and the nation. They were determined to achieve it through their hard work and eager to succeed in order to reach the level of professional advancement that would provide them with an entry into broader social networks so that they could be included into their adopted society on an equal basis to any other native citizen. In other words, they were seeking ways to belong through gaining acceptance by the host society. This indicated that the underlying feeling of uncertainty, of not fully belonging to their chosen society, was behind their striving to provide ontological security for their children.

In a similar way to the English interviewees, the Scots did not put much emphasis on the issue of national identity in their everyday activities. However, a striking difference from their neighbours south of the border was observed in how the Scottish respondents approached the subject of this research. The Scottish businesspeople were more strongly aware of their national belonging and were willing to talk about it much more extensively than their English counterparts. Their national identity discourse was often very emotionally charged, enriched by colourful descriptions and examples from real-life situations. Again, the issue of belonging and being associated with the nation was highlighted as one of the most significant in their national identity understanding; but in contrast with the English respondents, their expression of the awareness of these issues and appreciation of their importance for providing a stable psychological foundation was much more elaborated than in the English respondents' discourses.

The different emphases that English and Scottish interviewees put into national identity understanding and appreciation influenced their different approaches to articulating their thoughts during interviews. There was a noticeable difference in the way English and Scottish people expressed themselves. Although both were extremely polite and friendly, the ease of the conversation did not flow equally. The Scots were much more open in their responses, often verbally very fluid and taking the lead in their answers, and in some cases providing responses to questions that had not yet been asked. Interviews with the English businesspeople differed in character and could be described as more reserved and formal. In some cases, respondents' answers were rather brief and implicit, prompting me constantly to ask additional questions in order to access more fully people's understanding of their national identity. Some English respondents' interviews were rather sparse, which, to a certain extent, could serve as an additional descriptor of the nation's character. It also signified that national identity for them had no direct or immediate relevance to their everyday lives.

"The Other" in National Identity Claims

Positioning oneself against "the other" proved to be a useful instrument for conveying the essence of national identity. Almost every business traveller referred to comparisons with other nations when attempting to describe their own identity, demonstrating that understanding of what one is comes more easily and more clearly when it is understood what one is not. Hence, they were providing multiple real-life examples from interviewees' own experiences of communicating and working with people from other national backgrounds. It was mentioned several times that national differences and stereotypes were often the subject of conversations between international business travellers in hotel lounges as well as in the work environment. It was also highlighted that discussing national differences and peculiarities can act as an ice-breaker that helped to bring different people together. That was especially emphasised by the Scottish respondents who, having experienced the "power" and the "charm" of the Scottish identity overseas, learnt to use it in pursuing their business objectives.

The interviews also revealed the respondents' appreciation of national differences and the value they attach to the unity and power of diversity. There springs to mind respondent S12's recollection of working with colleagues from different countries on a large European project. Exploring differences and similarities of national features in their informal conversations during coffee breaks, they projected a fantastic future for Europe where all its policemen were German, all drivers were Swiss, all chefs were French, all chocolate was Belgian and all lovers were Italian. Undoubtedly, every nation has its unique features that are cherished by its people and, as was shown by the research data, the feeling of pride of being associated with one's nation was often much more strongly accentuated when the ways of creating and manifesting one's national identity were examined against "the other".

The Feeling of Pride as Part of the "Underlying Fabric" of National Identity Construction

The feeling of pride in the countries where the interviewees came from accompanied almost every interview. In some cases, it was a clearly articulated pride in the country's achievements and a personal association with them. In others, respondents were certainly proud to belong to their nation but found it difficult to explain the source of that feeling. At times, it was a combination of being proud of one's country on the one hand, and feeling embarrassed of certain elements of life in that country on the other. That particularly applied to the Russian and English interviewees. The Russians, for example, focused on Russian bureaucracy, the inefficiency of the state-run services, the undeveloped mechanisms of customer care and often rude and hostile attitude from officials and fellow citizens that one comes across in everyday situations. Some English people pointed out that they did not approve of the behaviour of certain groups of English holiday makers abroad (often in Spain) and showed no intention of being associated with them. British youth culture was also the subject of the English respondents' concern that caused the feeling of embarrassment for the disintegration of the British society and the country's former glory and uncertainty about the future of the British nation.

Nevertheless, despite some negative sentiment, the perception of national identity in the majority of cases was tightly intertwined with the inspiring feeling of pride. This emotional attribute underlined the understanding of national identity of all three national groups involved in this research. However, this should not be considered as a lone national identity marker. Appearing more tangible, the constructs of national identity are more observable than the feelings accompanying them. For example, culture as an expression of national belonging can manifest itself through music, published literary works, dancing and other forms of expression. Equally, people's behaviour is observable and can be copied or re-created by others. The feeling of pride can also be manifested, for example, through demonstrations of support for sports teams; however, as a psychological experience, it is very individual and cannot be re-lived or re-created by another person in exactly the same way. Therefore, the feeling of pride as a psychological condition accompanying the cognitive construction of one's national identity should be separated from the consciously constructed displays of national identity.

Overlapping (Multiple) National Identities

The English, Russian and Scottish respondents attributed different degrees of importance to the role of national identity in their everyday social experiences. The interview data also provided some evidence of overlapping identities when people felt that at the same time they belonged to more than just one nation. For example, they saw themselves as Russian/American (R13); Russian/British (R2); Scottish/British (S18, S12, S4); English/British (E10, E15) or Scottish/European (S15). Claiming overlapping (multiple) identities did not equate to "confused" identities, when English and British identities were intermixed and used interchangeably (i.e. E7). The explanation for this lies in the deeply rooted interconnectedness of historical, political, economic and cultural aspects of the relationship between England and Scotland since they formed their legal and political union in 1707. Within the Union, English identity has been absorbed and almost dissolved, resulting in a very weakly pronounced knowledge of Englishness by English people. In contrast to the English, the Scottish people were much more aware of their nation's distinctiveness, accentuated by the rise of nationalistic movements at the end of the 20th century and Scotland's devolution.

It was feared that the devolution of Scotland would evoke the rise of English nationalism in protest at the Scottish demands for more independent regulation of their political, economic and social affairs. However, those concerns proved ungrounded and the boundaries of Englishness are often not clearly defined and explained by people themselves. This was demonstrated by the interviews with the businesspeople in England, when even well-educated people, with the global reach of professional activities, sometimes could not explain the meaning of their national identity.

However, bearing in mind the flexible nature of national identity, it would be wrong to assume that in multinational states, like Russia and Britain, people's national identification would be sharply defined and firmly fixed. That particularly applied to those people whose ethnic background was not the same as that of the dominant population. In Russia, following the national policy of the USSR, every citizen of the state, despite their ethnic origin, was also Rossiyanin (a citizen of the Russian state). The interviews showed that, even after the collapse of the USSR in the early 1990s, non-ethnic Russians living in Russia, still perceived themselves as Russian (R11, R18), associating themselves with the collective culture of the whole country, sharing its people's mentality and being part of its history.

National self-identification was perceived differently by those Russian respondents who were in possession of another citizenship. These people, although firmly stating that their national identity was Russian, at the same time identified themselves with their adopted nation (e.g., the USA in case of interviewee R13). Simultaneous identification with more than one nation, although confusing for those who experienced it, was not surprising. Their lives were open not only to broader geographical areas in physical terms, allowing them to have homes in more than one country, but also to a wider range of social, cultural, professional and political aspects of life. Their ethical and cultural norms and values, formed in their childhood in their original environment, were built around their ethnic belonging. However, new experiences of living in other countries influenced their affinity with their new environment, often based on the cognitive choice to accept and associate themselves with civic institutions of those countries. Thus, the civic approach to identity comes to the fore when people identify themselves not so much with the nation but with a country's structures. This explains the apparent confusion that some of my Russian respondents commented on when they claimed that they felt at the same time Russian and American, or Russian and British.

Any form of identity is a lived experience, fluid and non-fixed. Multiple identities can be easily found, overlapping, complementing and enriching each other. They can also be the source of great confusion: Who am I: Russian or American? (R13). Here, understanding of the grounds on which people build their national identity is crucial (as well as the acceptance of mutual co-existence of different national identities within one character). Take for example interviewee R13, who sees herself as Russian when she thinks of herself in ethnic terms (when she passionately supports Russian sportsmen competing for the World Cup) and perceives herself as American when she is considering her national identity from the civic perspective (choosing to associate herself with the efficiency of the American health service rather than with the Russian bureaucracy).

Claims that one can feel British and English, or British and Scottish at the same time can be explained in a similar manner. It is worth pointing out that the prevalence of one identity over another can change depending on the individual's circumstances at the time when the identity hierarchy is being examined. This has been demonstrated by some of the English respondents who, depending on circumstances, could "twist" their identity from being English at home to being British when abroad. Similarly, the Scots often chose to be seen as Scottish abroad and as British in the UK, explaining that the Scottish identity is a great "door opener" overseas, which certainly is very helpful in pursuing business objectives abroad.

When available, the choice of national identity can be determined by either the ethnic or civic approach to the concept, or it can be influenced by circumstances in which one's identity is being displayed. It is due to identity's ambiguity that the way it is performed can be embraced in favour of one identity over another, or being absorbed into one, encouraging it to be a mixture, a confusion operating at different levels in different contexts and influenced by the choice of identity affiliations.

National Identity Constructs

Despite the differences to approaching and understanding the role and the meaning of their national identity by different national groups of international business travellers, the most significant constructs that the respondents employed in their attempts to categorise their national affiliation were often repeated. Thus, five national identity markers were broadly identified by all three groups of respondents to describe their national affiliation: national culture, place of birth, national history, national landscape and national characteristics of people. However, a different emphasis and a different weight were attached to this or that construct by different nations. For example, the most commonly mentioned national category for the Russians was their place of birth and belonging, whereas for the English, it was their country's history, and for the Scots, their association with the characteristics of the Scottish people.

The national landscape (or countryside) as a national identity signifier was commonly used by the Russian and the Scottish respondents and did not receive much attention from the English interviewees. The table below represents a summary of findings on the most commonly occurring national identity constructs identified by the research participants. The table also

Table 4.1 National identity constructs by each group of interviewees (1-most commonly used; 5-least commonly used). Numbers in brackets show how
many respondents discussed each construct.

	English	Scottish	Russian
1.	History (9)	People (14)	Place of birth (13)
2.	Culture (8)	Culture (11)	Culture (10)
3.	People's characteristics (8)	Place of birth (8)	People's characteristics (mentality) (10)
4.	Place of birth (7)	Countryside (7)	History (8)
5.	Countryside (2)	History (1)	Countryside (6)

demonstrates the order of priority that has been given to every national
identity marker by each national group of interviewees (Table 4.1.).

Table 4.1 clearly demonstrates that such national identity constructs as
place of birth, culture and people's characteristics (either general national
mentality or characteristics of businesspeople) have been adopted by all
three groups of respondents. National history was often used as a national
identity signifier by Russian and English businesspeople. As for their Scottish counterparts, history as a national identity construct was employed
to articulate the Scottish national character by only one respondent and
therefore history was not categorised as a prominent national feature in the
Scottish section. Countryside and the national landscape were quite often
adopted as a national identity construct by the Russian and the Scottish
businesspeople; this category was not prominently present in the English
people's discourse, having been mentioned by only two people.

Having identified the most commonly used categories, we should note
that they were not the only national identity claims employed by the respondents. Various other national identity markers were also used in the respondents' accounts on their national identity perception. Among less frequently
mentioned displays of national identity were such issues as class structure,
national institutions or international presence abroad. Below is a summary
of the major national identity categories that were identified in this research.
It is worth pointing out that the attributes of the national identity employed
by the respondents were closely interlinked and it would be wrong to treat
each of them individually in isolation from each other. However below they
are analysed individually for clarity. The sequence of categories in the discussion is organised in alphabetical order.

Countryside

Countryside as a national identity construct was mentioned by all three
national groups of respondents. However, it did not appear as a prominent identity marker for the English respondents as only two people in the

English research sample commented on the importance of countryside in their understanding of national identity. On the contrary, the Russian and the Scottish interviewees placed a very strong emphasis on the role that their country's nature, its landscape and character played in their relationship with the land to which they belong. Six Russian and seven Scottish interviewees talked about their affinity with their national countryside and the feeling of unity that they experienced when enjoying this connection, either by being in the countryside itself or even simply thinking and imagining it, a link that once established, is impossible to discontinue.

Comparing Russian and Scottish research participants' discourses, it becomes evident that the Scottish people were more explicit and passionate in sharing their feelings about their homeland. The statement of respondent S14 was particularly emotional and deeply touching when he claimed: "when I think about the happiest moments in my life it is standing somewhere on a golf course in Scotland or on the top of a mountain" (S14). It demonstrates how deep can be the connection between an individual and the landscape of his homeland. The Russians, referring to the natural beauty of their country, often mentioned traditional images of Russian white birches or the vastness and the openness of the Russian landscape. Thus, this research has identified that for the Russian and the Scottish businesspeople, the role of place in constructing their national identities represents deep significance, whereas the English businesspeople did not relate their understanding of their national self to the countryside with the same degree of attachment as their Scottish and Russian counterparts.

Culture

All three groups of business travellers mentioned national culture in their attempts to describe their national identity: ten Russian, eight English and 11 Scottish interviewees applied this category in their discourse. For the Russian businesspeople, this national identity construct manifested itself through my respondents' affiliation with Russian cinematography, literature, language, music and system of education. The English businesspeople, when discussing their national culture, highlighted their appreciation of their language, sport and stereotypical cultural images of people's behaviour, such as "having a sense of fair play, being polite and rational, not flustered, the stiff upper lip and not being over emotional about things" (E3). For the Scots, their understanding of their national culture and its significant place in their Scottish identity construction transpired through their discourses on the specific nature of their language, sport, the quality of Scottish education, national cuisine and, of course, Scottish cultural stereotypes. The interviews demonstrated that the Scots were fiercely proud of their distinctive form of dress and music, easily recognised around the world. My respondents spoke about these and other stereotypical features of their national character in a very enthusiastic manner.

Language as a cultural feature requires some deeper consideration. A common thread was noticed that united almost all (apart from two) of the Russian international business travellers I interviewed. It was their foreign language skills and predominantly the ability to communicate in English. That skill was identified as crucial for Russian businesspeople working in the international business arena and was mentioned by the majority of my respondents. Some of them had a very advanced level of English language proficiency, having studied in Western (primarily British and American) universities. They are constantly improving their linguistic knowledge through the advancement of their skills in routine business and life situations. Nevertheless, it was observed that those Russian businesspeople who live most of their time in Britain and are fluent in their oral and written English language skills, despite their advanced ability to communicate in English, often pointed out that it was not their native language, and they did not feel totally comfortable communicating in English.

This linguistic awareness, even though not preventing people from successfully operating in the international environment, nevertheless created an invisible barrier distinguishing one from "the other". On the extreme side, one respondent mentioned feeling discriminated on the grounds of her speaking "foreign" English while studying in the UK. The allegedly biased attitude of the lecturers at the UK university was not aimed particularly at the Russian student but applied to other foreign students in the course whose mother tongue was not English. For those living permanently in Russia, the ability to speak English, however, is seen as an invaluable asset and often works as a door opener into the world of the international business.

This was not the case for the British respondents who hugely benefited from their national language being the language of international communication. Appreciating the advantage of being a native English speaker, those British respondents who did not speak any other language stressed their lack of ability to communicate with their foreign colleagues in their language, admitting with regret the well-known reputation of the British as the nation who do not learn foreign languages. However, it would be wrong to assume that none of the UK interviewees could speak languages other than English. In both the English and Scottish samples there were people able to communicate in other languages. Unfortunately, they could very rarely apply their skills for business purposes due to the uniformly agreed preference for employing English for business use by their foreign colleagues. There was a disappointing comment from one of the English respondents who mentioned, referring to the decline of the former British supremacy in the world, that the English language was the only valuable thing left for English people.

The analysis of the interviews has shown that the businesspeople's perception of their national identity is heavily dependent on their understanding of their national cultures. Judging from the numbers of interviewees who employed national culture as a national identity marker, this applied almost equally to all three national groups of respondents. Thus, culture is an integrative element in national identity construction, uniting people who share equal understanding and appreciation of norms, values and behaviour expressed through various manifestations of the national "programming of the mind" (Hofstede, 2001: 9).

History

References to their countries' past and historical events commonly appeared in national identity discourses of the Russian and the English businesspeople. Mentioning of the Soviet regime and the USSR's achievements and failures during the communist rule was very prominent in the responses of eight Russian interviewees who used history to describe their national identity. Those nine English respondents who also employed history to explain their understanding of their national self mostly referred to their country's colonial past and the advancements and developments during its Imperial era.

The Scottish respondents, on the contrary, were less keen to assert their national identity through references to their country's historic past, perhaps avoiding the sensitive issue of the complex relationship between England and Scotland throughout the centuries. Owing to such a minimal mentioning of history as a national identity signifier in the rhetoric of the Scottish respondents, this category was not among the most significant national identity constructs identified by the research in the Scottish sample. However, for the Russian and particularly for the English interviewees, who used history more often than any other national identity attribute, national history was a magnifying glass through which they could see and understand the meaning of their national belonging with better clarity and enhanced precision.

People

Another very common resource that the business travellers used in order to convey the meaning of their national identity was the qualities generally applied to their fellow citizens. The Scottish businesspeople were particularly vocal depicting the Scottish character, with 14 of the respondents proudly sharing their thoughts on Scottish hospitality, sociability, warmheartedness, curiosity, solidness of the Scottish character and the importance of their family and friends. Talking about people's characteristics appeared the major articulator of the Scottish national identity in this study. Similarly, ten Russian respondents explicitly talked about the Russian people and their mentality, highlighting such features of the national character as openness, devotion to their family and friends, ability to build strong and deeply emotional connections, patience and bravery.

It was noted that the English research participants in this research did not directly comment on their people's characteristic features in order to explain their national identity, although characteristics such as stiff upper lip, dignity and reserve were mentioned by eight English respondents when national stereotypes were employed in explanations of their national identity. Both English and Scottish respondents also referred to national characteristics that they thought were typical of their business colleagues from their country. Such qualities of a businessperson as cunningness, innovativeness, fair play, doing business properly and for the right reasons, were attributed by the Scots to their Scottish colleagues. The English also mentioned fair play, respect for their partners and sticking to "level playing fields" when they described the business features characteristic of the English. Interestingly, the Russian respondents did not comment on the business qualities of Russian people which could be a reflection of a very young and evolving community of businesspeople in the country.

Russian respondents did mention in their discourse that since the early 1990s, when international travel (including travel for business purposes) became more accessible, new markets and collaboration with foreign counterparts have been explored that gave more international travel opportunities to Russian businesspeople than during the Soviet regime. The Russian market economy is still very young, the characteristics of the Russian business class are not clearly defined and the proportion of international business travellers in Russia appears relatively small. That was demonstrated during my preparations for fieldwork in Russia when trying to find and access Russian people with extensive experience of foreign business travel.

The transitional movement towards the open economy requires a new type of businessperson with knowledge and skills that would satisfy the demands of the contemporary business world. Russia's businesspeople, either self-starters or qualified business professionals, are adopting the rules of the new game, acquiring western business education and practices. However, the influences of Soviet managerial approaches are still noticeably present and the management style of Russian businesspeople is often quite distinct from that of the Western ones, as described by interviewee (R17) in her comparison of working with a Western and with a Russian manager in the same company:

> The business culture was different in the company where I worked. When the Russian boss was appointed, a lot of changes happened. Yes, there might be advantages in having a local Russian person in charge as he knows the environment and operates in it easily but democratisation disappears immediately. As an example, our American boss used to call the branches every week and he always started his conversations with his report on what is happening in the head office and not the other way around. He would tell everything I need to know in order to follow the main company line and what is happening in the company and only then he would ask me what is happening in my branch. As soon as a Russian boss took the executive position, with all his positive attributes

and degrees and MBA diplomas, I felt that I was pushed down as a manager of a lower level.

(R17)

The current economic climate has had an effect on the frequency of international business trips of some of my respondents. At least two Russian businesspeople mentioned that the limiting conditions of the economic environment have negatively affected the amount of international business travel and prompted deeper reliance on electronic communication with their foreign colleagues.

Frequent references to people and the general mentality of the respondents' nations signified the importance of the knowledge of, and association with, the national character in national identity construction. Thus, people and their national characteristics were another category explicitly articulating the construction of national identity as equally applicable to all three national groups of this research.

Place of Birth

Place of birth was another common feature that was widely used by all three national groups of respondents. For all of them, the association with the place where they were born and grew up was closely connected to the feeling of social and psychological security that the feeling of belonging provides to people of different ethnic origins or nationalities. Thirteen Russian respondents approached their understanding of their national identity from this perspective. The British businesspeople expressed a slightly weaker attachment to the geographical location where they were born than the Russian ones: seven English people adopted this category as their national identity construct, whereas among the Scottish interviewees, eight people referred to their place of birth as their national identity signifier.

For all of these people, the place where they were born was typically also the place where they grew up and where the fundamental views, values and principles of their social reality were formed and developed. That process was primarily influenced by the cultural and social order which was characteristic for the social environment they happened to be born in. Whether it was Russian, English or Scottish, it remained highly critical in people's understanding of their national self throughout the course of their lives. Slightly less frequent references to their place of birth by the English and Scottish respondents, perhaps, demonstrated a degree of distancing from their birthplace, especially when the individuals were extensively exposed to the international environment through their professional engagements. In the case of the Russian business travellers, the degree of their international exposure was less advanced as the frequency of their international travel was not as extensive as that of their British counterparts.

Thus, place of birth has been articulated as an important national identity category. People's experiences at the initial stages of their lives shaped their perception of the world and built the foundations of their fundamental principles and norms, moral values and patterns of behaviour. The social environment of people's birthplace, if the link had not been interrupted by a move at an early age and was continuing into people's adulthood, sustained its influence throughout people's lives and provided them with the feeling of belonging to their land.

To sum up, all three groups of respondents displayed similar approaches to identifying their national belonging. Despite their differing cultural, national, linguistic backgrounds and psychological relationship with the subject of this research, the dominating categories determining their understanding of their national identity were very similar. The diversity of degrees of involvement with the issue of national identity among different national groups of respondents did not significantly alter the choice of national identity constructs.

Thus, all three national groups claimed that national identity was manifested and performed through people's association with their place of birth, upbringing and the sense of belonging. Secondly, their national identity was shaped by people's association with and deep lived knowledge of their national culture. Thirdly, national identity was displayed through the qualities and behaviour of their nation's people. Less influential (nevertheless quite prominently present in the research dataset) national identity constructs were national history and the role and place of the national countryside. It is important to note that history was represented more weakly by the Scottish interviewees than by their English or Russian colleagues. In a similar vein, countryside was far less significant for the English businesspeople than for the Scottish or the Russian.

Having established major national identity signifiers in contemporary Russian, English and Scottish businesspeople's understanding of this concept, we shall now examine to what extent these findings reflect A.D. Smith's national identity theory (1991).

At its outset, the book set out to test the applicability of A.D. Smith's (1991) national identity theory to the national identity construction by international businesspeople at the beginning of the 21st century. Having established through the research data analysis what constitutes national identity in businesspeople's understanding of the concept, we can now correlate the findings with A.D. Smith's theory.

In his book *National Identity*, A.D. Smith (1991) claims that national identity consists of five fundamental features: a historic territory or homeland; common myths and historical memories; a common, mass public culture; common legal rights and duties for all members; and common economy with territorial mobility for members (p. 14). A.D. Smith argues that national identity is a complex and abstract phenomenon which can be combined with other types of identity: class, religious or ethnic. It can also be influenced by ideology and is "fundamentally multi-dimensional; it can never be reduced to a single element, even by particular factions of nationalists, nor can it be easily or swiftly induced in a population by artificial means" (p. 14).

Comparing the current research findings with A.D. Smith's national identity theory, it becomes obvious that at the beginning of the 21st century, national identity remains flexible and multi-dimensional. Furthermore, the research points to some divergence from A.D. Smith's structural composition of national identity. Thus, the international businesspeople interviewed constructed their national identity primarily in ethnic terms. Although there were some references to the civic approach to national identity construction in their discourses, they were not mentioned often enough to represent the majority of opinions and a significant influence on articulation of national identity. The businesspeople interviewed, when explaining their understanding of national identity, did not mention the "common legal rights and duties for all members" (apart from the two Russian interviewees who associated themselves with Britain and America rather than Russia) or "common economy with territorial mobility for members" identified by A.D. Smith (p. 14). Thus, in their national identity discourses the research participants adopted the ethnic component of the A.D. Smith's theory, largely avoiding the civic side of what he believes constitutes national identity.

This is an important finding characterising the nature of the contemporary post-modern social reality. Global forces, represented in this research by the international business environment in which the professional life of my interviewees takes place, do leave a mark on people's understanding of their social world. Discussing the issue of national identity outside any particular context but merely considering it as a concept, the participants of this research did not explicitly mention the unity of people based on common duties that they have to perform for their people or, indeed, the rights that they can exercise within their national society. Furthermore, they did not talk about their nations' economies as a significant attribute of their national identity. That perhaps arises due to the nature of their professional scope that opens their perception of the economy in a global rather than national scale. This suggests that those people who are extensively exposed to international business communication, collaboration and travel do not see their national identities through the lens of citizens' rights and responsibilities, tightly confined within the boundaries of their nation-states. Equally, they do not approach their understanding of national identity through the prism of their national economy operating within the national borders. Thus, it may be argued that A.D. Smith's national identity theory may not fully apply in the world of the international business traveller.

As mentioned in the introduction, the selection of categories in national identity construction by the respondents of this study is complex and far from being straightforward. The research findings highlight that the respondents' understanding of their national identity is not fully consistent with national identity categories identified by A.D. Smith. According to the current research, the understanding of national identity, when placed out of any particular context, is linked to people's association with their culture, people, history, landscape and the place of birth (ethnic perspective) and is not related to the institutional structures of their states expressed through national economy and citizens' rights and duties laid out within their national context (civic perspective).

Does this finding direct us to the assumption that the businesspeople's understanding of their national identity would be even less state-influenced if positioned in the context of the global business environment? Does it allow us to assume that the international business travellers' national self-identification would have even weaker attachment to their national boundaries if they were to consider their national association in the context of the global business arena? This aspect of the research will be addressed in the following chapter through consideration of the respondents' discourses on how (if at all) their international travel has affected their sense of national belonging.

References

Gill, F. (2005) Public and Private: National Identities in a Scottish Borders Community. *Nations and Nationalism*, 11 (1), pp. 83–102.

Hofstede, G. (2001) *Culture's Consequences: Comparing Values, Behaviours, Institutions, and Organisations Across Nations*. London: Sage Publications.

Hopkins, N. and Moore, C. (2001) Categorising the Neighbours: Identity, Distance, and Stereotyping. *Social Psychology Quarterly*, 64 (3), pp. 239–252.

McCrone, D. and Bechhofer, F. (2008) National Identity and Social Inclusion. *Ethnic and Racial Studies*, 31 (7), pp. 1245–1266.

Skey, M. (2010) 'A Sense of Where You Belong in the World': National Belonging, Ontological Security and the Status of the Ethnic Majority in England. *Nations and Nationalism*, 16 (4), pp. 715–733.

Smith, A.D. (1991) *National Identity*. London: Penguin Books.

Part Two
National Identity and the International Business Environment: The Analysis of Trends and Tendencies Towards Change

The analysis of national identity construction by English, Scottish and Russian international business travellers presented earlier identified that the research participants' understanding of national identity, when considered generally and outside any particular context, is linked to their association with their culture, people, history, landscape and the place of birth and is not related to the institutional structures of their states which can be expressed through national economy and citizens' rights and duties laid out within their national context. This finding suggests that A.D. Smith's (1991) national identity theory is not fully applicable to the international business traveller, a large proportion of whose professional life takes place in the international business environment. Can we assume that the shift away from the national institutional structures in businesspeople's national identity construction is due to the influences of the global business environment?

It appears useful to re-visit some of the definitions of globalisation offered by contemporary theorists. We are saying "some" as it would be impossible to bring together all definitions of globalisation from the vast sea of academic and popular literature within the scope of this thesis. Addressing the issue from a broad spectrum of varying perspectives, publications on globalisation differ significantly, perceiving it as a social, political, cultural or economic phenomenon. Thus, according to Baylis *et al.* (2008), globalisation is "the process of increasing interconnectedness between societies such that events in one part of the world more and more have effects on peoples and societies far away" (Baylis *et al.*, 2008: 8). Paul Hirst (2000) sees globalisation as "an ongoing process of the growth of international trade and investment, linking a growing number of countries in increasingly intense exchanges in an open world trading system" (p. 108). Richard Scase (2007) states that globalisation can be understood as Americanisation "in terms of not only global brands but also the music, films and television shows it has exported so successfully" (p. 14).

George Soros in his book *On Globalization* (2002) admits adopting a rather narrow definition of globalisation: "the free movement of capital and the increasing domination of national economies by global financial markets and multinational corporations" (p. vii). Also approaching globalisation from an economic perspective, Jagdish Bhagwati (2004) defines it as the "integration of national economies into the international economy through trade, direct foreign investment (by corporations and multinationals), short-term capital flows, international flows of workers and humanity generally, and flows of technology" (p. 3). As an economic process globalisation is characterised by being "uneven, with unequal distribution of benefits and losses" that leads to "polarisation between the few countries and groups that gain, and the many countries and groups in society that lose out or are marginalized" (Khor, 2001: 16).

However, globalisation is not all about economic interconnectedness. As observed by David Cromwell (2001), according to Anthony Giddens, globalisation demonstrates "strength, diversity and cross-fertilisation of cultures". It also "encapsulates the rise of the internet, increasing international travel, the meeting and mingling of different heritages" (p. 44). Globalisation can also be understood as the development of a common consciousness of human society on a world scale (Shaw, 2000). The discussion below aims to contribute further to our understanding of the depth of the development of a common consciousness on a world scale by looking at the dynamics of national identity perception by British and Russian business travellers.

Understanding of Globalisation

Interviews with the English businesspeople demonstrated that globalisation was understood through a wide spectrum of approaches highlighting the all-encompassing nature of the phenomenon. For some respondents, globalisation was understood as homogenisation of the world's cultures and people's ways of living. In their view, global flows of consumer products, people and cultures led to inevitable homogenisation of every corner of the world. They noted though that at the time when the interviews took place more developed areas were more advanced in this process than small provincial places. Nevertheless, the power of globalisation should not be underestimated. Respondent E11 believed that a huge level of cultural mix was happening at the moment and, although "some attempts of countries to preserve their nationalistic features will be made, homogenisation is inevitable, it cannot be avoided" (E11). E4 expressed an immense disappointment about cultural homogenisation eroding local languages:

> It is a great pity that languages are being lost. Nobody knows what to do to keep this going. I have just been on holiday in Chile and went to a desert in the North. There people used to have their indigenous language but it has almost disappeared now. Yes, that is a great pity.
>
> (E4)

Echoing E4, respondent E11 commented on homogenisation:

> With all the communication technologies, media and people and trade moving around it is almost too late. The world is getting too

homogenised. The business travel hotels are the same around the world, there are McDonald's everywhere, you can buy the same cameras every-where you go . . . perhaps except some tiny provincial places but it will catch up very soon.

(E11)

This vision of globalisation expressed the deepest concern for the future of our global society and the type of regulation that will be needed in order to preserve fair governance, order and justice for everyone. However, not all my respondents had thought about globalisation and its consequences before their involvement in this research. They admitted that they certainly had noticed significant changes around them that were the consequences of global influences, but considerations of globalisation and its effects on the world did not fall into the focus of their primary concerns:

It *[globalisation]* just happens around you, whether you are aware of it or not. I am sure when you go to other parts of the world or your own country, people are aware of things and events that are happen-ing, whether they are good or bad. I am where I am and I do not over-analyse it.

(E10)

While some respondents did not demonstrate much interest in globalisa-tion, preferring to concentrate on their daily routine, some others spoke of globalisation with a degree of personal feeling attached to it, both negative and positive. For example, quite a concerned approach to globalisation was expressed by respondent E8, who mainly perceived globalisation as an eco-nomic process. To him, globalisation exposed better understanding of the poorer quality of life of people in less developed countries. That provoked his forward thinking about the future of the developed economies if the power balance shifted from the West to the East as a consequence of global economic development:

My company have moved production of our machines from Russia to China. It is much cheaper and they can be transported anywhere in the world. First they went from Britain to Russia and then from Russia to China. There are four people in finance. Do you need four people? You can have one person here and one director, a couple of people there at a fraction of the cost. All of a sudden we are making profits. Rather than selling 70 machines more, I can re-organise my department. This is what globalisation means to me.

(E8)

A different vision of globalisation was provided by E8's counterpart E6, for whom globalisation was a positive advancement in travel and com-munication technologies, facilitating easy communication and affordable transportation of goods, services and people. This take on globalisation emphasised the advantages of conducting business across national borders that only became possible with globalisation and the ability of staying connected with people and places that had been only a dream a few decades ago:

> I think it is fantastic when people say good bye, they know they are not saying good bye for several years, which was two generations ago. It has become more affordable, faster, and more practical. As a result more people are moving around in a positive way. If you go in the centre of London, you will hear all sorts of different accents. And it is less true that a family would be born in Glasgow, raised in Glasgow, marry in Glasgow and have kids in Glasgow and ultimately die in Glasgow. It has all changed. People do not feel the need to be attached to one country. Personally, I would quite happily go and live elsewhere.
>
> (E6)

According to the research participants in England, globalisation provided them with enhanced opportunities and wider choices which had not been available not so long ago. Their discourses about the effects of globalisation on themselves and their businesses indicated that new possibilities became available at the micro and macro levels of the world society, providing new advantages to both individuals and structures. Globalisation was described as a social process that had made the life of individual people easier, for example by satisfying their commercial needs through provision of the same (global) products anywhere in the world, thus enhancing consumer homogenisation:

> It makes everything so much more accessible but the world is also becoming too small because everything is so much more accessible and nothing is quite much of a surprise. You go to a shopping centre in London and it is exactly the same somewhere else. You lose the difference between places.
>
> (E4)

From a structural perspective, globalisation was also seen as beneficial for businesses. It offered advanced opportunities for trading internationally and outsourcing businesses in order to pursue the interests of cost effectiveness. The labour market has become increasingly mobile and, as a result, companies are now employing staff from abroad seeking to attract best people for their business, which is crucial in the world of knowledge economy:

> We have multinational employees, we have Americans, we have European salesmen, so we are no longer. . . . We are a British company but we do not employ only British people. We have Russian people in the office, we have Americans, we have Poles, we have a whole myriad of

Europeans and people from further afield, we have Singaporean engineers, we have Singaporean managing directors . . .

(E2)

Such diversity, however, did not necessarily imply homogenisation of business. E2 in his discourse noted that all those international employees were bringing their national influences into their originally British business model, thus shaping a renewed character of the long-established culture of this British business.

Thus, globalisation from the English respondents' perspective was a process of global development characterised by advanced communication technologies, global travel and economic and cultural homogenisation and marked by a positive as well a negative impact on both micro and macro levels of the world society. The respondents' discourses on globalisation could be categorised as reflecting the positions of both sceptics and globalists, with the sceptical position being supported by those who saw globalisation as a natural process of world development. The globalist theoretical stance was reflected by those who perceived globalisation as the process of homogenisation of various spheres of social, economic and cultural life on this planet.

The conversations revealed that globalisation was perceived as a complex process that bred opportunities and threatened security; it opened wider avenues for development and erased existing structures and cultures. Whether it was seen as a positive or a negative process, constructive or destructive, it concerned everyone on this planet. Its effect on every human being was inevitable regardless of whether people expressed much interest in it or not.

Does Globalisation Influence the English Business Travellers' Understanding of Their National Identity?

The business travellers in the English group pointed out that the international business environment helped them to see one's reality from a different perspective, from outside. They noted that in their business practices worldwide their communication with foreign colleagues usually happened in English and this made English people realise how limited their linguistic abilities were, how insular British life was and that "Britain was a small island in a big world" (E1). This new understanding of themselves encouraged people to develop their linguistic abilities and learn foreign languages, travel more and experience different cultures in depth. This made them feel more part of a global society, rather than of a small island. Meeting people from other national and cultural backgrounds enhanced the English business travellers' perception of the world's diversity and influenced their understanding of their own identity:

I have become more international! I meet people from all cultures. Lots of British people resent foreigners as they have never mixed with other cultures and never travelled. They have very blinkered lives. I had many opportunities to meet very different people from many cultures. You become more open and it is great!

(E17)

International travel broadens people's minds through their exposure to new experiences and involvement in new activities (E5). This makes them realise that the same objective can be achieved through a variety of approaches; and the new knowledge gained via participation in international activities can be adopted for the benefits of their established business practices. At the same time, appreciation of typically British qualities and characteristics becomes even more pronounced and pride in being British becomes stronger (E5).

The international environment also teaches people different ways of negotiating and new behaviour, thus shifting the boundaries of what is already known and familiar:

I became more educated. You certainly notice how different communities operate, you meet people from different countries and start understanding how different negotiations and offices work, what accepted codes of behaviour are, which I would not have had a clue of if I stayed in Gosport.

(E16)

The educational effects of international travel range from acquiring new business knowledge to personal development, broadening people's understanding about various aspects of the lives of other nations. Respondent E12 found it

really fascinating to go to different places and see how they build houses or maintain streets (or do not maintain streets), how they behave towards each other, dress, eat at different time of day, calendar is different, languages, everything.

(E12)

From the point of view of some respondents, their international exposure, while broadening their experiences also re-emphasised people's awareness of their own national identity. Learning more about other peoples and countries, the business travellers become more international and at the same time they discover more about themselves, giving them more confidence and deepened knowledge (E15). Realising that there are national differences, people learn to compromise and perhaps "take something from each other" (E13).

For others, globalisation started a new era of internationalisation of markets, products, suppliers and consumers. In this new global marketplace, national boundaries are being erased as well as the national features of those who are involved in international business operations:

> When you are in business, you are actually selling or buying something. So, you can be working for a British company selling things produced in China, India or somewhere else. So, any feeling of nationality from a business point of view disappears. You are then very much a global businessperson. What has happened in the last 20 years and particularly in the last 10, perhaps, is that national identity has been driven out. It does not matter which country you are coming from. People travel all over the place to make money. That is the nature of capitalism. And they probably feel more international than they ever did before.
>
> (E9)

This view was opposed by respondent E3, who devoted many years of his life working for a company that went through being a truly British business to a genuinely cosmopolitan one. Despite his company's move towards internationalisation of their business, this respondent noticed no significant difference in his personal appreciation of his national identity. Acknowledging cultural blending on the one hand, he was fully aware of people's different backgrounds on the other:

> I think it is more of a blend now. Everybody is different and everybody has stories to tell and compare. It does not mean you are separated by it. These differences are diminishing. Everywhere you go the shops are the same. It is just a norm. I do enjoy talking to people from other countries. But on a day-to-day basis I do not even notice that Peggy is from Germany. But it is interesting to talk to her about the lifestyle where she grew up which was Eastern Germany. Her early days were quite different from ours, so it is nice to compare . . .
>
> (E3)

This view was firmly supported by respondent E8 who did not believe that a European (or indeed global) identity was in the making at the time of the interviews. From his point of view, the erosion of national identities was not something that he could envisage happening. To support his opinion, he used an example of various stereotypes attached to different nations and a famous rivalry between the English and the French:

> We know that the British do not like the French. Unless there is a massive mixing of races where one nationality married another and the whole region became multicultural, I do not think it will ever happen.
>
> (E8)

Speaking specifically about the influences of the global business environment on national identity, he applied an example from his practical approach to sales within different national territories. E8 specifically put his emphasis on the importance of national peculiarities and international relationships that prevail in the global business sphere today and will always sustain their influence:

> If you were to sell something from England to Ireland, you will never have an English person doing it. The Irish do not like the English. You'd rather have a Scottish person. I think people will always be nationalistic.
>
> (E8)

This view was supported by other respondents (e.g., E6, E11) who recognised the globalisation of international business but also believed that national identity within the international business context remained very strong:

> I happened to be British. I cannot change the fact that I have got my heritage, my culture, my traditions, customs and superstitions and everything that comes with it: family, education, lifestyle, background, everything. I am not British because I want to be British. It is just the way it is. It is just the fact of life. It is just there.
>
> (E6)

Some people do not notice any change in their perception of their national identity. They do acknowledge that their involvement in international business does require understanding of their foreign partners, their way of thinking and working and finding common grounds for mutual collaboration. This, however, does not influence their own understanding of their national belonging. This approach to national identity in the international business world was characteristic for respondent E7:

> Even if it was a Japanese company, I'd still be proud of where I am from. We have got the Queen. Afternoon tea, London buses, cabs. I always acknowledge to people where I am from. Does not matter where I work and who I work for. I am proud to be British.
>
> (E7)

The findings of the English research group suggest that globalisation is perceived as a powerful contemporary process which affects many spheres of people's lives and particularly the world's economic and business structures. It was noted that with globalisation of the world businesses, more international interaction takes place at both structural and individual levels. Within this process, better understanding of different cultures is developing and people who are exposed to business interaction with their foreign counterparts recognise their internationalisation that transpires through their better knowledge of (and interest in) different cultures. They admit to becoming more sensitive towards other national characteristics and ways of living and business conduct. This broadens people's horizons and teaches them (directly or indirectly) how the same issues and problems can be addressed in different ways. Very few respondents acknowledged that national identities were being "driven out" in the global business context.

The majority of interviewees in the English research group stated that with becoming more international and globally aware and experienced, they, nevertheless, did not lose their own national features. They did not feel they were being homogenised and clearly saw the distinctiveness of their own national character or, indeed, the cultural qualities of other nations. As noted by respondent E5, "national identity might get blurred around the edges"; however, firmly engraved in people's understanding of themselves through upbringing and attachment to a particular national environment, it retains its strong presence in people's minds. Respondent E11's statement illustrates this conclusion:

> Everybody is stuck with where they were brought up and where the vast majority of their life is. You cannot shake your culture off. You can get fresh perspectives but you are from where you were raised.
>
> (E11)

In order to appreciate more fully the trends in national identity construction and development in the era of globalisation, I shall now address the subject of this research from the Scottish businesspeople's perspective.

Understanding of Globalisation by the Scottish Business Travellers

From the point of view of the Scottish businesspeople, globalisation has internationalised the business world through the development of communication channels allowing us to "communicate globally, and suddenly people are not far away any more" (S18). It was noted that the Internet allowed people to adopt mobile work practices without being confined to their office space. Telephone communication has made business operations much easier and removed certain protocols previously attached to international business telephone calls. For example, telephone calls to America 15–20 years ago were still quite expensive and required careful preparation and planning. Now telephone communication is a very informal, affordable and easy type of business communication, as is email (S2).

Thus, globalisation with its communication advancement and easy and fast international travel has revolutionised businesspeople's work culture making their work pattern very flexible and mobile. For example, it is now possible for respondent S2 to alternate working two weeks in the USA and two weeks in the UK, where he works from his home in Scotland (S2). S15, discussing globalisation, also referred to the ease of his international travel. He passionately described the ease of travelling to his business meetings in Africa and perceived an eight-hour flight as the norm in his business practice. Seeking to provide a balanced approach to globalisation, he pointed out the advantages of easy travel and fast communication technologies. He also mentioned some negative effects of globalisation, such as the spread of fast food in poorer areas of the world, where it was associated with prestige. As a result, countries like Botswana increasingly face obesity problem among pre-school children (S15).

Focusing on the positive effects of globalisation, some other respondents commented on opportunities to choose the best products and services available from different parts of the world. Globalisation also made it possible to choose the best approaches to problem-solving and a variety of skills available from various countries. Owing to communication technologies, businesses can grow and develop much faster now than before the world entered the globalisation stage (S12).

According to respondent S19, among all spheres of life and business affected by globalisation, the financial world has globalised the most to the extent that governments are not able to control monetary flows. From this perspective, he perceived globalisation as a threat because of left uncontrolled, it could have a toxic effect on the global society:

It's like with medicine. Although it is good, it can have a toxic effect. There are always side effects. So, globalisation improved world trade but at the same time the toxic effect is that the risks are too high. You get speculation rather than investment. They are different things. Globalisation has become a factor that allowed some of the worst practices. So, there needs to be more regulation to stop this happening.

(S19)

On the other hand, some noticeable changes in the global regulatory system have been mentioned by the respondents. As an example, interviewee S6 discussed the evolution of the legal system which is already making international business easier and more regulated. "We now have international law and bodies on this" (S6).

Overall, globalisation was perceived as a complex process that made it impossible "to see things entirely in the national context" (S16). Various examples could illustrate this, from tackling climate change to developing cancer treatments. As it was pointed out in the course of the interviews, it is impossible to address these issues fully by working on them exclusively within a national context and without wider international collaborative communication and knowledge exchange with colleagues from other countries (S16). He also understood globalisation as development of commerce (S16) and the impact "in the way of the cost of goods and services and the way that they are provided". The contemporary world, that is largely driven by markets, is becoming smaller and "people are now doing business in areas where a few years ago they would not even think about" (S8). This opens up new learning experiences about other countries and cultures, making people more rounded in their understanding of the world.

Respondent S7, talking about her understanding of the global development of the world, pointed out greater homogenisation in the way people are working:

> there is greater understanding, there is greater productivity. . . . I think a lot of this is because of globalisation. People are motivated by core values in a business community (whether it is profit making a difference or speed) there are just some basic core values, does not matter what your origin is. It is a global approach.
>
> (S7)

The global business environment erases individuality: everywhere around the world businesspeople have adopted the Western dress code, English has become the language of business communication. Business hotels are the same around the world, Holiday Inn being just one example. As described by S4,

> Every single room everywhere is identical. So, if you wake up in the middle of the night with your eyes closed you still know where the shower room is, etc. Personally I think this detracts a great deal from an individual's national identity. It is becoming very identical, glam, vanilla, it is not necessarily great. On a small scale, all high streets are all looking the same. Starbucks is on every corner.
>
> (S4)

Thus, globalisation, from the Scottish businesspeople's perspective is understood as internationalisation of the business world enhanced through the development of communication channels, and fast and affordable international travel and characterised by development of commerce and financial systems that cannot operate entirely within the national context any longer. Globalisation is noted to have its positive and negative effects. On the one hand, it provides individuals and businesses with opportunities to choose the best available products, goods and services from all over the world and opens up new learning opportunities. On the other, it is homogenising the way people work and operate and, by doing so, erasing national individuality and the uniqueness of the world's cultures.

This vision of globalisation is supporting the globalist perspective of globalisation theory, highlighting that the advancement of communication technologies and global travel influence tight interconnection of global commerce, financial flows and consumer supply and satisfaction. On the other hand, the concern that has been expressed over the erosion of national and cultural peculiarities directs us towards the assumption that the global advancements, although influencing homogenisation of many spheres of human activities and traits, have not proceeded far enough to assume full homogenisation. The issue of national languages and preservation of local cultures was raised by many respondents of Scottish origin, something that lies dear to their hearts and perhaps is at the core of their desire to preserve their national character and cultural identity.

Therefore, despite seeing themselves as global professionals with an international outlook, skills and knowledge, the Scottish businesspeople at the same time were fiercely defensive of the values and attitudes that they have developed by growing up in Scotland and absorbing its national and cultural features. All this indicates that at the current state of the social development, the Scottish businesspeople, being very advanced in terms of global responsiveness to the challenges and opportunities of the global business sphere, nevertheless expressed their deep concern over keeping the attachment with their national roots, and the need to preserve their cultural distinctiveness and affiliation with Scotland.

The Scots also very cunningly use the popularity and the image associated with their country and culture in the world. They easily recognise the "ice-breaking" effect that their accent, national dress and stereotyped types of behaviour can have on the flow and result of business interactions with foreign colleagues. Therefore, they rightfully utilise these national peculiarities for the advantage of the business. In doing so, their own understanding of their national identity is being reinforced while also being promoted overseas. One might wonder whether in this process, Scottish national identity is turning into an effectively working national brand, something that Tony Blair initiated for Britain in 1995, being inspired by the idea of reinvented British identity (The Economist, 1997).

As in the case with the Russian and English respondents, their current stance on globalisation suggests that the world has made significant advancements towards becoming truly global. This can be exemplified by the internationalisation of the business traveller through interaction with foreign colleagues, international business travel and exposure to foreign business cultures. However, national differences are still shaping people's mindsets, determining their behaviour through the powerful influences of national and cultural features on the business traveller's character. Therefore, theorising the global business traveller's view on globalisation based on their discourses on globalisation, it is logical to assume that their vision of global processes falls between the globalist and sceptical theoretical perspectives.

Does Globalisation Influence the Scottish Business Travellers' Understanding of Their National Identity?

It was observed in the course of the interviews that globalisation was seen as a significant influencing factor in respondents' personal and professional growth leading to acquiring new international experiences, knowledge and skills. When asked whether globalisation has influenced their understanding of their national identity, some respondents used very definitive answers such as "absolutely" (S7) and "hugely" (S6). For the majority of them, their international business travel and interaction with foreign counterparts have developed their ability to operate with ease on the global arena and be more sensitive towards other cultures and ways of business conduct in other national and cultural environments. Sharing their global business experiences, they pointed out that they became more international through globalisation:

> globalisation is about internationalisation. We are one world rather than a number of communities within continents and a number of countries within each continent. From a business perspective there is globalisation in how people dress, how people communicate, how meetings are undertaken . . . in the approaches. And the fact that there is a lot of cross border interaction. . . . There are no boundaries, how can there be boundaries nowadays with communications from the Internet through to telephones, etc. That has created globalisation initially.
>
> (S7)

Despite acknowledging the greater international perspective that the respondents have noticed in their professional and personal visions of themselves, they also emphasised the solid presence of national influences that persist in their understanding of themselves. Characteristically for the Scottish sample, the national attachments of the respondents divided into two groups with quite a large degree of disparity. The first group was composed of those respondents who firstly associated themselves with being British and secondly saw themselves as Scottish. The second group claimed they were Scottish first and foremost, while in some cases mentioned that they perceived themselves as British secondly. There were no claims to solely international identities (European or global).

The majority of the Scottish interviewees identified themselves with Scotland. It is essential to note that for many of them, their sense of belonging to the Scottish nation was experienced alongside their awareness of being part of the wider international community and feeling international (S3). This is paradoxical as on the one hand, people felt that they had more chances to assert their Scottishness through their travelling and working with people from other parts of the world, talking about their home country and thus becoming even more Scottish:

> I think I have become more Scottish. I am far more aware that I am part of the international community, I suppose that is paradoxical in a way. I have more occasions to assert my Scottishness because I have been travelling and people say: where do you come from? And I say: I come from Scotland and the reason why I do this is to make sure people do

not think I am anything else: American or English even. I find that I am asserting my Scottishness in order to define who I am.

(S3)

On the other hand, their international business travel and collaboration made them feel part of a bigger social grouping that extended beyond national boundaries and united people under a global idea of belonging to the global society. This was seen as a "natural evolution and a natural progression of travelling abroad" (S8). Respondent S12, who identified himself as Scottish, commented on the evolution of national identity with further depth:

I think it *[national identity]* is changing but there are still some very strong underlying issues. What globalisation has brought about is that instant communication that has broken down so many barriers. Even between Britain and France. . . . It has always been a very interesting relationship. The French are very French and the British are very British. The French used to defend everything French to the absolute limit. Even they have relaxed a bit because they have realised it is not to their advantage to do it all the time. They began to realise that there is a much broader range of connections. But at the same time there are times when they'll stick with it and defend it. And you can see that quite a lot between Britain and France politically as well as business-wise these days. So, yes, interesting times.

(S12)

The evolution of Scottish national identity is a complex process. Some respondents have experienced its enhancement through being perceived as a brand, due to its popularity overseas and used it as an ice-breaker in business communication and negotiations (S2). Such use of national identity heightens the sense of people's national belonging (S18) and even strengthens it when it is exposed to other national cultures (S17). From the point of view of respondent S14, the Scottish identity has a unique character which is different from any other identity in its ability to resist global pressures towards homogenisation:

The Scottish identity is very robust. I do not know why . . . maybe because it stands the test of globalisation better than other identities. It is the way we are brought up, the values we are given. It is our Scottish conservatism: we do not show our hands, we keep our feelings to ourselves; we do it all the time. There is a lot of history in Scotland that is not going to be wiped out in a few years with globalisation at all. We have got centuries of history . . .

(S14)

At the same time, some interviewees felt that despite people's desire to preserve their national identity, it was "chipping away through globalisation"

(S15), and national identities around the globe "are eroding around the edges but it is making them glue better together" (S20). Thus, Scottish national identity appeared a highly complex social phenomenon. On the one hand, the Scottish respondents felt the globalising influences affecting it in a homogenising way, whereas on the other, they actively discussed the strengthening of the Scottish national image and character that is currently taking place in the global business environment.

These findings suggest that the current state of the Scottish identity is characterised by a natural evolutionary process of development which is happening in two directions: The Scottish identity is being strengthened at its core through re-emphasising its historically established features and cultural traditions; at the same time, it is being slightly "chipped" around the edges by absorbing and adapting to global changes.

Understanding of Globalisation by the Russian Business Travellers

The Russian business travellers largely perceived globalisation as a positive process of world development manifesting itself through growing global interconnectedness which became possible with the development of communication technologies. They pointed out that due to the growth of the Internet, every sphere of human life is being advanced and the boundaries of business are being pushed significantly. Communication technologies in this process provide an avenue for easy and fast exchange of information between business partners, making it possible for people to work more effectively, productively and dynamically without travelling. As R13 put it,

> The fact that I and many of my friends live and work across several countries is the effect of world development. The global business is pushing boundaries. I should never stop saying thank you to people who invented the Internet. Owing to it, it is possible to work on three, four or five projects without travelling anywhere. This was not possible before the 1990s. Now it is a reality.
>
> (R13)

Several Russian interviewees pointed out that it was not simply communicating, but also living and working across national boundaries that characterised globalisation. "The [national] boundaries are being merged" (R10) and with them absorption of smaller companies into bigger ones is actively taking place in the globalising Western economy.

However, this trend, according to respondent R9, was not typical for Russia. The Russian business environment has been created in peculiar Russian conditions when

> a few people have managed to absorb large industries and they are trying to keep control over them. There are, of course, companies like

MTS and Beeline *[mobile phone companies]* that are trying to buy smaller businesses because they need to grow. But in the production industry this is not common at all. Currently every production business is trying to modernise its own equipment and expertise learning from foreign experience. All forefront technology. . . . I looked into Norilskii Nikel', they are trying to modernise but I do not see any big merges in our country just yet. I do not think we will see big global changes here in Russia. I think that time will sort this all out.

(R9)

Sharing their thoughts on globalisation, the Russian businesspeople particularly emphasised "the opening of the world" (R6), the feature, perhaps, crucially important for their country which had been operating behind the Iron Curtain for decades during the communist rule. The boundary-less world did not only facilitate Russia's more advanced participation in global affairs, but also brought big political changes to the former socialist world:

If we some years ago were sitting behind some curtains of socialism, many of those socialist countries do not exist anymore. No boundaries.

(R6)

Discussions of the economic globalisation highlighted the role of global financial flows enveloping the world into a tight net of monetary transactions. The services of financial institutions and the flexibility provided by the Internet were seen to be gaining more open global reach offering opportunities for businesses and individuals to explore their advantages across national borders (R1, R6, R8, R13, R14, R15, R20). Despite some clearly positive changes that globalisation had brought into the contemporary society, some negative features of globalisation were also pointed out. The global intertwining of various aspects of human activities has resulted in an unavoidable dependency of every corner of this planet on changes or catastrophes happening on the other side of the world. Thus, globalisation was understood as a generic concept that united local events under the umbrella of global living:

Now everything is so interconnected that any catastrophe or problem immediately affects everybody else in the world through currency exchange, through prices . . . we are under some sort of a hat of globalisation and we cannot build a wall and say, "you, guys, do whatever you want, we are not interested in what happens". Well, maybe in Gibraltar it is different but in general we all are under the same "hat" of globalisation . . .

(R6)

Whether globalisation was seen as a "hat" (R6) or as "one big space" (R3), in the eyes of my Russian respondents it was a process of growing influences of various aspects of social reality on each other, regardless of the geographical location where they were actually taking place. Another example was given by respondent R3, for whom globalisation was approached through the unification of consumer products around the world. It was commented that almost everywhere people were offered the same products, they spoke the same language and they grew closer through accumulating the same experiences, such as through food, music or cinema.

> There are the same shops everywhere in the world. There are the same brands everywhere and the same things. People are becoming very much alike: people dress similarly, they use similar gadgets, and everyone speaks the same language. *[It]* Does not matter what language you speak, you'll still understand what people are talking about. New universal words appear. All aspects of our life are being influenced: food, music, cinema. . . . The world is actually very small.
>
> (R3)

Thus, from the Russian interviewees' perspective, globalisation is the natural development of the world facilitated by the advancement in communication technologies. In this process, the world is becoming more open, with consumer products and financial flows enveloping the globe and often disregarding [national] boundaries. This leads to global interconnectedness, unification and unavoidable dependency of current agencies, structures and individuals.

It has been highlighted that the speed of globalisation is not equal in different parts of the world and is specific to regional, economic and cultural peculiarities of the locale where it is taking place. For example, the Russian interviewees pointed out that economic globalisation in Russia did not fully mirror the flow of global economic forces elsewhere. The merger of smaller companies into larger ones was not typical for Russia at the time of the interviews, which was conditioned by the current stage of development of Russian business coupled with its young history of market conditions and reinforced by Russian business culture. However, the Russian respondents did not exclude the possibility of Russian businesses merging into larger ones in the future with further maturation of the Russian economy (R9).

The Russian respondents' discourses on globalisation could be related to both globalist and sceptical theoretical approaches to globalisation. On the one hand, the globalist perspective was supported by those respondents who associated globalisation with the growing economic and cultural interconnectedness of the global society facilitated by ever-advancing communication technologies and their role in this process. On the other hand, it was noted that local influences preserve their persistent presence in global developments. This observation acts in support of the sceptical theoretical stance. Therefore, it appears logical to conclude that, according to the findings of the Russian research data, the perception of globalisation is not exclusively supportive of either theoretical camp.

Indeed, this understanding of globalisation involves considering diverse manifestations of this phenomenon that have their theoretical underpinning in both globalist and sceptical theoretical positions. Thus, from the Russian businesspeople's point of view, globalisation is a "multifaceted, complex and multidirectional" (R7) concept combining elements of both the sceptical and globalist perspectives of the globalisation theory. This statement is, perhaps, best supported by quoting one of the Russian respondents who suggested that:

> globalisation in its active form, when everybody is moving freely around the globe, has not come yet. It is only a very small part of the population of every country that moves absolutely freely globally. That is why it is perhaps too soon to talk about universalism and mergers just yet. I think that Russia is not ready yet to join this international marriage. We shall still preserve our core and the majority of people will still be living here, carrying this culture. But I do not think it is a negative process as I love travelling myself. I have friends in many countries. Many of my Russian friends have moved abroad and lead very international lifestyles. I think this is a natural process that, if we remember history, has always been present. Different transnational corporations always existed as well as various international connections. There has always been some language as the language of international communication, perhaps not always English but nevertheless. . . . It is a natural process and we should not be scared of it. But to say that the whole world has come up from its national seats and started moving around is a bit premature.
>
> (R19)

Does Globalisation Affect the Russian Business Travellers' Understanding of Their National Identity?

The analysis of the interviews revealed that all the Russian respondents saw positive influences of globalisation on their professional and personal growth and development. Owing to their international professional exposure, they have been able to advance their careers through wider professional networking, learn new skills and acquire new knowledge through collaboration with foreign counterparts. They also developed their foreign language skills and a deeper understanding of the world and themselves. The international business environment opened up opportunities for joining a much broader international multicultural society and forging professional and personal relationships. Their extensive exposure to the international environment provoked deeper considerations of one's national belonging, reinforced by observations of how different norms, values and attitudes specific to other national and cultural settings, manifest themselves through people's behaviour.

The Russian respondents firmly stated that operating at an international level did not mean being "dissolved in some multinational mass" (R19). Acquiring and adopting new knowledge and skills through international experiences did not necessarily lead to forgetting or replacing the values, attitudes and behaviours that the Russians developed and solidly established through their upbringing and growing up in Russia. Indeed, they found the process of personal growth through internationalisation enriching and interesting. At the same time, they all stressed the importance of their cultural and national heritage in their lives.

> I shall always be Russian. It will never change and cannot be changed. There are things that are very dear to me. Wherever I go, I am very happy to come back home. Whatever one can say about Saratov, it is still my city, it is my home and I love coming back. A person has to have a place to come back to. I very happily come back home and also very happily go away. It is a very positive process for me.
>
> (R17)

Fifteen out of 20 respondents undoubtedly declared that their national identity was clearly Russian, even though some of those people admitted acquiring an international mindset:

> Even if I went abroad now, I'd still be Russian. I was born Russian and I'll die Russian. However, my mentality is very international. Yes, I am a member of that *[international business]* community. But I shall always be Russian.
>
> (R12)

> I feel I belong to one big planet but I was born in this particular geographical point and I respect the history of this point of this planet and of course I feel Russian.
>
> (R20)

Mirroring R12's approach, some other respondents also saw their national identity as their own distinctive feature filled with meaningful significance; it is lived and deeply understood, cherished and valued. The Russians carried their identity with pride and were keen to preserve it for themselves and future generations:

> Every person always remains a whole piece in a salad bowl and carries his/her traditions. All people are very different and carry their cultural identity in their way. It is very interesting.
>
> (R19)

> I think that identity needs to be supported and preserved. Your identity is your history. It is very important. You cannot get away from it.

Boundaries can be merged, everything can be mixed and intermixed but people will always be interested in where they come from.

(R1)

In this context, the concept of transnationalism was in some cases surrounded by a fiercely negative feeling and was seen as specific to people who did not know and did not respect their country and the history of its people:

Of course there are people who have no Motherland. They do not care where they are as long as there is some money there or whatever else drives them. If a child grows up without a Motherland, if a child does not know where she/he lives, if she/he does not know her/his history and ancestors that created that country. . . . When I got seriously interested in Russian history, I read history by Solovyev and other respected historians. I also read Karamzin's History of the Russian State. In its introduction it said: why is it necessary for politicians to know history? It is because life is short and it is important to absorb our ancestors' experience in a compressed form. In other words, if you do not know history and experience of your ancestors, how are you going to lead your country? It goes on saying: why do ordinary people need to know history? It is for them to know that their ancestors during the establishment of your state went through different stages and sometimes it was much harder for them than for you now and the knowledge of history is important for you to stoically go through those hard times your country is going through.

(R10)

The concept of motherland was stressed with particular weight as something sacred and as something that everyone should have and respect. In this context, transnationalism was seen by some of the Russian respondents as a negative characteristic applicable to people who have no special attachment to their place of birth and upbringing, and therefore who have no motherland. For the older generation of the Russian respondents, this was an especially topical issue. They were not willing to discuss it in depth. However, they very clearly, although briefly, expressed their negative attitude towards multinationalism. It felt that for them the idea of transnationalism appeared almost offensive:

What is transnational? Without belonging anywhere? Without a motherland? I do not understand that and do not accept it.

(R14)

Interestingly, respondent R14, while rejecting the idea of transnationalism, nevertheless did not discard the possibility of people having multiple identities. Being truly Russian did not limit his associations with other broader geographical places. Continuing to think in geographical terms, he also affiliated himself with Europe, of which Russia is a part. And taking the geographical span even further, R14 stated that he could see himself as a global person who is prepared to live in other countries and already operates on a global scale:

> Personally, I think I shall always remain Russian. However, I do not separate being Russian and being European. I think of myself as European. Being Russian and European, I can also say that I am a global person. I could live and work somewhere abroad for some time.
>
> (R14)

The Russian respondents highlighted on several occasions that Russia was an inseparable part of Europe. Russian history and culture had been closely intertwined with those of the European countries throughout centuries, bridging European nations through the process of their historic development. In that respect, Russian identity is part of a broader European identity. The two do not necessarily have to overlap but they certainly can co-exist within the same individual. Regarding oneself as belonging to a particular nation is about appreciating its virtues and accepting its shortcomings. There is no space for overheated nationalism arising from extreme affiliations with one's background, but a healthy pride in what it means to be part of that nation. R20 explained his vision of himself as Russian and European very simplistically but extremely effectively:

> Conducting your deepest thoughts such as love and hatred, and also conducting your written and oral communication in a particular language defines your national identity. So, I regard myself as Russian. I feel connection with this land, with Russian history. My family, going back up to five generations, were all living here. That is why I certainly regard myself Russian. The second point is that I am also European as I also feel connection with European culture and history as Russian history is closely intertwined with European history. I shall never be Slavophile or Slavophobe, I do not like extremes. I shall never be Nazi and I shall never be ultra-leftist. We say: "We are Europeans!" Of course we are but at the same time we want to feel Irish or British or French. . . . Anyway, what is negative about being Russian and European or German and European?
>
> (R20)

To summarise, the analysis of the Russian interviews has shown that globalisation was understood by the Russian respondents as a natural process of the development of society influenced by the advancement in communication technologies. It was characterised by economic interconnectedness, cultural and consumer unification and interdependency of current agencies, structures and individuals, spanning national boundaries. The global business environment provided business travellers with the opportunities for professional and personal growth through access to international collaboration and communication with foreign counterparts. In the global environment, the issue of national identity becomes highly sensitive for Russian businesspeople, as the natural quest for them to understand themselves is strengthened by the enhanced complexity of the global reality.

Acquiring cosmopolitan perceptions on work and life generally, the Russian businesspeople are becoming more internationalised, at the same time fully appreciating the value of the views, norms, attitudes and behaviour that they have developed through their upbringing in the Russian national environment. Becoming more international, they, therefore, preserve their national affinity with the country of origin. Thus, it is possible to conclude that in the global environment the Russian business travellers are at the forefront of global change. Those who are more involved with global living and in possession of more than one citizenship sometimes exercise their option of shifting away from their original national affiliation. As this study has demonstrated, some of these people do take a cognitive decision to associate themselves with their new "adopted" countries. They, however, retain their emotional affiliation with their country of origin through the cultural features gained through their original ethnic and national upbringing.

Those who do not have an option of choosing their citizenship remain attached to their nation state and firmly see themselves as Russian in both civic and ethnic terms. Nevertheless, globalisation opens up access to new knowledge and experiences that influence businesspeople's vision of themselves as part of a broader society. Being Russian does not prevent people from seeing themselves as European or international. Preserving their Russian national identity, Russian businesspeople also acknowledged growing global influences on their perceptions, views and behaviour. Thus, national identity in the Russian case remains firmly present in people's understanding of themselves but people are becoming more international through the advancements of globalisation. Therefore, regarding the Russian participants of this research, it would be too premature for globalists to claim the erosion of national identity at the current point in the development of society; on the other hand, the sceptics cannot ignore the fact that the global forces are accelerating the natural process of the world interconnectedness, leaving us somewhere between these two theoretical claims on globalisation at present.

The English, Scottish and Russian businesspeople saw globalisation as a process of world development, enhanced by advancements in communication technologies and global travel and characterised by economic and cultural homogenisation. Globalisation was noted to have a positive as well as a negative impact on both micro and macro levels of world society, affecting both individuals and structures. Despite differences in historical, cultural and, until recently, economic conditions in the Russian case, all three groups of respondents understood globalisation fairly similarly and referred in their discourses to a range of examples from their own practical experiences that they had encountered while working in the international business.

Aiming to provide a balanced assessment of globalisation, they focused on both positive and negative aspects of the process. On the one hand, globalisation was presented as a force that stimulates growth and development, and on the other, as an influence that has the potential to cause tight inter-dependence between the world's systems, structures and peoples, and to erase cultural differences and national traditions. Recognition of the latter makes people realise how fragile and malleable national and cultural traditions are and to appreciate more fully their value and role in people's everyday lived experiences. The interviews also demonstrated that for many respondents, globalisation was a process of internationalisation of the world society leading to the merger of national structures (e.g., business structures) into global organisations. At the same it was highlighted that the current global system of regulation (political, financial and legislative) is not fully developed yet and this is something that needs to be addressed in order to provide proper functioning of newly emerging global bodies and organisations and to secure their fair, just, safe and stable influence on the world's populations.

From the cultural perspective, globalisation was perceived as a powerful social force capable of influencing the world's societies in a homogenising way through provision of global consumer products and the all-encompassing influences of global media. It was noted that communication technologies were linking with ease individuals from all over the world, disregarding national borders. Easy and affordable travel to almost any geographical point on this planet makes the world very small. The reign of the English language in business operations and other spheres of life diminishes the use of local languages and dialects in many parts of the world. However, recognition of the consequences of the global cultural merger brings to the fore the issue of preserving local traditions. As a result, the heightened awareness of the importance and meaning of local traditions and cultures is becoming more strongly pronounced, as shown by this research.

It is worth mentioning that concern about the erosion of local languages, cultures and identities was more explicitly and vividly expressed by the Russian and the Scottish business travellers than the English ones. In the Russian case, the reason for this could lie in the burning nature of the Russian soul, which constantly seems to be on a quest for self-discovery and self-understanding. Providing answers to questions on national identity in the course of this study, the Russians often referred to Russian literature and art as the best reflections of typically Russian cultural traditions. Thus, the blending of Russian culture into the global cultural kaleidoscope would understandably represent a matter of concern for many educated Russians. Indeed, protecting the "purity" of the Russian language and tackling its "pollution" with foreignisms, especially among young Russians (The Telegraph,

2007), became high on the agenda of the Russian national government and the Russian president at the turn of the century.

Vladimir Putin's mission was to run a campaign for cleaning up the Russian language, minimising swearing and grammatical mistakes, and banning the use of foreign words. The idea behind this campaign was "to promote national pride in answer to widespread feelings of inferiority provoked by the loss of Russia's superpower status" (www.Russiajournal.com). Later in 2006, Putin welcomed UNESCO's decision to proclaim the year 2007 the Year of the Russian Language in Russia and Abroad (www.newsru.com). During that year a number of Russian language-related events were organised in Russia and abroad in order to promote interest in the Russian language and strengthen the international contacts (www.rlcentre.com). The official opening ceremony of the Year of the Russian Language took place in Malta on the eve of Orthodox Christmas. To name just a few events that took place that year, The International Congress of Russian Language, Day of Slavic Writing and Culture, the Festival of Russian Arts in Cannes, Week of Russian Language and Russian Education in Montenegro (www.rlcentre.com).

In a similar vein, the Scottish people appeared extremely appreciative of the unique character of their culture. For them preserving as many ways of manifesting the Scottish identity as possible was crucially important. In a world dominated by Starbucks and McDonald's, the emotional value of being associated with the Scottish peaty water and the Scottish character has become even more appreciated and cherished by the Scots. The rise of national awareness prompted by the Scottish nationalistic movement of the 1990s has also left a mark on people's recognition of the national qualities of which Scotland can be proud. Thus, Scottish patriotism is marked by its resilient character, able not just to sustain the pressures of globalisation but also to place more emphasis on and pride in Scottish music, national dress, language and many other manifestations of the unique Scottish identity.

It was observed that the attitude of my English respondents towards globalisation was much more muted. Consistently within the discourses on national identity, their expressions of their attitudes towards globalisation were far less emotional than those of the Russians and the Scots, once again emphasising the cultural divide between the English and the Scots observed by David Goodhart (2008). However, some degree of disappointment was noticed during the interviews when the respondents mentioned the English language becoming the language of global communication and thus losing its position as a unique national feature. This concern over the English language may be used as an example of how globalisation facilitates people's reassessment of their national values. Perhaps this finding signals the rebirth of the English national identity in the English respondents' cognition.

Summing up the respondents' views on globalisation, it is possible to conclude that globalisation for them is a multifaceted process that unites the world under its global umbrella, while at the same time exposing its differences and celebrating its diversity. Using one of the research respondent's analogies, our world is a big salad bowl where individual pieces do not blend (R19). Thus, the globalisation debate within this research accepts the position of the sceptics while at the same time supporting the ideas of the globalists. These findings leave us somewhere between these polarised theoretical stances and direct us towards adopting the transformationalist theoretical approach to globalisation.

An understanding of the dynamics of national identity in the global business environment may be used to explain the transformationalist theoretical stance. As the analyses of the interviews with the global business travellers demonstrated, national identity is undergoing some evolutionary changes under the influences of globalisation in general, and in the global business environment in particular. From the point of view of global business travellers, national identities are homogenising on the one hand and proclaiming their individuality on the other.

This homogenisation may, however, be subconsciously perceived as a threat. It became apparent through the interviews that national identity was becoming more strongly expressed in terms of the nation's past, its local language and culture when the international business traveller was exposed to foreign interactions. This strengthens national identity's ethnic manifestations. At the same time, the development and globalisation of structural systems and institutions, such as financial markets, businesses corporations and global governance systems, weakens national identity's civic positions. The majority of interviews showed that the business travellers did not relate their understanding of their national identity to the structural features of their nation states, already widely operating at the global level. And only in the case of a few respondents, who were in possession of more than one citizenship, was their national belonging determined by a cognitive association with state structures and their functioning.

This book has revealed different degrees of involvement of the English, Russian and Scottish respondents with the issue of national identity, and different depths of articulating their national belonging. For the Russian businesspeople, the issue of their unique national culture and character appear to have become becoming extremely sensitive in this era of globalisation and especially in the global business environment. Doing business internationally for the Russian people means reaffirming their own understanding of who they are, what is particular about them and how, whilst being different from other nations, they can participate on equal terms in the global business game.

The interviews have demonstrated that for the Russians, the meaning of their national belonging is a highly topical matter which occupies people's minds and causes a constant reassessment of its value, role and place in people's lives. Very often these considerations of national identity are related to an emotional and psychological understanding of one's belonging, acceptance and understanding of the place one is born and grew up rather than with the structures that create the operational environment for society. There was a tendency among the Russian respondents eagerly to share their thoughts on national identity. They were extremely open, explicit and passionate in their discourses. The results suggest that the national identity of the Russian business travellers is being strengthened and reaffirmed during their international business operations. On the other hand, their exposure to the international business environment makes the respondents feel more international and open to wider participation in the global society.

The Scots, in their discussions of the dynamics of their national identity in the global business environment, were closer to the Russian respondents rather than the English. They highlighted the globalising power of the international business environment that made them feel more international in the global business arena. At the same time, they defensively expressed their appreciation of their Scottish identity supporting their discourses with numerous examples of the value of their national identity in their business operations and its importance in their everyday lived experiences.

It transpired that in the era of globalisation and particularly in the context of the political self-determination of Scotland within the United Kingdom, the Scottish national identity has become reinforced. This is not to say that the revival of Scottish identity leads to Scottish isolation from the global community. On the contrary, the Scots (at least in the context of the global business) have managed to negotiate a unique place for their identity. Reaffirmation of the unique Scottish national character helps the Scottish businesspeople to integrate better in the global business world using their national identity as a very successful national brand.

The English respondents in general, acknowledging that their national identity was not a primary focus of their daily lived experiences, openly admitted that they had never considered the issue of their national identity before. It is possible that for this reason they found it challenging to articulate its meaning and place in the global business arena. However, when prompted with questions regarding national identity at the beginning of the 21st century, the English businesspeople in general expressed a feeling of disappointment that their national identity is being lost in the global world (e.g., the loss of English language as a specific English feature as discussed above). This leads us to conclude that English national identity, although not explicitly debated on a day-to-day basis among the business travellers, is nonetheless not absent in their understanding of their social reality. And although, according to Susan Condor (2010), the rise of Scottish nationalism at the turn of the last century did not provoke the rise of English national movement, debating issues of English national identity can awaken people's recognition and appreciation of their national belonging.

The interchange of English and British identities observed during the course of the interviews signified the inseparable association of the dominance of English in the British context that takes its origin in the colonial context of the British past. Historically seeing themselves as part of a larger social, political and economic Imperial formation, the English business travellers saw themselves as international people in addition to recognising their English (or British) identity.

Thus, national identity, as a complex social construct, is undergoing significant developments in the era of global evolution and particularly under the influences of the global business environment. With political, economic, technological and cultural global transformation, national identity in the global business context is changing and adapting to the contemporary environment. With globalisation of the world economy and development of global institutions, the importance of civic categories such as "common national economy" and "national rights and duties" identified by A.D. Smith in his national identity theory (1991), is becoming less prominent in businesspeople's understanding of their national identity. As demonstrated by the interviews, more emphasis in the respondents' discourses is being paid to an ethnic understanding of national identity expressed through associations with national territory, history and culture.

The weakening of the civic aspects of national identity is signified by people's association with the global and recognition of themselves as international people, the citizens of the world. On the other hand, the strengthening of the ethnic categories of national identity reaffirms a deepening attachment to national roots. This consideration is important if we are to understand the contemporary nature of national identity. In the context of the global business environment, national identities are influenced by global and local forces simultaneously. As argued by respondent R20, "on the one hand the integration is happening, on the other the walls are being raised" (R20). Hence, being shaped by a two-way evolution of their national identities, the global businesspeople are constantly growing globally while becoming more firmly local.

References

Baylis, J., Smith, S. and Owens, P. (2008) *The Globalization of World Politics* (4th Ed). New York: Oxford University Press.

Bhagwati, J. (2004) *In Defence of Globalization.* New York: Oxford University.

Condor, S. (2010) Devolution and National Identity: The Rules of the English (Dis) Engagement. *Nations and Nationalism*, 16 (3), pp. 525–543.

Cromwell, D. (2001) *Private Planet: Corporate Plunder and Fight Back.* Charlbury: Jon Carpenter Publishing.

The Economist (1997) A New Brand for Britain. *The Economist*, 344 (8031), pp. 43–44.

Goodhart, D. (2008) *A Mild Awakening, England's Turn?* Available at: http://www.opendemocracy.net/article/ourkingdom-theme/post-post-nationalism-englands-turn.

Hirst, P. (2000) The Global Economy: Myth or Reality? In Kalb, D., van der Land, M., Staring, R., van Steenbergen, B. and Wilterdink, N. (eds.) *The Ends of Globalization.* Maryland: Rowman and Littlefield Publishers, Inc.

Khor, M. (2001) *Rethinking Globalization*. London: Zed Books Ltd.

Scase, R. (2007) *Global Remix: The Fight for Competitive Advantage*. London: Kogan Page.

Shaw, M (2000) *Theory of the Global State: Globality as Unfinished Revolution*. Cambridge: Cambridge University Press.

Smith, A.D. (1991) *National Identity*. London: Penguin Books.

Soros, G. (2002) *On Globalization*. Oxford: Public Affairs Ltd.

The Telegraph (2007) English Invades Russian Language. *The Telegraph*, September 12, 2007. Available at: www.telegraph.co.uk/news/worldnews/1562947/English-invades-Russian-language.html.

5   Erosion of National Identity?— Searching for Answers

This concluding chapter returns to the original research question of the book. The purpose of the book was to contribute to a better understanding of social processes in the era of globalisation. It sought to explore the interrelation between the global business environment and international businesspeople's construction and understanding of their national identity. In doing so, it attempted to provide an answer to the question whether national identities are being eroded in the global business environment and what role globalisation plays in shaping the national identities of international businesspeople. The book makes a contribution to the advancement of our knowledge on the global business reality and international business travel in particular, the "omnipresent practice in the twenty-first century, but also a practice that is only partially understood and that increasingly causes concern for workers and employers alike" (Beaverstock *et al.*, 2009).

Studies on national identities have not extensively explored the understanding of national self by international business travellers, the social group perhaps most exposed to the influences of globalisation. Consequently, this book contributes to two specific fields of contemporary sociological thought. Firstly, to the field of area studies through providing an insight into how the perceptions of national identity by international business travellers from Great Britain and Russia are constructed, how they differ and in what ways they are affected by globalisation. Our better understanding of these processes will shed light on the dynamic of national identity within the global business world and what significance it has on erosion of national identity in our globalising society. Secondly, the book aims to contribute to the sociology of business that extends beyond understanding the function of international business travel in international business operations.

The findings of the study that informed the book identify the international business traveller as an upwardly striving manager, in a middle or senior-management position, more often a male than a female, in his/her forties, married, educated to a degree level or higher, not necessarily possessing foreign language skills in the case of a native English speaker and usually with a good command of business English in the case of any other mother tongue.

He/she operates with ease and feels comfortable in any part of the world, apart from dangerous places. However, the feeling of being a foreigner persistently stays with him/her regardless of the extent of foreign travel experience. This person eagerly and easily communicates with his/her foreign colleagues and usually forms friendships with his/her overseas counterparts which are often sustained even when business relationships cease, growing into personal relationships. He/she fully appreciates the challenges that arise as a consequence of international business travel but, nevertheless, enjoys his/her busy lifestyle and its enriching experiences.

Bearing in mind the qualitative nature of this study and the sample size of 60 interviews, care needs to be taken with extrapolating this image onto all international business travellers. Nevertheless, this finding is consistent with the image of the international business traveller portrayed by Adler and Bartholomew (1992a) and Gustafson (2009). Having recognised cosmopolitan orientations and global connections as important features of the international business traveller's image, the book was concerned with the assessment of local attachments of the business travellers and their construction and understanding of national identity in particular.

National Identity Construction by the International Business Traveller

The analysis of international business travellers' discourses on national identity exposed the five most frequently mentioned constructs: culture, people and their characteristics, history, landscape and place of birth. Thus, it is evident that the understanding of national identity, when placed out of any particular context, is linked to people's ethnic understanding of the concept. Additionally, only in several cases national identity was related to the institutional structures of their states, expressed through national economy, citizens' rights and duties established within their national context. However, references to states' institutions and structures did not appear in the business travellers' discourses frequently enough to be classed as a valid identity attribute. Thus, in terms of A.D. Smith's (1991) model of national identity, we found that national identity construction by the international business travellers was based primarily on ethnic and more rarely on civic foundation, suggesting that the business travellers' mentality regarding economic activities and social responsibility was not strictly limited by the boundaries of their nation-states.

It was noted that the interplay between ethnic and civic domains changed depending on the context in which national identity was discussed. When considered as a general concept without any conditioning factors, national identity was articulated through the ethnic approach (i.e. culture, language, people, landscape) in the *majority* of cases, with *some* involvement of civic components of the notion (i.e. state structures and institutions). When national identity was discussed in the global business context, *almost all* respondents approached it from the ethnic perspective, placing a strong emphasis on ethnic signifiers (e.g., cultural stereotypes, language, people's traits and behaviour) and *extremely rarely* mentioning its civic attributes.

This finding represents a generalised overview of the respondents' approach to constructing their national identity. However, noticeable differences were observed in their depth of involvement with the subject of this research, which varied between national groups. Therefore, national identity construction was considered in a cross-cultural perspective, followed by the assessment of globalisation as an influencing factor in national identity construction.

National Identity Construction in a Cross-Cultural Perspective

It was found that the global business environment stimulates its actors' affiliation with the global through universal application of international business skills, the use of English language as the means of business communication and consumption of universal business-related services, provided, for example, by travel, hotel and communication industries. Extensive involvement in international business facilitates further businesspeople's ability to operate at a global level, regardless of their ethnic or national origin.

At the same time, their relationship with their national identity did not show any tendency towards weakening. On the contrary, as demonstrated in this book, while the business travellers from all three national research samples developed similar international skills through their involvement in similar international experiences of their businesses and thus "globalising" in an equal way, the degree of their engagement with their national identity became more strongly pronounced through their exposure to international business interactions. However, the depth of reassessment of the meaning of national identity differed for the English, the Scottish and the Russian research participants, reflecting these people's "initial" degree of immersion with the issue.

For the English business traveller's national identity, when considered as a concept which is not limited by any specific context, was not an issue of high importance. It represented an inseparable part of an individual's life and understanding of oneself. When not made the focus of attention, it did not require further pontificating and was accepted as a fact of life. On a number of occasions, the English business travellers highlighted that they had never thought about their national identity before and found it challenging to explain the meaning of their identity. Nevertheless, they acknowledged experiencing a heightened sense of being English/British when they noticed national and cultural differences in their international business interactions.

National identity was perceived in a slightly different manner by the Scottish business travellers. In contrast to their English counterparts, the Scots willingly shared their thoughts on what constitutes their national identity, what it means to them and what role it plays in their lives. In a similar manner to their English counterparts, their national identity was much more strongly appreciated when placed in the international business context in which cultural and national differences became more vividly expressed and acknowledged.

Even tighter engagement with the issue of national identity was found in the interviews with the Russian business travellers. For many of them national identity was a topical issue that occupied an important position in their cognitive processes and was often considered a tool for better understanding of oneself. As with the findings from the English and the Scottish samples, national identity of the Russian research participants was reinforced through contrast with other cultures and nations observed during international business engagements.

A particularly strong engagement with one's national identity is experienced by those business travellers who lived in national and cultural environments other than their country of origin. Permanently exposed to the foreign environment, these people were highly concerned with their feelings of belonging and national identity as they were seeking to determine and define their place in their host society. For these businesspeople this issue appeared crucial in their search for ontological security, essential for one's emotional, psychological and social well-being. This suggests that people who were born and grew up outside their current permanent place of residence experienced some degree of discomfort, originating from the uncertainty of continuity and belonging.

This implies that the different degrees of immersion in the issue of national identity by different national groups that happen simultaneously with the rapid globalisation of the international business traveller, point to a highly complicated picture of the interrelationship between national and global belonging. For international business travellers, becoming global is a uniting factor that emphasises the power of global forces to bring people together and build supranational social formations such as the TCC above and beyond national attachments. However, at the same time, national belonging is still playing a highly important role in developing people's sense of self and, as the study found, for different nations it happens with different degrees of depth. This finding reinforces our appreciation of national influences and diversity, which results in people's life-long commitment to the places they originally come from.

Globalisation as an Influencing Factor in National Identity Construction

The interpretations of the international business travellers' discourses have implications for understanding globalisation as an influencing factor in national identity construction. The book has demonstrated that globalisation, largely perceived as an economic, political and cultural process, is able to affect people's lived experiences and their understanding of themselves. Under the influences of global development and particularly the global business environment, international business travellers are indeed becoming more global; however, at the same time, they are becoming more strongly aware of their national belonging. This contradictory process is affecting national identities in two ways. On the one hand, it facilitates business travellers' affiliation with the global world, thus weakening civic positions of the national identity. On the other hand, it reinforces people's attachment to their national roots, emphasising the importance of ethnic components of national identity. Thus, in the global business context, national identity is becoming more blurred in some aspects and reinforced in others.

From the theoretical perspective on globalisation, neither the sceptical nor globalist positions can currently accommodate the contemporary stage of global influences on national identity. This finding supports P. Gustafson's (2009) claim that "more cosmopolitanism does not necessarily mean less localism" (p. 44). In the process of a global social transformation, local attachments and cosmopolitan orientations can be (and indeed are) complementary. By no means mutually exclusive, they create much richer conditions for deep appreciation and preservation of local traditions on the one hand, and exciting opportunities of exploring global openness on the other.

This book has sought to provide insight into how international business travel influences businesspeople's understanding of themselves in terms of their national identity, and whether erosion of national identity is taking place in the era of globalisation. It has been demonstrated that globalisation in the face of international business travel does affect international business travellers' understanding of their national identity: in becoming more cosmopolitan they also grow more aware of their national belonging. As one of the business travellers observed, erosion of national identity is happening around the edges, but only so that different cultures can be better glued together.

References

Adler, N.J. and Bartholomew, S. (1992a) Managing Globally Competent People. *The Executive*, 6 (3), pp. 52–65.

Beaverstock, J.V., Derudder, B., Faulconbridge, J. and Witlox, F. (2009) International Business Travel: Some Explorations. *Geografiska Annaler: Series B, Human Geography*, 91 (3), pp. 193–202.

Gustafson, P. (2009) More Cosmopolitan, No Less Local. *European Societies*, 11 (1), pp. 25–47.

Smith, A.D. (1991) *National Identity*. London: Penguin Books.

Index

37–9; definitions of 39–40; education
46; enjoyment/dissatisfaction with
a busy lifestyle 63–4; feeling a
foreigner whilst abroad 56–7; feeling
comfortable/uncomfortable abroad
54–6; friendship with foreigners
59–62; gender 44–5; integration/
assimilation 52–4; national identity
construction 172–3; proficiency in
foreign languages 46–9; religion 46;
travel abroad 49–50

Jang, Y.S. 23–4
Jenkins, J. 47
Jones, R. W. 96

Kellner, D. 19
Kentor, J. 23–4
Kumar, K. 12, 79

landscapes 28, 81–2
language: barriers 52–3, 60; English
47–8, 58, 78, 83, 136, 165–6, 168,
173; foreign language proficiency
24–5, 46–9; identity and 30; learning
local 57–8; national 38–9
lifestyle 63–4
Lonner, W.J. 26
Lovell, S. 118

McCrone, D. 69, 95, 96
Malpass, R.S. 26
Mandler, P. 6, 11, 12
Martin, D. 19–20
Marx, K. 16
migration 24, 103–4
Moore, C. 91
Morgan, G. 24, 31
motherland: Russian 110, 116, 119–20,
162; Scottish 93, 98
Muldoon, O.T. 29
multiple identities 8, 10–11, 131–5
Munck, R. 20

national clichés 101
national identity: academic publications
27–31; challenges in studying 11–12;
collective identity and 9; as concept
83; constructs 133–5; English
68–76; in era of globalisation 15–17;
force in policy making and nation-
building 30–1; multiple 10–11,
131–5; nation (state) and 12–13;
negotiation 72; "the other" in 130;

as part of public culture of modern
state 10; psychology and 26; role of
landscapes signifier of 28; role of "the
other" in understanding 12; Russian
107–9; Scottish 87–9; significance
in English businesspeople's lives
128–30; significance in Scottish
businesspeople's lives 128–30;
significance Russian businesspeople's
lives 128–30; "taken-for-granted"
70; theory 14–15; types of 9–10;
see also identity
national identity construction: in
cross-cultural perspective 173–4;
English international business
travellers 67–84; globalisation as
an influencing factor in 174–5;
by international business traveller
172–3; Russian international
business travellers 107–24; Scottish
international business travellers
87–105; *see also* identity; national
identity
nationality 7, 26, 29–30, 71, 78, 89,
108, 115, 118, 149
Neugarten, B.L. 40
"new imperialism" 16
Northern Ireland 29

"the other" 130

Papadopoulos, D. 30
Paterson, L. 96
patriotism: Russian 119–24, 124;
Scottish 100, 104
Peters, B. 8, 9–11
Pittock, M. 71
place of birth: English 84, 134, 139–42;
Russian 109–11, 122, 134, 139–42;
Scottish 95–7, 134, 139–42
political apathy 68–9
pride: English 80–1, 130–1; Russian
120–1, 130–1; Scottish 93, 104
psychology: academic publications
27–31; as branch of science 26;
national identity and 25–6; role of
"cultural dimension" 28–9
Putin, V. 166

quality of life 41, 71, 145

Reicher, S. 26–8
religion 29, 46
Ricoeur, P. 6–7

For Product Safety Concerns and Information please contact our EU
representative GPSR@taylorandfrancis.com
Taylor & Francis Verlag GmbH, Kaufingerstraße 24, 80331 München, Germany

www.ingramcontent.com/pod-product-compliance
Ingram Content Group UK Ltd.
Pitfield, Milton Keynes, MK11 3LW, UK
UKHW020944180425
457613UK00019B/514